AI in Hospital Administration
Revolutionizing Healthcare

David Mhlanga
The University of Johannesburg
College of Business and Economics
Auckland Park, South Africa

CRC Press is an imprint of the
Taylor & Francis Group, an **informa** business

A SCIENCE PUBLISHERS BOOK

First edition published 2025
by CRC Press
2385 NW Executive Center Drive, Suite 320, Boca Raton FL 33431

and by CRC Press
4 Park Square, Milton Park, Abingdon, Oxon, OX14 4RN

© 2025 David Mhlanga

CRC Press is an imprint of Taylor & Francis Group, LLC

Reasonable efforts have been made to publish reliable data and information, but the author and publisher cannot assume responsibility for the validity of all materials or the consequences of their use. The authors and publishers have attempted to trace the copyright holders of all material reproduced in this publication and apologize to copyright holders if permission to publish in this form has not been obtained. If any copyright material has not been acknowledged please write and let us know so we may rectify in any future reprint.

Except as permitted under U.S. Copyright Law, no part of this book may be reprinted, reproduced, transmitted, or utilized in any form by any electronic, mechanical, or other means, now known or hereafter invented, including photocopying, microfilming, and recording, or in any information storage or retrieval system, without written permission from the publishers.

For permission to photocopy or use material electronically from this work, access www.copyright.com or contact the Copyright Clearance Center, Inc. (CCC), 222 Rosewood Drive, Danvers, MA 01923, 978-750-8400. For works that are not available on CCC please contact mpkbookspermissions@tandf.co.uk

Trademark notice: Product or corporate names may be trademarks or registered trademarks and are used only for identification and explanation without intent to infringe.

Library of Congress Cataloging-in-Publication Data (applied for)

ISBN: 978-1-032-74673-9 (hbk)
ISBN: 978-1-032-75826-8 (pbk)
ISBN: 978-1-003-47580-4 (ebk)

DOI: 10.1201/9781003475804

Typeset in Times New Roman
by Prime Publishing Services

Acknowledgements

Writing a book is a journey that requires the support, encouragement, and contributions of many individuals and institutions. As I reflect on the completion of *AI in Hospital Administration: Revolutionizing Healthcare*, I am deeply grateful to all those who have played a part in bringing this work to fruition. First and foremost, I would like to express my profound gratitude to the University of Johannesburg, particularly the College of Business and Economics, for providing me with the academic and professional environment necessary to conduct my research and compile this book. The resources, facilities, and intellectual community at the university have been indispensable in my work. I am deeply indebted to the numerous scholars and experts whose research and writings have informed and inspired this work. I also acknowledge the valuable input from the extensive body of literature cited throughout this book, which has provided the theoretical and practical underpinnings for my analysis. To my family and friends, your unwavering support and encouragement have been my source of strength throughout this journey. Your patience, understanding, and belief in my work have been a constant source of motivation. A special mention goes to my editor and the publishing team whose expertise and attention to detail have ensured that this book meets the highest standards of quality and readability. Your dedication and professionalism have made this process a smooth and rewarding experience. Lastly, I am grateful to the readers of this book. It is my hope that *AI in Hospital Administration: Revolutionizing Healthcare* will serve as a valuable resource and inspire further exploration and innovation in the integration of artificial intelligence in healthcare. Your interest and engagement are what ultimately bring purpose and relevance to this work. Thank you all for your contributions and support. This book is as much a product of your efforts as it is of mine.

Preface

The healthcare sector is on the cusp of a profound transformation, one driven by the accelerating adoption of artificial intelligence (AI) across various domains. As a researcher deeply invested in the intersection of technology and healthcare, I have had the privilege of witnessing how AI is beginning to reshape hospital administration—optimizing processes, improving patient outcomes, and fundamentally altering how care is delivered.

This book, "AI in Hospital Administration: Revolutionizing Healthcare," is a culmination of my research, insights, and observations gathered over years of studying the application of AI in healthcare settings. My motivation for writing this book stems from a desire to bridge the gap between the theoretical potential of AI and its practical application in hospital management. I hope to provide a comprehensive guide for healthcare administrators, professionals, and policymakers who are navigating the complex and rapidly evolving landscape of AI.

The journey of writing this book has been both challenging and rewarding. It has involved extensive research, consultation with experts, and the exploration of numerous case studies that illustrate the transformative power of AI in hospital settings. Along the way, I have been fortunate to receive support and encouragement from colleagues, family, and friends, to whom I owe a debt of gratitude.

This book is not just a scholarly endeavor; it is a call to action. The healthcare industry is at a critical juncture, where the thoughtful integration of AI can lead to unprecedented advancements in patient care and operational efficiency. However, this transformation is not without its challenges. Ethical considerations, data security, and the need for robust governance frameworks are just a few of the issues that must be addressed as we move forward.

In writing this book, my goal has been to provide readers with a balanced perspective—highlighting both the opportunities and the challenges associated with AI in hospital administration. I hope that this book will serve as a valuable resource for those looking to harness the potential of AI to revolutionize healthcare.

Finally, I would like to extend my deepest thanks to the University of Johannesburg, particularly the College of Business and Economics, for providing the academic environment that has enabled me to conduct this research. I am also grateful to the many scholars, healthcare professionals, and AI experts whose work has informed and inspired my own.

As you read this book, I encourage you to approach the content with an open mind and a forward-thinking perspective. The future of healthcare is being written today, and AI will undoubtedly play a central role in shaping that future.

Prof. David Mhlanga
University of Johannesburg
South Africa

Contents

Acknowledgements	*iii*
Preface	*v*
About the Book	*ix*
1. Introduction to AI in Hospital Administration	1
2. Basics of Artificial Intelligence	6
3. Enhancing Patient Management and Scheduling through AI Solutions	28
4. The Synergy of AI and Electronic Health Records: Revolutionizing Data Management and Patient Care	49
5. Medical Imaging and Diagnostics: The Fundamentals of Medical Imaging and AI	68
6. AI and Predictive Analytics and Risk Assessment in Healthcare	89
7. Revolutionizing Resource Allocation and Optimization in Hospitals with AI	105
8. Redefining Clinical Decision Support Systems through AI: A Futuristic Perspective	120
9. Disease Diagnosis and AI Applications in Hospital Administration	143
10. AI in Healthcare Finance and Billing: Enhancing Efficiency and Accuracy	159
11. Ethical Considerations in AI-Enabled Healthcare	180
12. Overcoming Barriers to AI Adoption in Healthcare	194
13. AI in Hospital Administration: Revolutionizing Healthcare. A Conclusion	215
Index	221

About the Book

AI in Hospital Administration: Revolutionizing Healthcare by Professor David Mhlanga is a comprehensive exploration of the transformative impact of artificial intelligence (AI) on the healthcare sector, specifically within hospital administration. This book delves into the numerous ways AI technology is reshaping healthcare management, from patient care to resource optimization, ultimately aiming to enhance both operational efficiency and patient outcomes. At the heart of this book lies the premise that AI has the potential to address some of the most pressing challenges faced by hospital administrators today. With the rapid advancements in AI technology, hospitals are increasingly capable of improving patient scheduling, managing electronic health records, enhancing medical imaging, and supporting clinical decision-making processes. Professor Mhlanga provides a detailed analysis of these applications, showcasing how AI can streamline operations and elevate the standard of care provided to patients. The book is structured to guide readers through a journey that begins with an introduction to the basic principles of AI. It explains fundamental concepts such as machine learning, deep learning, and natural language processing, establishing a solid foundation for understanding subsequent chapters. Professor Mhlanga then delves into specific AI applications within hospital settings, providing a thorough examination of how these technologies are being implemented and the benefits they bring.

One of the key features of this book is its emphasis on real-world case studies. Prof. David Mhlanga includes numerous examples of successful AI integration in hospitals around the world. These case studies highlight practical insights and demonstrate the tangible benefits of AI, such as reduced waiting times, improved diagnostic accuracy, and an effectual resource allocation. By presenting these examples, the book not only illustrates the potential of AI but also offers a roadmap for healthcare administrators looking to implement similar solutions in their own institutions. In addition to exploring the technological aspects, *AI in Hospital Administration: Revolutionizing Healthcare* also addresses the ethical and practical challenges associated with AI integration. Professor Mhlanga discusses concerns related to data privacy, security, and the human-machine interface. He underscores the importance of maintaining ethical standards and ensuring that AI technologies are used responsibly to protect patient confidentiality and trust. *AI in Hospital Administration: Revolutionizing Healthcare* is an essential resource for healthcare professionals, administrators, policymakers, and researchers. It provides a comprehensive understanding of AI's role in hospital administration and offers practical guidance on leveraging these technologies to drive innovation and improvement in healthcare delivery. Prof.David Mhlanga insightful analysis and forward-thinking perspective make this book a valuable addition to the field of healthcare management literature. In summary, this book offers a thorough exploration of how AI is revolutionizing hospital administration. Through a blend of theoretical foundations, practical applications, and ethical considerations, Prof. David Mhlanga provides a holistic view of the future of healthcare management in the age of artificial intelligence.

1 Introduction to AI in Hospital Administration

This chapter provides a comprehensive overview of the transformative impact of artificial intelligence (AI) in hospital administration, exploring its application across various aspects of healthcare management. As AI technology continues to evolve, its integration into hospital settings is revolutionizing processes from patient care to resource management. This chapter outlines the book's structure, highlighting key chapters that discuss the integration of AI in areas such as patient scheduling, electronic health records, medical imaging, and clinical decision support systems. The chapter also discusses the challenges and ethical considerations of implementing AI in healthcare settings. By offering a preview of the insights and detailed discussions within the book, this chapter sets the stage for understanding how AI technologies can enhance operational efficiency and patient outcomes in hospital administration.

Introduction

The book *AI in Hospital Administration Revolutionizing Healthcare* explores the transformative potential of artificial intelligence (AI) in hospital administration and its substantial impact on reshaping healthcare. AI has emerged as a powerful tool in the healthcare sector, with the ability to enhance and optimize several aspects of healthcare administration (Le et al., 2018; Santosh and Gaur, 2022; Harry, 2023; Mhlanga, 2024). These aspects encompass the provision of medical treatment, distribution of resources, decision-making methods, and operation effectiveness (Mhlanga, 2021; Santosh and Gaur, 2022; Mhlanga, 2022). The widespread adoption of AI in hospital management presents significant opportunities and challenges for healthcare systems on a global scale (Li et al., 2021; Yaqoob et al., 2021). Healthcare organizations necessitate effective management and decision-making procedures to optimize patient outcomes and efficiently allocate resources, given their intricate and ever-changing nature. However, traditional administrative approaches sometimes face challenges in meeting these criteria, resulting in prolonged waiting times, inefficient scheduling, inaccurate forecasts, and suboptimal allocation of resources.

Researchers in the academic literature have extensively explored the potential applications of AI in the healthcare sector. More precisely, their attention has been directed towards the potential uses of AI in medical imaging, clinical decision support systems, and illness detection. Studies by Yan et al. (2006), Malmir et al. (2017), Sutton et al. (2020), and Mhlanga (2023a, b, c) have explored these applications. While significant advancements and achievements have been made in these fields, the extent of AI's influence on hospital administration has not been thoroughly investigated. This book aims to address the information gap by offering valuable insights into the specific challenges faced by hospital management and exploring the potential of AI to address these problems effectively. This book thoroughly examines the current hospital management methods by scrutinizing the available academic literature and pinpointing pressing challenges and limitations. This book examines the complexities of managing patient transportation, optimizing resource allocation, ensuring effective staff scheduling, and establishing data-driven decision-making processes. Moreover, it explores how AI-powered solutions might alleviate these challenges and revolutionize the healthcare industry. The book employs a multidisciplinary research and extensively explores cutting-edge AI technologies, such as machine learning, natural language processing, and predictive analytics, and their practical applications in hospital administration. It also analyzes the ethical ramifications and potential challenges associated with integrating AI in healthcare, including concerns around privacy, data security, and the human-machine interface.

This book provides practical insights by showcasing real-world case studies and successful examples of AI implementations in hospital administration. This publication equips healthcare professionals, administrators, legislators, and academics with the necessary knowledge and tools to efficiently harness AI, foster innovation, and facilitate positive transformation in healthcare organizations. The book *AI in Hospital Administration: Revolutionizing Healthcare*" addresses the lack of scholarly literature on the use of AI on hospital management, providing a comprehensive analysis of its impact. It aims to stimulate more research, promote well-informed decision-making, and establish the groundwork for a future when AI plays a crucial role in enhancing hospital management. It accomplishes this by highlighting the problem description and offering pragmatic solutions.

The book *AI in Hospital Administration: Revolutionizing Healthcare* explores the transformative potential of AI in the field of hospital administration and its profound impact on healthcare. This book employs existing scholarly literature and interdisciplinary research to provide a comprehensive overview of cutting-edge AI technology and its applications in hospital administration. It begins by explaining the basic principles of AI and then explores the pressing challenges faced by hospital administrators, such as long waiting times, ineffective scheduling, inaccurate forecasting, and insufficient resource allocation. It emphasizes the significance of employing effective management and decision-making procedures to optimize patient outcomes while also ensuring the proper utilization of resources. Despite significant advancements in AI in areas like medical imaging and clinical decision support systems, there has been limited research focus on its implementation in hospital management. This book aims to rectify this inadequacy by examining the complexities of managing patient travel, enhancing resource allocation, ensuring efficient staff scheduling, and implementing data-driven decision-making processes. It explores several AI-driven solutions, including machine learning, natural language processing, and predictive analytics, and their capacity to tackle these challenges. Furthermore, they tackle ethical considerations and potential hurdles associated with the integration of AI in healthcare, encompassing concerns of privacy, data security, and the interaction between humans and machines. Pragmatic perspectives that are integrated by tangible case studies and illustrations of triumphant AI implementations in hospital management are provided. This initiative offers healthcare practitioners, administrators, policymakers, and researchers the necessary information and resources to efficiently utilize AI, foster innovation, and implement advantageous transformations in healthcare organizations. The objective of *AI in Hospital Management: Revolutionizing Healthcare* is to address the lack of scholarly literature on the influence of AI on hospital management. This resource offers a comprehensive understanding of this field's challenges, limitations, and opportunities, promoting further exploration and aiding informed decision-making. A futuristic scenario where AI greatly enhances healthcare administration has been depicted.

This book thoroughly analyzes the significant influence that AI can have on hospital management. The text explores the diverse applications of AI, its potential repercussions, and the future of healthcare management. The tale begins by summarizing the basic principles of AI, including important concepts such as machine learning, deep learning, and natural language processing. These foundational elements offer the structure for understanding how AI can be employed to enhance hospital management and patient care. Following the introductory chapter, the book explores in-depth discussions on various uses of AI in healthcare. The Book examines state-of-the-art AI systems for patient management and scheduling, highlighting their capacity to improve efficiency and optimize resource allocation. This analysis examines the mutually beneficial connection between AI and electronic health records (EHRs), emphasizing how their integration enhances data management and enables more knowledgeable patient care choices. Furthermore, the book delves into the crucial importance of AI in the realm of medical imaging and diagnostics, emphasizing its profound impact on improving diagnostic accuracy and operating efficiency.

The passage then shifts to examining the application of AI in predictive analytics and risk assessment, demonstrating how these technologies might forecast health outcomes and enhance the proactive management of patient care. Furthermore, the Book delves into the significant influence of AI on the distribution and enhancement of resources in hospitals, offering case studies and instances of successful implementations. The integration of AI into clinical decision support systems, illustrating how AI aids physicians in making more informed decisions on patient care has been explored in the book. The text discusses disease diagnosis and the use of AI in hospital management, emphasizing the use of AI to improve operations and increase the accuracy of diagnoses. AI is employed in healthcare finance and billing to enhance efficiency, accuracy, and compliance with regulatory standards. The book also explores the ethical implications and challenges associated with the integration of AI in healthcare, analyzing issues such as privacy, data security, and the need for transparency. It examines the challenges that arise when using AI in healthcare and suggests strategies to overcome these hurdles in the concluding parts. This article predicts forthcoming advancements and developing trends in AI-powered healthcare, projecting the possible influence of these enhancements on hospital operations and the wider healthcare sector. Here is a detailed summary of the book.

    Section 1 focuses on the fundamental principles and concepts of Artificial Intelligence in the Context of Hospital Administration. Within this section, the chapters establish the fundamental principles necessary for comprehending the function of AI in the field of healthcare. Chapter 1 establishes the context by presenting the capacity of AI to improve efficiency and patient care. It also gives a summary of the next chapters and the significant knowledge they provide. Chapter 2 explores the fundamental principles of AI, including machine learning, deep learning, and natural language processing. These concepts lay the groundwork for the more complex applications that will be explored in following chapters. Section 2 specifically addresses the implementation of Artificial Intelligence (AI) in the Field of Hospital Administration. This section, spanning from Chapter 3 to Chapter 8, centers on the specific applications of AI in improving hospital operations. Chapter 3 explores the transformative impact of AI on patient management and scheduling, emphasizing the ways in which these technologies enhance operational efficiencies. Chapter 4 scrutinizes the use AI in EHRs, improving data administration and patient treatment quality. Chapter 5 delves into the profound influence of AI on medical imaging and diagnostics, while Chapter 6 examines the use of AI and predictive analytics in healthcare, namely, evaluating risks and detecting diseases at an early stage. Chapter 7 studies the impact of AI on resource allocation and optimization in hospitals. It explores how AI technology may improve the efficiency of resource distribution in healthcare facilities. Chapter 8 focuses on the improvement of clinical decision support systems using AI. It demonstrates how AI can assist in making more precise and informed decisions in clinical settings.

    Section 3 specifically addresses Ethical Considerations and Challenges. Chapters 9 through 11 of the book discuss the wider consequences and difficulties associated with implementing AI in healthcare. Chapter 9 centers on using AI in disease detection, demonstrating how AI improves the effectiveness and precision of medical diagnostics. In Chapter 10, the book explores the impact of AI on healthcare finance and billing, specifically focusing on how it can simplify administrative duties and enhance financial processes. Chapter 11 examines the ethical implications of AI in healthcare. It explores the difficulties, worries about privacy, and the necessity of openness and responsibility in using AI. In addition, Section 4 which includes the concluding chapters, namely, Chapters 12 and 13, focus on envisioning the future and surmounting existing obstacles. Chapter 12 delineates the impediments to implementing AI in the healthcare sector and offers tactics to surmount these challenges. The book concludes with Chapter 13, which summarizes the debates and emphasizes the pivotal role of AI in transforming hospital administration.

Conclusion

This chapter concludes by reiterating the significant role of AI in transforming hospital administration. It has set forth a detailed roadmap of the book's content, highlighting how each subsequent chapter will delve into specific AI applications and their impacts on healthcare management. The discussion emphasizes AI's ability to address traditional hospital challenges, such as inefficient resource allocation and patient management. It also points out the necessity for ongoing research, ethical considerations, and strategic implementation to fully leverage AI's potential. This foundational chapter not only introduces readers to the concept of AI in hospital administration but also prepares them for a deeper exploration of its practical applications throughout the book, ultimately demonstrating how AI is pivotal in shaping the future of healthcare.

References

Harry, A. (2023). The Future of Medicine: Harnessing the Power of AI for Revolutionizing Healthcare. *International Journal of Multidisciplinary Sciences and Arts*, 2(1), 36–47.

Le, D.N., Van Le, C., Tromp, J.G. and Nguyen, G.N. (Eds.). (2018). *Emerging Technologies for Health and Medicine: Virtual Reality, Augmented Reality, Artificial Intelligence, Internet of Things, Robotics, Industry 4.0*. John Wiley and Sons.

Li, J.P.O., Liu, H., Ting, D.S., Jeon, S., Chan, R.P., Kim, J.E., ... and Ting, D.S. (2021). Digital technology, tele-medicine, and artificial intelligence in ophthalmology: A global perspective. *Progress in Retinal and Eye Research*, 82, 100900.

Malmir, B., Amini, M., and Chang, S.I. (2017). A medical decision support system for disease diagnosis under uncertainty. *Expert Systems with Applications*, 88, 95–108. Mhlanga, D. (2024). Generative AI for Emerging Researchers: The Promises, Ethics, and Risks. *Ethics, and Risks* (February 24). SSRN.

Mhlanga, D. (2023a). Artificial Intelligence in Elderly Care: Navigating Ethical and Responsible AI Adoption for Seniors. *SSRN* (January), 4675564.

Mhlanga, D. (2023b). Financial Technology, Artificial Intelligence, and the Health Sector: Lessons We are Learning on Good Health and Well-Being. In: *FinTech and Artificial Intelligence for Sustainable Development: The Role of Smart Technologies in Achieving Development Goals* (pp. 145–170). Cham: Springer Nature Switzerland.

Mhlanga, D. (2023c). FinTech and Financial Inclusion: Application of AI to the Problem of Financial Exclusion What Are the Challenges. In: *FinTech and Artificial Intelligence for Sustainable Development*. Sustainable Development Goals Series. Cham: Palgrave Macmillan. https://doi.org/10.1007/978-3-031-37776-1_14.

Mhlanga, D. (2022). Human-centered artificial intelligence: The superlative approach to achieve sustainable development goals in the fourth industrial revolution. *Sustainability*, 14(13), 7804.

Mhlanga, D. (2021). A Dynamic Analysis of the Demand for Health Care in Post-Apartheid South Africa. *Nursing Reports*, 11(02), 484–94.

Yan, H., Jiang, Y., Zheng, J., Peng, C. and Li, Q. (2006). A multilayer perceptron-based medical decision support system for heart disease diagnosis. *Expert Systems with Applications*, 30(2), 272–81.

Yaqoob, I., Salah, K., Jayaraman, R. and Al-Hammadi, Y. (2021). Blockchain for healthcare data management: Opportunities, challenges, and future recommendations. *Neural Computing and Applications*, 1–16.

2 | Basics of Artificial Intelligence

The chapter will include an overview of and comprehensively examine the fundamental principles of artificial intelligence (AI), machine learning, deep learning, and natural language processing. This will elucidate crucial terminology and establish a solid foundation for understanding the subsequent parts of the book. Readers will thoroughly understand how these advanced technologies work and their importance in hospital administration. This chapter will explore the core principles, methodology, and applications of AI in healthcare. It will establish the groundwork for a comprehensive examination of the significance and potential of AI in transforming hospital management and enhancing patient outcomes.

Introduction

In this chapter, we aim to lay the groundwork for our inquiry into artificial intelligence (AI) by introducing the reader to the core concepts, theories, and methods underpinning AI as a scientific and technical discipline. The development of AI, often associated with the goal of replicating human intellect, is driven by the need to create computational systems capable of performing activities that typically require human cognition (Kasap, 2021; Mhlanga, 2023). The initial objective of AI, which focused on functionalism, has now shifted to highlight the progress, interaction, and emotional dimensions of cognitive systems (Genesereth and Nilsson, 2012). Despite challenges and ethical considerations, AI has been applied in various industries, including manufacturing, healthcare, and finance (Kasap, 2021). The primary goal of AI was to create artificial beings with capabilities similar to those of humans (Langley, 2006: Mhlanga, 2020, 2022). Over the years, significant progress has been made in expert performance and understanding human cognition (Leake, 2004). However, the subdivision of subfields within the AI field has led academics to take a narrow and precise approach (Langley, 2006; Mhlanga, 2021). The emergence of the AI revolution, driven by machine learning and big data, has led to the development of AI systems that have smoothly blended into our daily lives (Burchardt, 2021). The concept of AI has its roots in human desires and has been shaped by logical and intellectual pursuits (Trzęsicki, 2020).

These tasks range from simple pattern recognition to complex decision-making processes. However, the key to understanding AI lies in a problem statement that poses a twofold challenge and provides direction to researchers and practitioners: How can we create machines that not only mimic human intelligence but also improve upon it, thereby making valuable contributions to advancements in various fields such as healthcare, education, and environmental sustainability? To address this matter, this chapter explores the fundamental concepts of AI, starting with its definition and historical context, and then delving into an examination of the several types of AI systems, ranging from narrow or weak AI to general or strong AI. We will examine the underlying principles that enable machines to acquire knowledge from data, make judgments, and improve their performance over time. Specifically, we will focus on machine learning, deep learning, and neural networks. Furthermore, the chapter will familiarize the reader with the ethical considerations and societal impacts of AI, highlighting the importance of responsible innovation and the role of AI in shaping our future.

This chapter aims to elucidate AI by building a solid foundation, fostering curiosity, and facilitating a deeper understanding of its potential and limitations. Let us commence this journey together as we explore the fascinating domain of AI. We should undertake this exploration with a receptive and perceptive mindset, striving for a future in which technology and humanity seamlessly integrate. Burgsteiner et al. (2016) said that AI has already become an integral part of our everyday life, demonstrated by intelligent household appliances, smartphones, Google, Siri, and AI in computer games. Although AI-based services and products are well-known to most people, just a few are knowledgeable about the underlying technology that drives them. This chapter also explores the widespread misconceptions and false beliefs around AI, providing a clear and unbiased viewpoint on its potential and limitations. We analyze the impact of AI on many industries, such as healthcare and banking, and also explore the ethical considerations linked to these advancements. By the end of this chapter, you will have a thorough understanding of the fundamental principles of AI. This will allow you to completely understand its wonders and efficiently navigate its challenges.

Artificial Intelligence

Bajwa et al. (2023) define artificial intelligence (AI) as "the discipline that concentrates on advancing computers that employ algorithms or rules to replicate human cognitive capabilities, such as learning and problem-solving". AI systems are created to predict and tackle obstacles via deliberate, intelligent, and flexible actions. One significant advantage of AI is its ability to effectively evaluate vast quantities of intricate and varied data, facilitating the detection of patterns and correlations. AI has the ability to summarize a patient's complete health record into a single data point that suggests a likely diagnosis, thereby greatly aiding medical personnel in saving time (Mhlanga, 2020, 2021). Furthermore, AI systems can adapt and operate independently, allowing them to develop and improve their performance when exposed to novel information. The term "artificial intelligence" embraces a wide array of technologies, rather than being restricted to a single tool. The distinct subdomains of "machine learning" and "deep learning" make individual or collective contributions to the progress of intelligent systems.

Historical Overview of AI

The historical overview of AI encompasses a number of decades, each of which is characterized by the occurrence of major moments, pioneering research, and substantial advancements.

The Genesis of AI (1940s–1950s)

The emergence of AI in the 1940s–1950s marked a crucial time that laid the groundwork for the development of computational theories and technologies with the goal of replicating human intelligence. This period was characterized by the shift from abstract ideas to the early real-world applications of machines that can carry out tasks that usually necessitate human intelligence. Through their innovative and influential work, the pioneers of this era established the fundamental principles of AI in terms of philosophy, mathematics, and engineering, which form the basis of our current understanding of the field. Alan Turing, a British mathematician, logician, and computer scientist, had a significant role in the early advancement of AI. Turing is widely recognized and praised for his fundamental contributions to the science of computation and his crucial involvement in deciphering the Enigma code during World War II. Nevertheless, one of his most long-lasting contributions is his investigation into the capacity of robots to engage in cognitive processes. In his 1950 work titled "Computing Machinery and Intelligence", Turing proposed that a machine may be considered capable of thinking if it could converse with a human without the human being aware that they were communicating with a machine. The Turing Test is a concept that has subsequently become a fundamental element in talks about AI and its capacities.

The Turing Test served as more than just a theoretical concept; it established a concrete objective for advancing AI research and development. Turing's research proposed that the capacity of a machine to imitate human intelligence could be methodically evaluated and quantified, offering a distinct goal for early AI investigations. This concept ignited a surge of ingenuity and exploration in the domain. The Turing Test, introduced by Alan Turing, has played a crucial role in stimulating AI research and advancement, offering a distinct goal for the discipline (Korukonda, 2003). It has been utilized in many settings, such as computer gaming bots (Hingston, 2009) and healthcare (Ashrafian, 2015). Nevertheless, the test has faced criticism due to its shortcomings, including its emphasis on verbal responses (Michie, 1993) and its failure to fully encompass the intricacies of human intelligence (Maguire, 2015). Notwithstanding these concerns, the test remains a fundamental benchmark in AI assessment (Brodić, 2019) and is anticipated to influence the trajectory of AI development persistently (French, 2000).

In addition to Turing, the period of the 1940s–1950s witnessed several notable progressions that had a role in the emergence of AI. The emergence of the first electronic computers, such as the Electronic Numerical Integrator and Computer (ENIAC) and the Electronic Delay Storage Automatic Calculator

(EDSAC), facilitated the initiation of investigations into computational methods for intelligence. These machines were pioneers in showcasing the feasibility of automating intricate computations and operations, thereby establishing the foundation for future AI systems. Moreover, during this period, interdisciplinary cooperation was notable between mathematicians, psychologists, engineers, and other scientists. This collaboration resulted in the creation of initial neural network models. These models aimed to replicate the neurological processes of the human brain, providing insights into the potential design of machines capable of learning and adapting. The McCulloch-Pitts neuron model, introduced by Warren McCulloch and Walter Pitts in 1943, was a simplified mathematical representation of biological neurons. This model established a theoretical basis for comprehending the utilization of networks consisting of artificial neurons to perform logical operations, hence impacting subsequent investigations in neural networks and machine learning.

The initial investigations into AI in the 1940s–1950s were accompanied by philosophical discussions over the essence of intelligence and awareness, the capacity of computers to acquire these attributes, and the moral consequences of developing intelligent robots. These discussions persist in lasting impacting current AI research and conversations. To summarize, the emergence of AI in the 1940s–1950s was a time characterized by innovative concepts and fundamental advancements. Pioneers such as Alan Turing laid the groundwork for the continuous study of AI and the development of the first computers. This era laid the foundation for the extensive and diverse area of AI, including various disciplines and impacting numerous elements of society and technology.

The Birth of AI as a Field (1956)

The emergence of AI as a discipline in 1956 was a significant milestone in the technological landscape, signifying the shift of AI from the realms of imagination and conjecture to a well-defined field of scientific investigation. The Dartmouth Conference, a gathering of eminent intellectuals, served as a symbol for this transformation, as it convened to explore the capacity of machines to imitate human intelligence. The symposium, organized by John McCarthy, Marvin Minsky, Nathaniel Rochester, and Claude Shannon, is where the phrase "Artificial Intelligence" was first introduced. These four persons played a crucial role in establishing the fundamental principles for the future of AI. The Dartmouth Conference commenced with an audacious and sanguine agenda. The conference proposal, authored by McCarthy and his colleagues, suggested that it is theoretically possible to provide such detailed descriptions of all aspects of learning and intelligence that a machine can replicate. The optimism was driven by the recent progress in computational machinery and a growing comprehension of how logic could be utilized to address intricate difficulties. The conference participants believed that they were on the verge of a significant development that would enable machines to imitate human cognitive capabilities within a single generation.

The Dartmouth Conference had a major impact by creating a community of researchers committed to investigating AI's potential. This community subsequently made numerous crucial discoveries in the subsequent decades. For instance, within the field of machine learning, a branch of AI that concentrates on creating algorithms that allow computers to learn from data and make predictions or judgments, the conference established the foundation for upcoming advancements. During this era, there were also conceptualizations of early versions of neural networks, which are systems designed to imitate the human brain's cognitive processes in analyzing and processing information. Another significant domain that experienced progress following the Dartmouth Conference was natural language processing (NLP), a field of AI that concentrates on the interaction between computers and humans through natural language. The initial discussions focused on the ability of machines to comprehend and analyze human languages, which eventually led to the creation of early chatbots and translation systems. The field of robotics also experienced positive outcomes due to the fundamental research conducted during the Dartmouth Conference. The concept that machines possess the ability to think and act independently has resulted in notable progress in robotics. This encompasses the advancement of robotic appendages for industrial production, self-driving vehicles, and using robots such as the Mars Rovers for space exploration. The progress of autonomous robots has greatly enhanced many domains, such as manufacturing, space exploration, and daily existence (Nesnas, 2021). These robots can autonomously think and act, allowing them to carry out intricate tasks, including navigating across great distances in situations that lack structure (Chatila, 1998). Space exploration has greatly contributed to scientific advancements and has served as a source of inspiration for future generations (Chien, 2017). Intelligent robots have enhanced efficiency and safety in the manufacturing industry (Gruver 1994). Nevertheless, the growing independence of robots gives rise to ethical and moral quandaries and the possibility of employment displacement (Finkelstein, 2022).

Despite the initial optimism, the progress of AI has been characterized by cycles of notable gains followed by periods of decreased funding and interest, commonly referred to as "AI winters". Despite these limitations, the impact of the Dartmouth Conference is unquestionable. It served as the catalyst that propelled AI from an abstract concept to a well-defined area of research, paving the way for creating technologies that have profoundly impacted society. The impact of AI is pervasive, ranging from voice-activated assistants to recommendation systems in e-commerce. This influence can be traced back to the vision and ambition of the early pioneers at Dartmouth in 1956.

The Golden Years and Early Successes (1956–1974)

The time span from 1956 to 1974 is commonly considered as the golden era of AI, characterized by first achievements and fervent research that established the foundation for the discipline. This era succeeded the Dartmouth Conference in

1956, a crucial event where a consortium of scientists, including John McCarthy, Marvin Minsky, Nathaniel Rochester, and Claude Shannon, convened to deliberate on the capacity of machines to replicate all facets of learning and other attributes of intelligence. Their vision ignited a surge in AI research, resulting in notable progress and the development of pioneering systems that demonstrated the potential of AI. During this period, AI research predominantly concentrated on creating algorithms capable of executing tasks that demanded intellect at a level comparable to that of humans. These tasks included solving algebraic problems, demonstrating theorems in geometry, and comprehending spoken language. The initial accomplishments were mostly attained through rule-based methodologies, in which the functioning of AI systems was regulated by an extensive collection of rules and decision trees. This methodology sought to replicate human intelligence by directly incorporating expert knowledge and logical reasoning abilities into the program.

An outstanding accomplishment of this time period was the creation of ELIZA, computer software for NLP, by Joseph Weizenbaum in the mid-1960s. ELIZA was created to imitate a conversation with a psychiatrist, involving users in a dialogue that replicated human-like replies. ELIZA utilized pattern matching and replacement methodology to assess the user's input and generate responses according to a predefined script. Despite being simple, ELIZA was capable of generating an illusion of comprehension and compassion, captivating users and showcasing the capacity of computers to analyze and engage in communication using human language. During this period, a significant example was the General Problem Solver (GPS), created by Allen Newell, Cliff Shaw, and Herbert A. Simon. GPS aimed to simulate human problem-solving methods using a computer program. The program employed means-ends analysis, a technique that involved identifying disparities between the current and desired states and applying a sequence of operators to minimize these disparities. GPS was a multifaceted system that could be utilized for a range of purposes, including solving puzzles such as the Tower of Hanoi and demonstrating mathematical theorems. Within the realm of theorem proving, the Logic Theorist, also created by Newell, Shaw, and Simon, was another significant milestone. This application was specifically developed to demonstrate mathematical theorems by utilizing symbolic logic, successfully emulating the cognitive processes of a human mathematician. The Logic Theorist effectively demonstrated the computer's ability to engage in abstract thinking by proving multiple theorems from Principia Mathematica, a fundamental text in mathematical logic. The initial achievements in AI were crucial in showcasing the possibility of machines carrying out intelligent activities, establishing the groundwork for future progress. Their impact generated significant interest and hope in the possibilities of AI, resulting in a rise in funding and research endeavors. Nevertheless, the dependence on rule-based methods also exposed certain constraints, such as the challenge of capturing intricate human knowledge and the inefficiency of handling extensive decision **trees.** As a result, alternative approaches were investigated in the following years.

The AI Winters (1974–1980 and 1987–1993)

The progress of AI over the latter half of the 20th century encountered various obstacles. The field saw two notable periods of stagnation and disappointment, popularly known as the "AI winters". During 1974–1980 and 1987–1993, there was a significant decrease in funding, interest, and optimism in AI research and development. The decline in performance was mostly ascribed to the excessive promises and inadequate delivery of AI capabilities, resulting in scepticism and reassessment of methodologies in the field. The initial AI winter, which occurred in the mid-1970s, directly resulted from the exaggerated expectations established in the preceding decades. In the early stages of AI research, the creation of programs such as ELIZA and the General Problem Solver gave the impression that machines with human-like reasoning and communication abilities were on the verge of being developed. Nevertheless, when the intricacy and constraints of these systems based on rules became evident, it became clear that the ambitious objectives of AI were still far from being accomplished. A pivotal moment occurred in 1973 when the British government commissioned the Lighthill Report to evaluate the status of AI. The report strongly criticized the advancements made in AI, emphasizing the inability to fulfill the ambitious claims of the field. As a result, there have been significant reductions in financing for AI research in the UK, with similar decreases in support happening elsewhere.

During the initial period of decline in AI, numerous promising AI projects were put on hold, and researchers encountered challenges in securing financial support for their work. In the 1980s, the focus switched to goals that were more attainable and could be accomplished in the short term, such as creating expert systems. These systems, which aim to imitate the decision-making capabilities of human experts in specialized fields, take a more limited approach to AI. They prioritize practical uses instead of trying to replicate general intelligence. The second AI winter between 1987–1993 was triggered by several variables, one of which was the constraints of expert systems. Although they achieved initial success, these systems proved costly to create, challenging to upkeep, and constrained in their ability to adapt and scale. The enthusiasm surrounding AI in the early 1980s resulted in substantial financial commitments, particularly in expert systems. However, as the decade advanced, the limitations of these technologies became apparent. The unfulfiled potential of AI led to a decrease in financial support from both governmental and corporate entities, resulting in a period of stagnation in the field.

Additionally, in the late 1980s, the Lisp machine market experienced a decline, resulting in the downfall of specialzsed hardware specifically built to execute the Lisp programming language efficiently. This hardware was strongly linked to the advancement of AI. The advancement of more affordable and advanced general-purpose computing hardware rendered these specialized machines obsolete, exacerbating the decline in the AI industry. Throughout these winters, the area of AI saw substantial self-reflection and reassessment. Researchers initiated investigations into alternative methodologies, including neural networks and machine learning, which established the foundation for the revival of AI in the late 1990s and early 21st century. These periods of decreased funding and diminished interest were a stark reminder of the difficulties in developing intelligent machines, prompting the field to pursue more practical objectives and approaches. Although AI research and development faced challenges during the AI winters, the knowledge gained has played a crucial role in shaping the current state of AI. These experiences have emphasized the significance of setting realistic goals and maintaining a well-rounded understanding of the capabilities and constraints of AI technologies. The AI winters, marked by intervals of diminished funding and confidence, have played a crucial role in establishing the present AI ecosystem. The need to establish attainable goals and keep a well-rounded viewpoint regarding the capabilities and constraints of AI technology has been emphasized (Hagendorff, 2019: Mitchell, 2021). The problems and constraints of AI, such as methodological errors, social context, and technical restraints, have been important lessons derived from these times (Hagendorff, 2019). Udupa (2021) has emphasizd the necessity of ethical and responsible advancement and use of AI, along with the significance of diversity and accountability in AI ethics principles. Integrating AI research into clinical practice, namely in healthcare, has been recognized as a significant obstacle that necessitates rigorous review, performance measures, and regulation (Kelly, 2019). Russell (2015) has stressed the significance of ensuring the resilience and positive impact of AI systems and the necessity for interdisciplinary study in this field. Shneiderman (2020) emphasized the importance of adopting a human-centered approach in AI research, specifically emphasizing the significance of emulation and application. A 20-year community roadmap (Gil, 2021) has described the future of AI research and development, emphasizing the necessity for a profound transition and continuous investment. Finally, the discourse has revolved around the chronicles of AI and its capacity to avert another period of stagnation, emphasizing the acquisition of knowledge from previous experiences and the projection of forthcoming developments (Toosi, 2021).

The Emergence of Machine Learning (1980s–Present)

The renaissance of AI was driven by the emergence of machine learning (ML), which transformed the approach from rule-based to data-driven methodologies. Geoffrey Hinton, Yann LeCun, and Yoshua Bengio are notable figures who established the fundamental principles of deep learning, a specific branch of ML. Deep learning has played a significant role in recent AI advancements. Neural networks have greatly advanced picture and audio recognition, NLP, and autonomous vehicles through deep learning techniques. The revival of AI in recent decades may primarily be credited to the rise and development of ML, signifying a fundamental change from conventional rule-based systems to more flexible, data-driven methodologies. This transformation commenced in earnest during the 1980s and has persistently evolved, profoundly influencing the terrain of AI research up to the present day.

ML is creating algorithms that allow computers to learn from data and use that knowledge to make predictions or judgments. This technique starkly contrasts the previous rule-based systems, which necessitated explicit instructions from programmers for every possible case. The shortcomings of rule-based systems became apparent as the tasks became more complicated, requiring a more adaptable and efficient approach to information processing and problem-solving. The foundation for this transition was established by trailblazers in the domain, including Geoffrey Hinton, Yann LeCun, and Yoshua Bengio, whose efforts have played a crucial role in advancing deep learning, a subset of ML. Deep learning utilizes neural networks that consist of multiple layers (thus the term 'deep') to analyze extensive quantities of data. These neural networks are designed based on the structure and function of the human brain. They can learn hierarchical representations of data, making them highly successful for tasks that include complicated patterns and datasets. The emergence of deep learning has catalyzed significant breakthroughs in various disciplines of AI. Deep learning systems in picture identification have demonstrated exceptional accuracy rates, surpassing human ability in certain instances. One instance of this is the advancement of convolutional neural networks (CNNs), a category of complex neural networks, which are particularly efficient in handling pixel input and are extensively employed in facial recognition systems, medical image analysis, and several other applications.

Deep learning has made great progress in the field of speech recognition. Recurrent neural networks (RNNs), which belong to a different category of neural networks, have demonstrated exceptional ability in processing sequential input, such as audio or text. As a result, there has been progress in creating speech recognition algorithms that are more precise and effective. These systems provide the foundation for voice-activated assistants, now found in smartphones, smart speakers, and other gadgets everywhere. Deep learning approaches have significantly enhanced the ability of machines to comprehend and interpret human language, leading to substantial advancements in NLP. These advancements have allowed for more powerful chatbots, improved machine translation systems, and sophisticated sentiment analysis tools. As a result, the connection between people and robots has been greatly strengthened. ML is also applied in creating self-driving cars, which is a significant use case. ML algorithms may utilize data from several sensors and cameras to enable vehicles to identify impediments, understand traffic signals, and make judgments. This advancement contributes to the development of transportation systems that are safer and more efficient. The progression of ML from the 1980s to the present has been characterized by technological improvements and an increasing acknowledgement of its capacity to revolutionize industry, society, and everyday existence. As researchers further investigate novel techniques and uses, the impact of ML and its deep learning subset is set to grow, bringing about advancements and transforming the future of AI.

The Modern Era of AI (2010s–Present)

Over the past ten years, there has been a significant increase in the powers and uses of AI. The proliferation of extensive datasets, enhanced processing capabilities, and advancements in deep learning have resulted in notable accomplishments. AI systems currently surpass human performance in some domains, including intricate game playing (such as Go and chess), language translation, and medical diagnosis. The influence of AI is seen in various sectors, including healthcare, banking, transportation, and entertainment. The Modern Era of AI, which began in the 2010s and continues to the present, signifies a notable advancement and widespread adoption of AI technologies. This period is distinguished by three main factors contributing to the expansion of AI: the accessibility of extensive datasets, a large rise in computer capacity, and notable progress in deep learning techniques.

1. Availability of Large Datasets

In the digital age, there is a constant and unprecedented generation and collection of data. Massive datasets are generated through the utilization of social media platforms, internet transactions, and IoT (Internet of Things) devices. These datasets are essential for training AI models, allowing them to acquire knowledge and enhance their performance progressively. Image recognition artificial intelligence (AI) has substantially profited from datasets comprising millions of labelled photos. These datasets have enabled the systems to attain and even exceed human-level accuracy in the identification and categorization of objects inside images.

2. Increased Computational Power

Over the past ten years, there has been a significant rise in processing power, primarily due to developments in hardware technologies like GPUs (Graphics Processing Units) and TPUs (Tensor Processing Units). These specialized processors excel in managing the simultaneous processing demands of deep learning algorithms, greatly decreasing the time required to train intricate AI models. The significant increase in computer capacity has enabled handling more complex jobs and larger datasets than possible. For example, the creation of GPT-3, which is currently one of the biggest and most advanced language models, was made achievable by utilizing these improvements in computer infrastructure. The advancement of GPT-3, a robust language model, was facilitated by the significant increase in computer capacity, allowing for processing larger datasets and more intricate tasks (Barlas, 2015). The transformer design, introduced by Staal in 2009, improved the model by enabling it to learn more intricate long-range connections. By including a sparsely activated mixture-of-experts' architecture, the GLaM language model was able to increase its capacity and decrease training costs (Du, 2021, 2024). The growing need for CPU capacity in language processing jobs is fueled by the vast quantity of textual data (Agerri and Rodrigo, 2015). The capabilities of extensive language models such as GPT-3 in generating and manipulating material have been investigated, along with the ethical considerations and their misuse (Saravanan, 2022).

3. Advances in Deep Learning

Deep learning, a subset of ML, has played a crucial role in the current revolution of AI. Neural networks, specifically deep neural networks, have demonstrated remarkable efficacy in acquiring knowledge from extensive datasets. These networks have the ability to autonomously identify the necessary representations for detecting features or classifying, without requiring explicit programming for particular tasks. This talent has resulted in significant advancements in multiple fields. For instance, in the realm of Complex Games, AI systems like AlphaGo have triumphed over world champions in games like Go, a game that was previously seen as an impossible obstacle because of its great complexity and the need for strategic depth. Moreover, AI has demonstrated exceptional proficiency in chess and poker, demonstrating its capacity to navigate predictable and uncertain contexts.

Language Translation: Neural machine translation systems have significantly enhanced the caliber of automated language translation, enabling more authentic and precise translations. AI-powered tools such as Google Translate offer immediate translation in multiple languages, thereby overcoming linguistic obstacles and facilitating worldwide collaboration.

Medical Diagnosis: Artificial intelligence (AI) is advancing in the field of healthcare and can diagnose diseases with a level of accuracy comparable to, and often even exceeds, that of human professionals. AI-driven diagnostic systems can examine medical pictures, such as X-rays or MRIs, to identify abnormalities such as tumors or fractures. In certain instances, these technologies have exhibited the capacity to detect illnesses at earlier stages than human doctors, which could potentially enhance patient outcomes.

The Modern Era of AI is characterized by swift progressions that have broadened the potential of what AI can accomplish. The combination of extensive datasets, enhanced processing capabilities, and deep learning techniques has not only expedited the advancement of AI but has also expanded its utilization across other sectors, marking the advent of a new era of innovation and change.

Core Technologies and Algorithms

Developing a comprehensive understanding of the core technologies and algorithms in AI is crucial for grasping how AI systems work and the scope of their applications. Below, we delve into ML, deep learning, NLP, and robotics, highlighting their foundational principles, typical applications, and current limitations.

Machine Learning (ML)

Machine Learning (ML) stands at the forefront of advancements in AI, embodying a powerful suite of techniques that enable computers to learn from data, make predictions, and support decision-making processes across various domains. This field leverages algorithms and statistical models to allow machines to improve their performance on a specific task with experience, learning from past data to predict future events or understand complex patterns.

Supervised Learning

Supervised learning is one of the pillars of ML, characterized by its use of labeled datasets to train algorithms. These datasets consist of input-output pairs, where the input data is tagged with the correct output. The goal of supervised learning is to train a model on this data to accurately predict the output for new, unseen inputs. Supervised learning applications are vast, ranging from email filtering systems that distinguish between spam and non-spam messages to voice recognition systems that convert spoken words into text. Consider a real estate app that estimates house prices based on features like location, size, and the number of bedrooms. The app uses a supervised learning algorithm trained on a dataset of houses with known prices (labels). By learning the relationship between house features and prices, the algorithm can predict the price of a new house listing.

Unsupervised Learning

Unlike supervised learning, unsupervised learning algorithms deal with unlabeled data. These algorithms aim to identify inherent patterns or structures within the data without the guidance of a specific output variable. Clustering and dimensionality reduction are common techniques used in unsupervised learning. Clustering involves grouping data points that are similar to each other, while dimensionality reduction focuses on simplifying the data without losing its essential characteristics. For example, a music streaming service uses unsupervised learning to group songs into different genres without pre-labeled genre information. The algorithm analyzes the features of each song, such as tempo, beat, and lyrics, to cluster them into genres, helping in personalized music recommendations.

Reinforcement Learning

Reinforcement learning is distinct from both supervised and unsupervised learning. It involves training algorithms to make decisions by interacting with an environment. The algorithm, or agent, learns to achieve a goal in an uncertain, potentially complex environment by trial and error, receiving rewards or penalties for actions. It's about learning what actions to take and when to take them to maximise some notion of cumulative reward. Robotics is a field where reinforcement learning has been successfully applied. A robot learning to navigate through a maze can use reinforcement learning to make decisions at each intersection it encounters. The robot receives positive feedback when it moves closer to the exit and negative feedback when it hits a wall or takes a longer path, thus learning the optimal route through trial and error.

ML's capacity to improve automatically through experience makes it a cornerstone of AI. Its applications span numerous fields, from healthcare, where it helps diagnose diseases and suggest treatments, to finance, where it is used for credit scoring and algorithmic trading. As data continues to grow in volume and complexity, the role of ML in extracting value and insights from this data will only become more pivotal, driving innovation and efficiency across industries. Current limitations are that it requires large amounts of labeled data for supervised learning. Difficulty in interpreting the models, especially in unsupervised learning. Reinforcement learning can be computationally expensive and slow to converge.

Deep Learning (DL)

Fundamental Principles: Deep learning (DL) is a subset of ML based on ANNs with representation learning. These neural networks have multiple layers (hence, 'deep') that can learn increasingly abstract features from data. DL represents a revolutionary approach to AI, particularly in how machines learn and make decisions. At its core, DL is a subset of ML, which itself is a subset of AI. The fundamental principles of DL are rooted in its architecture—artificial neural networks (ANNs) designed to simulate how human brains operate, albeit in a simplified manner. These networks are 'deep' because they consist of multiple layers of nodes or neurons, each capable of learning different aspects of the data it processes.

The Architecture of Deep Learning

The architecture of DL is inspired by the biological neural networks in the human brain. An ANN consists of input, hidden, and output layers. The input layer receives the data, the hidden layers process the data through various neurons and functions, and the output layer produces the final result or prediction. The 'deep' in DL refers to multiple hidden layers that allow these networks to learn complex patterns in large datasets. In image recognition, an input layer might first identify basic features such as edges and colors. Subsequent layers might recognize more complex features like shapes or specific objects (e.g., faces, cars). When the information reaches the output layer, the network can classify the image with remarkable accuracy. For instance, based on the features it has learned, a DL model trained on a dataset of animal photos can accurately identify a given image as that of a specific animal, such as a dog or a cat.

Representation Learning

One of the key principles of DL is representation learning. This means the system can automatically discover the representations needed for feature detection or classification directly from raw data. This contrasts with traditional ML techniques, which often require manual feature extraction. DL, a subset of ML, has revolutionized the field by enabling the automatic discovery of representations from raw data, eliminating the need for manual feature extraction (Goodfellow, 2020). This is particularly evident in text mining, where DL has successfully automatically learned feature representations from big data (Liang, 2017). The practicality and learning ability of DL, compared to traditional methods, have made it increasingly popular (Du, 2018). The development of data representation learning, from traditional feature learning to DL, has been reviewed, highlighting the application of deep architectures in tasks such as image classification and object detection (Zhong, 2020). DL has also shown impressive performance in object recognition, detection, and segmentation, outperforming conventional computer vision systems (Xu, 2021). The technique's ability to automatically learn hierarchical representations in deep architectures for classification has been emphasized (Firdaus, 2024). In the context of text categorization, unsupervised deep feature representation methods have been compared, with a focus on their application in text clustering (Wang, 2019). Lastly, DL has been applied to image classification, with preliminary results showing its potential in developing robust classification systems (McCoppin, 2014; Mhlanga, 2024). In speech recognition, DL models process raw audio clips and learn to recognize speech patterns, such as phonemes and words, without needing explicit instructions on what sound features to pay attention to. Over time, these models can transcribe spoken language into text with high accuracy, understanding different accents, tones, and even background noise.

The Power of Deep Learning

The effectiveness of DL comes from its ability to process and learn from enormous amounts of data. The more data the model is exposed to, the better it can perform. This capacity to improve with data, coupled with the increasing availability of large datasets and powerful computing resources, has led to significant advancements in computer vision, NLP, and autonomous vehicles. Autonomous vehicles use deep learning to process the massive influx of sensory data from their environment, allowing them to make decisions in real-time. The models learn to recognize traffic signs, pedestrians, other vehicles, and road conditions, enabling these vehicles to navigate safely through complex environments. DL's multilayered approach and ability to learn from large datasets have made it a cornerstone of modern AI. Its applications, from enhancing computer vision to enabling real-time speech recognition and autonomous navigation, demonstrate the transformative potential of DL across various sectors.

Natural Language Processing (NLP)

Fundamental Principles: NLP enables computers to understand, interpret, and generate human language. This involves speech recognition, sentiment analysis, and language translation. NLP represents a critical and vibrant field within AI and computational linguistics, focusing on bridging the gap between human communication and computer understanding. At its core, NLP aims to enable computers to understand and interpret human language and generate responses in a manner that mimics human-like interactions. This capability opens up many applications and possibilities across various sectors, including healthcare, education, customer service, and many more.

Understanding and Interpretation

One of the fundamental principles of NLP is enabling machines to understand and interpret human language. This process involves several key tasks, such as speech recognition, parsing, and semantic analysis.

Speech Recognition: This is the process of converting spoken words into text. Voice-activated assistants like Siri and Alexa are prime examples of speech recognition technologies. These systems are trained on vast datasets of spoken language, allowing them to recognize and interpret speech from users with diverse accents and patterns.

Parsing: Parsing involves analyzing the grammatical structure of sentences to understand the relationships between words. For instance, parsing helps differentiate between the subject and object in the sentence "The cat chased the mouse", ensuring that the machine understands who is doing the chasing.

Semantic Analysis: This goes beyond the literal interpretation of words to understand their meaning within the context of the sentence. For example, in the sentence "I left my heart in San Francisco", semantic analysis helps the machine understand that the speaker is expressing fondness for San Francisco, rather than implying a literal action.

Sentiment Analysis

Sentiment analysis is another critical task within NLP, enabling computers to identify and categorize opinions expressed in text. This is particularly useful in social media monitoring, market research, and customer service, where understanding public sentiment is crucial. For example, companies use sentiment analysis to gauge customer opinions on products and services by analyzing reviews and social media posts. This helps in identifying trends, improving products, and addressing customer concerns more effectively.

Language Translation: This is perhaps one of NLP's most challenging yet impactful applications. It involves converting text or speech from one language to another while preserving the meaning and context. Services like Google Translate demonstrate the capabilities and challenges of language translation, enabling users to communicate across language barriers but sometimes struggling with idiomatic expressions or context-specific meanings. Despite significant advancements, NLP faces challenges such as understanding context, idiomatic expressions, and the nuances of human language. Future directions in NLP research focus on improving context awareness, handling diverse languages and dialects more effectively, and making NLP models more efficient and accessible. The integration of NLP in everyday applications continues to grow, transforming how we interact with technology. From simplifying tasks through voice commands to breaking down language barriers and providing insights from data, NLP remains at the forefront of creating more natural and intuitive interactions between humans and machines.

Robotics

Fundamental Principles: Robotics combines computer science and engineering to design, build, and operate robots. AI algorithms, particularly in ML and computer vision, enable robots to perform tasks autonomously or semi-autonomously. Robotics is an interdisciplinary field that merges principles from computer science and engineering to create robots capable of performing various tasks. At the heart of robotics is the goal to design, build, and operate robots that can assist humans in various contexts, ranging from industrial manufacturing to healthcare, and even space exploration. The integration of AI algorithms, especially those in ML and computer vision, has significantly advanced the capabilities of robots, enabling them to execute tasks with a level of autonomy previously unattainable.

Fundamental Principles

The foundational principles of robotics revolve around several key areas: mechanical design, electrical engineering, computer science, and AI. The mechanical design focuses on robots' physical structure and mobility, allowing them to navigate and manipulate their environment. Electrical engineering contributes to developing circuits and power systems that drive the robot's sensors, actuators, and processors. Computer science provides the algorithms that enable robots to process information, make decisions, and execute tasks. Lastly, AI, particularly ML and computer vision, endows robots with the ability to learn from their environment and adapt to new challenges, enhancing their autonomy.

Machine Learning in Robotics

ML, a subset of AI, plays a crucial role in robotics. It allows robots to learn from experience, improving their performance without explicit programming for every conceivable situation. For example, industrial robots in manufacturing plants use ML to optimize their movements for efficiency and precision. By analyzing data from previous tasks, these robots identify patterns and refine their algorithms to perform tasks faster and with fewer errors.

Computer Vision in Robotics

Computer vision is another critical robotics component, enabling robots to interpret and understand the world visually. This capability is essential for tasks requiring identification, classification, and object interaction. Autonomous vehicles, for instance, rely heavily on computer vision to navigate roads safely. They use cameras and sensors to detect obstacles, read traffic signs, and recognize pedestrians, making real-time decisions to avoid accidents.

Industrial Robotics: In automotive manufacturing, robots equipped with AI algorithms perform various tasks, such as welding, painting, and assembly. These robots can adapt to different car models and configurations, reducing production times and increasing safety by taking over dangerous tasks from human workers.

Medical Robotics: Surgical robots, such as the da Vinci Surgical System, utilize AI to assist surgeons with high precision and control. These robots can learn from surgical procedures, enhancing their performance and providing surgeons with real-time information to improve patient outcomes.

Exploration Robotics: NASA's Mars rovers, like Perseverance, are equipped with AI-driven systems that enable them to navigate the Martian terrain autonomously. They collect samples, analyze data, and send valuable information back to Earth, contributing significantly to our understanding of the Red Planet.

The fusion of computer science and engineering in robotics, bolstered by advancements in AI, has led to the creation of robots that can perform increasingly complex and varied tasks. Integrating ML and computer vision has been particularly transformative, enabling robots to learn from their environments and make decisions with minimal human intervention. These developments have wide-ranging implications, improving efficiency, safety, and capability across numerous industries and research areas. AI's core technologies and algorithms represent a vast and rapidly evolving field. While they offer transformative potential across numerous sectors, their limitations underline the importance of ongoing research and development. Addressing these challenges is crucial for the next generation of AI advancements.

Types of AI

Classifying AI systems into narrow AI, general AI, and artificial superintelligence (ASI) helps in understanding their capabilities, limitations, and potential future developments. This classification also sheds light on the evolutionary path of AI technology from performing specific tasks to potentially surpassing human intelligence.

Narrow AI (or Weak AI)

Capabilities: Narrow AI is designed to perform a specific task or a set of closely related tasks with intelligence. These systems are programmed to follow explicit rules and algorithms, enabling them to excel in their designated functions without possessing consciousness, emotion, or self-awareness. Voice Assistants like Siri and Alexa are prime examples of narrow AI, excelling in speech recognition and natural language understanding within a defined scope. Recommendation Systems used by Netflix or Amazon analyze user behavior and preferences to suggest movies, products, or services. Autonomous Vehicles use AI for navigation, obstacle detection, and decision-making within the driving context. However, it is limited to specific, predefined tasks. A weak AI lacks of adaptability to tasks or problems outside their programmed domain and does not possess general reasoning or problem-solving capabilities.

General AI (or Strong AI)

Capabilities: General AI refers to systems that possess the ability to understand, learn, and apply knowledge across a wide range of tasks, mimicking human intelligence. Such systems can generalize their learning to new tasks, showing flexibility and adaptability not seen in narrow AI. The development of general AI is a major goal in AI research, but it remains theoretical at this point. Achieving general AI would require breakthroughs in understanding human cognition, learning, and emotion. Such systems would revolutionize fields by performing any intellectual task that a human being can, with potential applications ranging from advanced problem-solving in science and engineering to creative arts. Currently, no existing systems meet the criteria for general AI. Ethical and safety considerations become significantly more complex, given the potential for such systems to make autonomous decisions.

Artificial Superintelligence (ASI)

ASI represents a hypothetical stage of AI where systems would surpass human intelligence across all fields, including creativity, general wisdom, and problem-solving. Such systems would be capable of self-improvement, leading to rapid advancements beyond human control or understanding. ASI remains a speculative concept, with debates around its feasibility and timeline for development. If achieved, it could lead to unprecedented changes in society, with both positive applications and significant risks. Potential applications could include solving complex global challenges, such as climate change, disease, and poverty, by identifying solutions beyond human capability. The primary concern with ASI is the potential for it to act in ways that are not aligned with human values and interests, leading to scenarios where its actions could be detrimental to humanity. Ethical, governance, and control mechanisms are central to discussions about ASI, to ensure that such intelligence, if developed, would benefit humanity.

The classification of AI systems into narrow AI, general AI, and ASI provides a framework for understanding AI technology's current state and potential future. While narrow AI has seen significant advancements and applications, general

AI and ASI remain theoretical. Each step forward brings both opportunities and challenges, underscoring the importance of ethical considerations and safety in AI development. The classification of AI systems into narrow AI, general AI, and ASI provides a framework for understanding AI technology's current state and potential future (Chen and Decary, 2020). While narrow AI has seen significant advancements and applications, general AI and ASI remain largely theoretical (Hanssen and Nichele, 2019). The development of AI systems raises ethical considerations and safety concerns, particularly in AI alignment and the potential for superintelligent systems (Iklé et al., 2018). The practical and philosophical case for AI ethics, including regulation and public trust, is emphasized in the context of narrow AI (Rees, 2020). The lack of a well-defined material scope for AI ethics principles is a major obstacle to their operationalization (Mökander et al., 2022). The behavior of AI systems, particularly those based on modern ML methods, raises concerns about transparency, explainability, bias, and accountability (Shadbolt, 2022). The potential for AI safety, particularly in the context of AGI, is explored through General Collective Intelligence (GCI) (Williams et al., 2021). The challenges and opportunities of AI technologies in the economy and society are discussed, focusing on the need for further research and the expansion of AI applications (Mukhamediev et al., 2022).

Conclusion

This chapter has established the foundation for a comprehensive comprehension of AI and its constituents, encompassing ML, DL, and NLP. Through an in-depth exploration of fundamental concepts and terminology, we have laid a strong groundwork for thoroughly examining the function and influence of AI, specifically in hospital management. The knowledge acquired from this introduction clarifies the functioning of these modern technologies and emphasizes their ability to bring about significant changes in healthcare. In the next chapters, we will expand on this basis and explore how AI can transform hospital management and greatly improve patient outcomes.

References

Agerri, R., Agirre, E., Aldabe, I., Aranberri, N., Arriola, J. M., Atutxa, A., ... and Soroa, A. (2023). State-of-the-Art in Language Technology and Language-centric Artificial Intelligence. In European Language Equality: A Strategic Agenda for Digital Language Equality (pp. 13-38). Cham: Springer International Publishing.

Ashrafian, H. (2015). Artificial intelligence and robot responsibilities: Innovating beyond rights. Science and engineering ethics, 21, 317–26.

Bajwa, M. H. A., Richards, D. and Formosa, P. (2023). Providing alternative ethical perspectives through intelligent agents in a serious game for cybersecurity ethical training. Games for Change Asia-Pacific Journal, 2, 149–78.

Barlas, P. (2015). Automating simulation: an open source software for automated input data in discrete event simulation projects (Doctoral dissertation, University of Limerick).

Brodić, D. and Amelio, A. (2019). The CAPTCHA: Perspectives and Challenges: Perspectives and Challenges in Artificial Intelligence.

Burchardt, A., Lommel, A. and Macketanz, V. (2021). A new deal for translation quality. Universal access in the information society, 20, 701–15.

Burgsteiner, H., Kandlhofer, M. and Steinbauer, G. (2016, March). Irobot: Teaching the basics of artificial intelligence in high schools. In: *Proceedings of the AAAI Conference on Artificial Intelligence*, *30*(1).

Chatila, J.G. and Townsend, R.D. (1998). Modeling of pollutant transport in compound open channels. Canadian water resources journal, *23*(3), 259–71.

Chen, M. and Decary, M. (2020, January). Artificial intelligence in healthcare: An essential guide for health leaders. In *Healthcare management forum* (Vol. 33, No. 1, pp. 10-18). Sage CA: Los Angeles, CA: SAGE Publications.

Du, S. and Xie, C. (2021). Paradoxes of artificial intelligence in consumer markets: Ethical challenges and opportunities. Journal of Business Research, 129, 961–74.

Du, X.L., Li, W.B. and Hu, B.J. (2018). Application of artificial intelligence in ophthalmology. International journal of ophthalmology, *11*(9), 1555.

Du, Y., Niu, J., Xing, Y., Li, B. and Calhoun, V.D. (2024). Neuroimage Analysis Methods and Artificial Intelligence Techniques for Reliable Biomarkers and Accurate Diagnosis of Schizophrenia: Achievements Made by Chinese Scholars Around the Past Decade. Schizophrenia Bulletin, sbae110.

Finkelstein, M., Cha, J.H. and Langston, A. (2022). Optimal preventive switching of components in degrading systems. Reliability Engineering & System Safety, 219, 108266.

Firdaus, A. and Nawaz, S. (2024). Viewpoints of Teachers about the Usage of Artificial Intelligence in ELT: Advantages and Obstacles. University of Chitral Journal of Linguistics and Literature, *8*(I), 82–93.

French, R.M. (2000). The Turing Test: the first 50 years. Trends in cognitive sciences, *4*(3), 115–122.

Genesereth, M.R. and Nilsson, N.J. (2012). *Logical Foundations of Artificial Intelligence*. Morgan Kaufmann.

Gil, Y., Garijo, D., Khider, D., Knoblock, C.A., Ratnakar, V., Osorio, M. ... and Shu, L. (2021). Artificial intelligence for modeling complex systems: taming the complexity of expert models to improve decision making. ACM Transactions on Interactive Intelligent Systems, *11*(2), 1–49.

Goodfellow, I., Pouget-Abadie, J., Mirza, M., Xu, B., Warde-Farley, D., Ozair, S., ... and Bengio, Y. (2020). Generative adversarial networks. Communications of the ACM, *63*(11), 139–144.

Gruver, G.W. and Xu, D. (1994). Optimal location and production: a profit function analysis in cartesian space. Journal of Urban Economics, *35*(1), 46–70.

Hanssen, A.B. and Nichele, S. (2019). Ethics of artificial intelligence demarcations. In: *Nordic Artificial Intelligence Research and Development: Third Symposium of the Norwegian AI Society, NAIS 2019*, Trondheim, Norway, May 27–28., Proceedings 3 (pp. 133–42). Springer International Publishing.

Hingston, P. (2009). A Turing test for computer game bots. *IEEE Transactions on Computational Intelligence and AI in Games*, *1*(3), 169–86.

Iklé, M., Franz, A., Rzepka, R. and Goertzel, B. (2018, August). Artificial general intelligence. In: *11th International Conference on Artificial General Intelligence*, Prague (pp. 22–25).

Kasap, G.H. (2021). Can Artificial Intelligence ("AI") Replace Human Arbitrators? Technological Concerns and Legal Implications. *J. Disp. Resol.*, 209.

Kelly, C.J., Karthikesalingam, A., Suleyman, M., Corrado, G. and King, D. (2019). Key challenges for delivering clinical impact with artificial intelligence. BMC medicine, 17, 1–9.

Korukonda, A.R. (2003). Taking stock of Turing test: A review, analysis, and appraisal of issues surrounding thinking machines. *International Journal of Human-Computer Studies*, *58*(2), 240–57.

Leake, D., Maguitman, A. and Reichherzer, T. (2004). Understanding knowledge models: Modeling assessment of concept importance in concept maps. In Proceedings of the Annual Meeting of the Cognitive Science Society (Vol. 26, No. 26).

Langley, P. (2006). Cognitive Architectures and General Intelligent Systems. *AI Magazine*, 27(2), 33. https://doi.org/10.1609/aimag.v27i2.1878

Liang, Y. and Lee, S. A. (2017). Fear of autonomous robots and artificial intelligence: Evidence from national representative data with probability sampling. International Journal of Social Robotics, 9, 379–84.

Maguire, P., Moser, P. and Maguire, R. (2015). A clarification on Turing's test and its implications for machine intelligence. In Proceedings of the 11th International Conference on Cognitive Science (pp. 318–323).

McCoppin, R. and Rizki, M. (2014, June). Deep learning for image classification. *In: Ground/Air Multisensor Interoperability, Integration, and Networking for Persistent ISR V, 9079,* 218–27. SPIE.

Mhlanga, D. (2023). Artificial Intelligence in Elderly Care: Navigating Ethical and Responsible AI Adoption for Seniors. *SSRN,* 4675564.

Mhlanga, D. (2021). Financial inclusion in emerging economies: The application of machine learning and artificial intelligence in credit risk assessment. *International Journal of Financial Studies, 9*(3), 39.

Mhlanga, D. (2020). *Artificial Intelligence (AI) and Poverty Reduction in the Fourth Industrial Revolution (4IR).* Preprints 2020, 2020090362. https://doi.org/10.20944/preprints202009.0362.v1.

Mhlanga, D. (2022). The role of artificial intelligence and machine learning amid the COVID-19 pandemic: What lessons are we learning on 4IR and the sustainable development goals. *International Journal of Environmental Research and Public Health, 19*(3), 1879.

Mhlanga, D. (2024). Generative AI for Emerging Researchers: The Promises, Ethics, and Risks. *Ethics and Risks* (February 24). *SSRN.* 4675564.

Michie, D. (1993). Knowledge, learning and machine intelligence. In Intelligent Systems: Concepts and Applications (pp. 1-19). Boston, MA: Springer US.

Mitchell, M. (2021). Abstraction and analogy-making in artificial intelligence. Annals of the New York Academy of Sciences, 1505(1), 79–101.

Mökander, J., Juneja, P., Watson, D.S. and Floridi, L. (2022). The US Algorithmic Accountability Act of 2022 vs. The EU Artificial Intelligence Act: What can they learn from each other? *Minds and Machines, 32*(4), 751–58.

Mukhamediev, R.I., Popova, Y., Kuchin, Y., Zaitseva, E., Kalimoldayev, A., Symagulov, A., ... and Yelis, M. (2022). Review of artificial intelligence and machine learning technologies: Classification, restrictions, opportunities, and challenges. *Mathematics, 10*(15), 2552.

Nesnas, I.A., Hockman, B.J., Bandopadhyay, S., Morrell, B.J., Lubey, D.P., Villa, J. ... and Bhaskaran, S. (2021). Autonomous exploration of small bodies toward greater autonomy for deep space missions. Frontiers in Robotics and AI, 8, 650885.

Rees, C. (2020). The ethics of artificial intelligence. Unimagined futures–ICT opportunities and challenges, 55–69.

Russell, S., Dewey, D. and Tegmark, M. (2015). Research priorities for robust and beneficial artificial intelligence. AI magazine, 36(4), 105–114.

Saravanan, S., Ramkumar, K., Adalarasu, K., Sivanandam, V., Kumar, S.R., Stalin, S. and Amirtharajan, R. (2022). A systematic review of artificial intelligence (AI) based approaches for the diagnosis of Parkinson's disease. Archives of computational methods in engineering, 29(6), 3639–3653.

Shadbolt, N. (2022). "From So Simple a Beginning": Species of Artificial Intelligence. *Daedalus, 151*(2), 28–42.

Shneiderman, B. (2020). Human-centered artificial intelligence: Reliable, safe & trustworthy. International Journal of Human–Computer Interaction, 36(6), 495–504.

Toosi, A., Bottino, A.G., Saboury, B., Siegel, E. and Rahmim, A. (2021). A brief history of AI: how to prevent another winter (a critical review). PET clinics, 16(4), 449–469.

Trzęsicki, K. (2020). Idea of artificial intelligence. Studia Humana, 9(3-4), 37–65

Udupa, S., Hickok, E., Maronikolakis, A., Schuetze, H., Csuka, L., Wisiorek, A. and Nann, L. (2021). Artificial intelligence, extreme speech and the challenges of online content moderation.

Wang, P. (2019). On defining artificial intelligence. Journal of Artificial General Intelligence, 10(2), 1–37.
Williams, S., Layard Horsfall, H., Funnell, J.P., Hanrahan, J.G., Khan, D.Z., Muirhead, W., ... and Marcus, H.J. (2021). Artificial Intelligence in Brain Tumour Surgery—An Emerging Paradigm. *Cancers*, *13*(19), 5010.
Xu, Y., Liu, X., Cao, X., Huang, C., Liu, E., Qian, S. ... and Zhang, J. (2021). Artificial intelligence: A powerful paradigm for scientific research. The Innovation, *2*(4).
Zhong, H., Xiao, C., Tu, C., Zhang, T., Liu, Z. and Sun, M. (2020). How does NLP benefit legal system: A summary of legal artificial intelligence. arXiv preprint arXiv:2004.12158.

3 | Enhancing Patient Management and Scheduling through AI Solutions

This chapter explores the revolutionary capacity of Artificial Intelligence (AI) in reconfiguring patient management and scheduling within healthcare systems. AI technologies have been proven to increase operational efficiency, optimize the allocation of resources, and boost patient outcomes by utilizing predictive analytics, tailored treatment plans, and automating administrative duties. Integrating AI into patient scheduling systems enables more precise and efficient appointment arrangements, decreased waiting times, and improved patient flow. Furthermore, the utilization of AI in decision-making processes contributes to the creation of customized treatment strategies and enhances the overall standard of healthcare provision. This chapter delves into the practical applications of AI and the ethical aspects and necessity for strong data protection measures when using AI solutions in healthcare settings.

Introduction

This chapter comprehensively analyzes how Artificial Intelligence (AI) can significantly improve patient management and scheduling in the healthcare industry. In the current healthcare environment, which is marked by difficulties such as increasing numbers of patients and limited resources, AI emerges as an essential partner. This narrative does not solely focus on advancements in technology; rather, it exemplifies a significant transition towards a healthcare delivery system that places a high importance on meeting the needs and preferences of patients. The existing modern healthcare environment poses substantial difficulties for organizations in efficiently overseeing patient management and scheduling, such as increasing patient numbers, restricted resources, and superior and exceptional treatment requirements (Gupta, 2018). The complexity of healthcare delivery systems adds to the difficulties, necessitating the importance of efficient patient scheduling (Gartner, 2016). The efficacy of scheduling in ambulatory settings relies heavily on the smooth integration of patient and resource management (Ross, 1998). Several patient scheduling alternatives have been suggested, such as software agent-based systems (Mageshwari, 2012). Nevertheless, the scarcity of capable healthcare administrators and the necessity to prepare for forthcoming leadership transitions present further difficulties (Baker, 2001). Public hospital managers encounter political pressures, resource limitations, and the responsibility to function within a public setting (Boufford, 1991). Efficient management of patient flow and capacity is essential. The proposed techniques include overbooking and minimizing unnecessary follow-up sessions (Bahalkeh, 2021). To effectively manage hospital patient scheduling, adopting a decentralized and flexible strategy is crucial. One such method is to employ agent-based systems, as suggested by Paulussen in 2006.

Conventional approaches frequently lead to prolonged waiting periods, inefficient distribution of healthcare resources, and reduced patient contentment. Moreover, the fluctuation in the frequency at which patients do not attend their appointments, which is impacted by various socioeconomic, demographic, and access-related factors, exacerbates these difficulties, leading to adverse consequences on clinic productivity, revenue, and the overall effectiveness of healthcare delivery. The exhibited capability of AI and ML technologies in diverse fields suggests their potential to offer inventive solutions in healthcare scheduling and management. Nevertheless, incorporating these technologies into healthcare practices faces other obstacles, such as moral dilemmas, worries regarding data security, and the requirement for substantial organizational modifications. This chapter aims to explore using AI and ML to optimize healthcare scheduling and management operations, enhance patient experiences, and improve health outcomes. Moreover, it will address the practical and ethical difficulties arising from adopting these technologies. This chapter is a thorough and informative guide that imparts knowledge and serves as a source of inspiration. It showcases the vast potential of AI to transform patient care and scheduling. This book presents solid evidence of the effectiveness of AI when used with understanding and empathy, to greatly improve efforts to achieve improved health and well-being for all humans. This work is essential for a wide-ranging audience, including physicians, healthcare administrators, and politicians. This study showcases the deliberate fusion of research and practical knowledge to use the potential of AI in creating a healthcare system marked by improved efficiency, efficacy, and patient-centeredness.

Patient Management

Patient management is a comprehensive approach encompassing all aspects of healthcare, beginning with the patient's initial contact with the healthcare system, progressing through diagnosis, treatment, and follow-up, and extending to discharge planning and beyond. The procedure begins with patient registration and gathering medical history, laying the foundation for all subsequent interactions and treatments. An effective approach to managing patients requires a comprehensive and inclusive strategy, as Hunter (1997) and Shakhabov (2020) highlighted. This approach should prioritize the requirements and welfare of the patient, considering their biological, personal, and environmental factors (Leigh, 1986). Efficient disease management is essential to patient care, as it has been proven to improve patient outcomes and save costs (Montague, 1997). To effectively manage patients before, during, and after surgery, it is essential to assess their condition promptly, follow consistent clinical protocols, and provide standardized care after the operation (Kerridge, 2006). Integrating primary care with case management is crucial for effectively managing chronic disorders (Phillips-Harris, 1996). Implementing disease management efficiently requires the use of a systems approach, as recommended by Todd (2012). Patients should be given the chance to acquire their health information so that they can actively participate in their own healthcare (Leonard, 2007). This information provides the foundation for the initial session, in which healthcare specialists assess the patient's current health problems and decide on the next steps to take. Following the assessment, a thorough diagnosis is performed, which usually requires additional tests such as laboratory analysis, imaging studies, and physical examinations. This leads to the development and implementation of an individualized treatment plan, which may involve a combination of medications, therapies, surgeries, and lifestyle adjustments. The technique is flexible, with ongoing monitoring and subsequent evaluations to ensure its effectiveness and make necessary adjustments based on the patient's progress and feedback. Education plays a vital role in this process, as it imparts patients and their families with knowledge about the ailment, treatment alternatives, and preventive actions. This enables individuals to thoroughly understand and actively engage in their healthcare. Discharge planning is crucial for individuals requiring hospitalization. It includes devising strategies for subsequent appointments, arranging for home healthcare providers, and instructing both the patient and caregiver on how to handle care beyond the hospital setting. This is implemented to facilitate a smooth and uninterrupted shift from hospital-based treatment to care provided at home.

Efficient care coordination is essential, especially for patients with complex conditions that require collaboration among numerous specialists. This coordination ensures that all aspects of a patient's treatment are considered, with seamless communication among doctors to deliver comprehensive and consistent care. The integration of technology, such as electronic health records (EHRs) and telemedicine, has significantly enhanced the manner in which patients are supervised. These tools optimize the efficiency of providing treatment, promote enhanced communication among healthcare teams, and enable the remote monitoring of patients, thereby broadening the range of healthcare services. Regular assessment of the quality of care and patient satisfaction is a crucial part of managing patients. It helps determine the effectiveness of therapy and identifies areas that need improvement. By placing a high importance on ongoing enhancement, healthcare professionals may maintain extraordinary levels of care and efficiently adapt to the evolving needs of their patients. An essential component of patient care requires following ethical and legal standards to ensure that individual rights, privacy, and autonomy are respected when providing healthcare. Healthcare providers meticulously navigate these concerns, ensuring that their decisions and actions emphasize the welfare of the patient. The management of patients is a multifaceted and dynamic process that places importance on the patient's involvement in healthcare. An all-encompassing, multidisciplinary approach is essential for addressing the medical and non-medical aspects of patient care, including their emotional and social needs, in order to enhance overall health and well-being.

Patient Scheduling

Effective patient scheduling is a vital component of healthcare management as it significantly influences patient flow, minimizes waiting times, and facilitates healthcare workers in delivering timely and efficient care. Effective patient scheduling is crucial in healthcare administration, as multiple studies have highlighted its significance in optimizing patient flow, reducing wait times, and ensuring efficient service delivery (Hall, 2012; Borglum, 2014; Braaksma, 2020; Blanken, 1981; Hm, 1990; Cayirli, 2012; Huang, 2018). Operations research techniques, such as forecasting, mathematical modeling, and optimization, are commonly used in scheduling systems (Hall, 2012). These methods can be enhanced by incorporating patient classification systems (Blanken, 1981; Hm, 1981) and developing intelligent scheduling systems that consider patient waiting periods, physician idle time, and individual no-show rates (Huang, 2010). Despite some advancements, there is still a requirement for more universally applicable concepts to develop appointment systems (Cayirli, 2003). Effective patient scheduling systems and strategies are essential for maximizing resource allocation, enhancing patient satisfaction, and guaranteeing smooth operations in healthcare organizations. Now, let us go into the intricacies of patient scheduling and the tactics employed to achieve these goals. The patient scheduling process begins with appointment booking, where patients are allocated specific time slots for their consultations with healthcare experts.

This approach can be expedited by several means, including telephonic communication, online scheduling platforms, and in-person inquiry. The goal is to synchronize the needs of patients with the available healthcare resources, such as doctors, nurses, medical equipment, and examination rooms, in a way that optimizes the usage of these resources and reduces patient waiting times. A crucial tactic in patient scheduling entails differentiating between various types of appointments. For instance, first consultations with new patients usually require longer time intervals in comparison to follow-up meetings with existing patients. Healthcare facilities can enhance appointment scheduling and reduce patient flow problems by classifying appointments based on their nature and anticipated duration. Another method involves using advanced scheduling software that uses algorithms to predict the most beneficial arrangement of appointments. This application possesses the capacity to take into account variables such as the precise nature of care required, the degree of urgency for the appointment, and the accessibility of specialized medical personnel and equipment. Moreover, it possesses the ability to adjust schedules in real time to accommodate unexpected situations or abrupt cancellations, hence enhancing flexibility and responsiveness.

Telehealth has emerged as a crucial element of patient scheduling, offering a convenient substitute for in-person appointments for certain types of consultations and follow-ups. By integrating telehealth appointments into the scheduling system, healthcare practitioners can offer patients enhanced flexibility, potentially reducing the necessity for in-person appointments and lowering the burden on facility resources. To improve efficiency, some healthcare providers implement open access scheduling or same-day scheduling, where a portion of the daily appointment slots are reserved only for same-day appointments. This approach is particularly beneficial for urgent medical needs and can lead to higher patient satisfaction by providing timely access to care when it is most essential. Optimal patient scheduling requires clear and efficient communication with patients regarding their appointments, including reminders and instructions for preparation or cancellation procedures. This helps to reduce occurrences of clients not showing up for appointments and cancelling at the last moment, therefore allowing for more effective use of scheduled time slots. While patient scheduling may pose challenges, it is not exempt from issues. Maintaining equilibrium between the need for appointments and the existing supply of healthcare resources requires continuous monitoring and adjustment. Unanticipated events such as the absence of healthcare professionals, equipment malfunctions, or sudden surges in demand for care can disrupt carefully planned arrangements, necessitating the use of flexible and adaptable scheduling methods. In summary, patient scheduling is a complex yet vital process that directly impacts the efficiency of healthcare delivery and the overall contentment of patients. Healthcare practitioners can enhance the effectiveness of patient scheduling systems by employing advanced scheduling technologies, strategic appointment classification, and innovative methods like telemedicine and open access scheduling. These efforts not only improve the effectiveness of healthcare resources but also ensure that patients have timely and convenient access to the required care. Multiple studies have highlighted the potential of utilizing sophisticated scheduling technology and targeted appointment classification to enhance patient scheduling systems. Borglum (2014) and Hm (1981) both emphasize the importance of improving scheduling methods, with the latter proposing a patient classification system comprising three tiers. Kane (2024) asserts that automating scheduling is a crucial factor in improving patient experience and staff satisfaction. Matulis (2020) and Gingrass (2015) suggest that using innovative approaches such as telemedicine and open access scheduling can improve operational efficiency and expand patient access. These efforts not only improve the effective utilization of resources but also ensure timely and convenient healthcare for patients.

Literature on Enhancing Patient Management and Scheduling through AI Solutions

AI and ML are acknowledged as disruptive technologies in the healthcare sector, significantly influencing patient care and operational efficiency. Li et al. (2022) highlighted the utilization of AI to enhance the efficiency of hospital operations.

They specifically concentrated on implementing the shortest-consultation time (SCT) paradigm in order to reduce patient waiting times. This strategy enhances the caliber of healthcare services in facilities lacking appointment systems. Their research validates the feasibility of utilizing AI-powered interventions to improve service delivery by identifying barriers and reconfiguring healthcare protocols. Similarly, Knight et al. (2023) investigated the consequences of AI and ML on scheduling inside medical practices across many fields. Their thorough literature study focuses on the practical applications of these technologies in optimizing scheduling. It emphasizes their ability to decrease effort, increase stakeholder satisfaction, and enhance operational efficiency. Among the 3,415 citations identified in their comprehensive search, only 11 papers were deemed to satisfy their precise requirements. This underscores the fact that this region is still in its nascent phase of advancement. Ala and Chen (2022) did a comprehensive examination of the problems related to Appointment Scheduling (AS) in the healthcare industry. They conducted a comprehensive analysis of over 150 research publications and formulated feasible solutions to improve patient satisfaction. Their analysis emphasizes the importance of utilizing simulation models, mathematical optimization, Markov chains, and AI as essential strategies for addressing scheduling difficulties. They stress the need of matching patient flow and preferences with service capabilities. Patil and Shankar (2023) analyzed the broader implications of integrating AI into healthcare, emphasizing the significance of collaboration between AI developers and healthcare professionals. Supporters argue that these partnerships can lead to advancements in customized medicine, clinical decision support systems, and healthcare process optimization, ultimately enhancing patient outcomes by bolstering diagnostic precision and treatment strategizing.

Wahl et al. (2018) examined the application of AI in resource-constrained settings, emphasizing its potential to significantly improve health outcomes despite its current underutilization. They advocate for increasing research efforts and investing additional resources to develop AI systems tailored for these unique environments. They stress the significance of tackling ethical issues pertaining to patient safety and privacy. According to Alowais et al. (2023), AI has the ability to revolutionize healthcare by improving disease identification, therapy selection, and clinical testing. The authors outline the advantages of AI, such as increased accuracy, reduced costs, and enhanced healthcare for patients, while also acknowledging challenges such as protecting data privacy and the importance of human expertise. These studies emphasize the profound influence that AI and ML could have on healthcare, encompassing improvements in operational efficiency through schedule optimization and advancements in clinical practices for diagnosis and treatment. The increasing consensus underscores the need for ongoing collaboration, research, and ethical deliberation to fully realize the benefits of AI in improving healthcare delivery and patient outcomes.

Enhancing Patient Management and Scheduling through AI Solutions

When it comes to patient management and scheduling, the application of AI has the potential to greatly improve both the efficiency and effectiveness of healthcare services. In this context, AI can be utilized in a number of different ways, as seen in Figure 1 below.

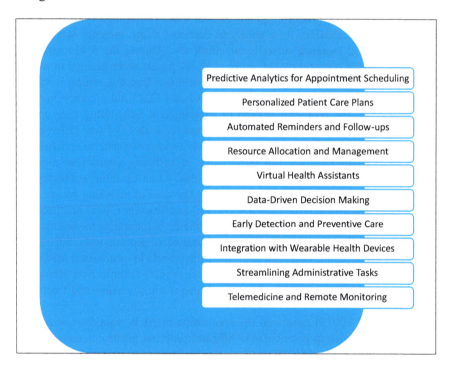

Fig. 1   Enhancing Patient Management and Scheduling through AI Solutions.

Integrating AI in patient management and scheduling can greatly improve the efficiency and effectiveness of healthcare services, as shown in Figure 1.

Predictive Analytics for Appointment Scheduling

AI has the capability to examine patterns in the cancellation, non-attendance, and rescheduling of appointments in order to enhance the efficiency of appointment slots. This can result in improved patient flow and decreased waiting times. Various research has investigated the application of AI and data-driven methods to enhance the efficiency of appointment scheduling in the healthcare sector. Cubillas (2014) and Green (2008) employed predictive models to enhance scheduling, resulting in a significant time reduction of 21.73% achieved by Cubillas. Salazar (2021) and Wang (2011) conducted research on patient no-show prediction and adaptive appointment systems, respectively. Salazar achieved a recall rate of 0.91. Xue (2024) and Wang (2014) both examined the influence of no-shows on scheduling. Xue emphasized the significance of overbooking, while Fiems suggested a scheduling method based on data analysis. Safdar (2021) proposed an innovative method for creating timetables for physicians that aimed to limit the amount of time patients have to wait. In Wijewickrama's (2005) study, simulation was employed to determine optimal appointment schedules. These studies collectively illustrate the capacity of AI and data-driven strategies to enhance appointment scheduling, optimize patient flow, and decrease waiting times in healthcare environments. AI-driven predictive analytics revolutionizes healthcare appointment scheduling systems by examining past data on cancellations, instances of patients not showing up, and rescheduling. This analysis enables the recognition of patterns and the anticipation of future trends, resulting in optimal appointment slots and enhanced patient flow. For example, clinics can utilize AI to evaluate the possibility of patients not showing up for their appointments and then schedule additional appointments with patients who have a lower likelihood of not showing up. This method greatly decreases the amount of time that the practitioner spends not doing anything. Furthermore, dental offices and clinics have the ability to utilize predictive analytics in order to anticipate and predict future cancellations in advance. By identifying these time slots in advance, medical staff can take proactive measures to reach out to people and verify, cancel, or reschedule their appointments. This allows for the possibility of accommodating individuals on the waiting list. In addition, AI systems excel at identifying optimal times for particular services and patient demographics, allowing healthcare professionals to efficiently adapt their schedules to suit demand.

Another inventive application entails customizing the duration of appointments according to the individual requirements and medical background of each patient, rather than adhering to a standardized method. The meticulous planning of schedules results in a more precise and effective distribution of time during the day. Predictive analytics is used in situations when emergencies can cause disruptions to typical schedules. It helps to foresee possible delays and automatically reschedule appointments, ensuring that patients are kept informed and minimizing any disturbance. AI is also essential in identifying patients who are at a high risk and would benefit from more frequent monitoring or check-ups. Healthcare professionals can optimize patient care and efficiently organize their schedules by proactively booking appointments for these individuals, thereby mitigating the risk of sudden surges in emergency situations. These methods demonstrate how predictive analytics may transform appointment scheduling, enhancing its efficiency and user-friendliness. Through the utilization of AI, healthcare professionals have the ability to not only optimize operational efficiency but also greatly boost patient satisfaction and improve the results of patient treatment.

Personalized Patient Care Plans

AI algorithms can analyze patient records to create personalized care plans. This involves considering the patient's medical history, current conditions, and even genetic information to propose the most effective treatment plans. AI algorithms are increasingly being used to analyze patient records and create personalized care plans. These algorithms consider a range of data, including medical history, current conditions, and genetic information, to propose the most effective treatment plans (Ivanović, 2022; Lella, 2021; Gifari, 2021). They are also used for prognosis and diagnosis in personalized healthcare services, with a focus on major diseases such as cancer, neurology, and cardiology (Mehra, 2020). Furthermore, AI solutions are being developed to analyze patient trajectories and predict disease progression, with a particular focus on chronic diseases (Allam, 2024; Ed-Driouch, 2022; Mhlanga, 2023a, b, c). These advancements are transforming patient-clinician relationships and enabling the provision of personalized health information services (Nov 2020; Shin, 2018; Mhlanga, 2021, 2022). Personalized patient care plans, facilitated by AI algorithms, represent a transformative approach in healthcare, tailoring treatments to the individual needs of patients. By analyzing extensive patient records, AI can take into account a patient's medical history, current health conditions, and genetic information, among other factors, to craft the most effective and customized treatment plans. This personalized approach ensures that each patient receives care that is specifically designed to address their unique health profile, potentially improving outcomes and patient satisfaction. For instance, in managing chronic diseases such as diabetes, AI can predict how different individuals respond to various treatment regimens based on their genetic makeup, lifestyle, and disease progression.

This allows healthcare providers to adjust medications, diet, and exercise plans in a way that is most likely to be effective for each patient. In cancer treatment, personalized care plans become even more critical. AI algorithms can analyze genetic mutations in cancer cells from patient samples to identify targeted therapies that are likely to be more effective based on the specific characteristics of the cancer. This precision oncology approach helps in avoiding the one-size-fits-all treatments and focuses on therapies with the highest likelihood of success for the patient's specific type of cancer. Moreover, AI's role in personalized medicine extends to preventive care. By analyzing a patient's genetic predisposition to certain conditions, lifestyle factors, and family history, AI can help healthcare providers recommend personalized preventive measures. This might include tailored advice on diet, exercise, and screenings for early detection of diseases for which the patient is at high risk. AI also enhances the continuity of care by monitoring patient progress over time and adjusting care plans as needed. For example, wearable devices that track vital signs can feed data back into AI systems, enabling real-time adjustments to treatment plans based on the patient's current health status. Furthermore, personalized patient care plans are not limited to physical health. Mental health treatments can also benefit from AI's insights, with algorithms analyzing patterns in behavior, mood changes, and response to previous treatments to suggest customized mental health interventions. By leveraging AI to analyze the vast amounts of data contained in patient records and other sources, healthcare providers can offer a level of customization in care plans that was previously unattainable. This approach not only promises to improve treatment efficacy and patient outcomes but also represents a shift towards more patient-centered healthcare.

Automated Reminders and Follow-ups

AI systems can automatically send reminders to patients for upcoming appointments, medication intakes, and routine check-ups. This not only improves patient compliance but also helps in reducing no-shows. Automated reminders and follow-ups, powered by AI systems, are enhancing the way healthcare providers engage with patients, leading to improved patient compliance and reduced no-show rates. Automated reminders, particularly those delivered by clinic staff, have been shown to significantly reduce no-show rates in healthcare settings (Parikh et al., 2010). These reminders can be cost-effective, especially for high-risk patients. Reminder phone calls have also been effective in reducing no-show rates, with a 50% decrease reported in one study (Woods, 2011; Mhlanga, 2023d; Ndhlovu and Mhlanga, 2024). However, the effectiveness of reminder systems can vary, with some studies showing no significant difference in appointment adherence rates (Maxwell, 2001). Despite this, a systematic review found that patient reminders, particularly electronic notifications, consistently reduce missed appointment rates and improve clinic attendance (Opon, 2020). These AI-driven systems can efficiently manage the task of reminding patients about upcoming appointments, when to take their medications, and the need for routine check-ups, ensuring that patients stay on top of their health management with minimal effort. This automation extends beyond simple reminders. AI can analyze patient engagement and follow-up on missed appointments by suggesting new times, thus reducing the gap in care. For medications, AI systems can not only remind patients to take their pills but also provide important information on dosage and potential side effects, personalized to each patient's treatment plan. This is particularly useful for managing chronic conditions, where adherence to medication schedules is critical for effective management.

In the case of routine check-ups, AI can assess a patient's health records and predict when they should schedule their next visit, based on their health status, history of conditions, and outcomes from previous appointments. This proactive approach ensures that patients receive timely care, potentially preventing the escalation of conditions that could be managed or mitigated with early intervention. Moreover, these automated systems are capable of personalizing communication methods to match patient preferences, whether it's through SMS, email, or phone calls, making it more likely that the reminders are seen and acted upon. For elderly patients or those with chronic conditions requiring frequent medication,

AI-driven reminders can be a lifeline, helping them maintain their health regimen without overwhelming them with the need to remember numerous appointments and medication schedules. Additionally, AI algorithms can identify patterns in no-shows and cancellations, enabling healthcare providers to target specific groups with additional reminders or alternative scheduling options, like telehealth appointments, to accommodate their needs better. The integration of AI in sending automated reminders and follow-ups not only streamlines administrative processes for healthcare providers but also plays a crucial role in enhancing patient care and engagement. By leveraging technology to keep patients informed and involved in their health management, healthcare systems can improve outcomes, reduce the burden on healthcare facilities, and foster a more proactive and preventive approach to health and wellness.

Resource Allocation and Management

AI can help in the efficient allocation of resources such as hospital beds, equipment, and staff based on the predicted patient inflow, thereby optimizing hospital operations. Resource allocation and management, enhanced by AI, are pivotal in optimizing hospital operations by ensuring the efficient use of resources such as hospital beds, equipment, and staff. AI systems can predict patient inflow with remarkable accuracy, allowing healthcare facilities to prepare for varying levels of demand and significantly improve service delivery and patient care. For example, AI can forecast the number of patients expected to visit emergency departments or require hospitalization, enabling the strategic allocation of beds and ensuring that critical resources, like intensive care units, are available for those in urgent need. This predictive capability is crucial during flu seasons, epidemics, or other healthcare crises when demand can surge unpredictably. In terms of equipment utilization, AI algorithms analyze usage patterns and patient needs to optimize the scheduling of diagnostic tools and operating rooms. By predicting periods of high demand, hospitals can ensure that equipment like MRI machines and CT scanners are available when needed, reducing wait times for patients and improving the efficiency of diagnostic processes.

Staffing is another area where AI-driven resource allocation can make a significant impact. By analyzing data on patient admissions, procedural needs, and historical staffing patterns, AI can help hospital administrators forecast staffing requirements. This ensures that enough healthcare professionals are on hand during peak times while avoiding unnecessary staffing during quieter periods. For nurses and doctors, this can mean more manageable workloads and better patient care. Moreover, AI can assist in inventory management, predicting the need for medical supplies and medications to prevent shortages or overstock situations. This aspect of resource management is especially critical in ensuring that treatments are not delayed due to the unavailability of necessary medical supplies. AI's role in resource allocation extends beyond the day-to-day operations to long-term planning. Hospitals can use AI insights to identify trends in healthcare demands, guiding decisions on where to invest in new equipment, additional staff training, or facility expansion. The integration of AI into resource allocation and management not only enhances operational efficiency but also directly contributes to patient satisfaction by minimizing wait times and ensuring that quality care is delivered promptly. For healthcare administrators, AI offers a powerful tool to navigate the complexities of hospital management, enabling them to make informed decisions that balance patient care needs with available resources. This intelligent approach to healthcare operations is transforming the way hospitals and clinics meet the demands of patient care in an increasingly dynamic environment.

Virtual Health Assistants

AI-powered chatbots or virtual assistants can provide 24/7 support to patients, answering queries, providing health tips, and even helping in symptom assessment. Virtual health assistants, empowered by AI, are revolutionizing patient support by offering round-the-clock assistance, answering queries, providing health tips, and aiding in symptom assessment. These AI-powered chatbots or virtual assistants represent a significant leap forward in making healthcare more accessible and personalized. These virtual assistants can engage in natural language conversations with patients, answering questions ranging from medication schedules to pre-appointment preparations. Their ability to provide instant responses to a wide array of queries enhances patient experience and engagement, ensuring that individuals have access to reliable health information at any time. Beyond answering queries, virtual health assistants can serve as proactive health coaches, offering personalized health tips and reminders for medication intakes, hydration, and exercise. By analyzing user data, these assistants can tailor their advice to each individual's health goals and needs, supporting patients in managing chronic conditions, improving lifestyle choices, and promoting overall wellness. Symptom assessment is another crucial area where virtual health assistants excel. By guiding users through a series of questions about their symptoms, these AI tools can offer preliminary assessments, suggesting possible conditions and advising when to seek professional medical advice. This feature is particularly valuable for individuals uncertain about the severity of their symptoms and whether they warrant a visit to the doctor. The availability of virtual health assistants 24/7 ensures that patients have continuous support, especially outside of regular healthcare service hours. This constant availability can alleviate anxiety for patients who might otherwise feel isolated with their health concerns during off-hours. Moreover, virtual health assistants can effectively triage patient queries, directing them to appropriate healthcare resources or escalating issues to human professionals when necessary. This not only improves the efficiency of healthcare services but also ensures that patients receive the right level of care at the right time. The integration of AI into virtual health assistance is a testament to the potential of technology to enhance healthcare delivery. By providing reliable, accessible, and personalized support, virtual health assistants are paving the way for a future where healthcare is more responsive to the needs and preferences of patients, making it easier for individuals to manage their health and well-being.

Data-Driven Decision-Making

By analyzing vast amounts of healthcare data, AI can assist healthcare providers in making informed decisions about patient care, treatment modalities, and management strategies. Data-driven decision-making, enhanced by the analytical power of AI, is significantly improving the quality and efficacy of healthcare provision. By sifting through vast amounts of healthcare data, AI assists healthcare providers in making informed decisions about patient care, optimizing treatment modalities, and devising effective management strategies. This data-driven approach enables a more nuanced understanding of patient conditions, leading to highly personalized treatment plans. AI algorithms can analyze patterns in patient data, including medical history, genetics, and lifestyle factors, to recommend treatments that are most likely to be effective for individual patients. This level of customization ensures that care is tailored to meet the unique needs of each patient, potentially improving outcomes and patient satisfaction. In the realm of treatment modalities, AI's capability to process and learn from a plethora of research studies, clinical trials, and patient outcomes worldwide offers an unprecedented advantage. Healthcare professionals can leverage AI to stay abreast of the latest advancements in medicine and incorporate evidence-based practices into their care protocols. For instance, AI can identify which cancer treatment regimens have shown the most promise for specific genetic profiles, helping oncologists choose the most effective therapy options.

AI also plays a crucial role in managing healthcare resources and strategies. By predicting patient inflow, identifying high-risk patients, and forecasting trends in disease outbreaks, AI enables healthcare facilities to allocate resources efficiently and prepare for future challenges. This proactive approach ensures that healthcare systems can maintain high standards of care even in the face of fluctuating demand and evolving healthcare landscapes. Furthermore, AI-driven analytics can uncover insights into public health trends, helping policymakers and healthcare administrators develop targeted intervention strategies to address issues such as chronic disease management, mental health, and preventive care. By analyzing data on a population level, AI can highlight areas where healthcare services need to be expanded or improved, guiding investments in public health initiatives. In the clinical setting, AI aids in diagnostic processes by analyzing images, lab results, and other diagnostic data with high accuracy and speed, often identifying patterns that may not be immediately apparent to human observers. This support not only enhances the diagnostic accuracy but also speeds up the process, allowing for earlier intervention and treatment. The integration of AI into healthcare decision-making is transforming the sector into one that is more informed, efficient, and patient-centered. By leveraging the vast amounts of data available in the healthcare sector, AI is enabling healthcare providers to make decisions that are not only data-driven but also more aligned with the individual needs and outcomes of patients. This marks a significant step forward in the pursuit of optimal healthcare delivery, where decisions are made with a deep understanding of the complexities and nuances of patient care.

Early Detection and Preventive Care

AI tools can analyze medical records and diagnostics to detect early signs of diseases, allowing for timely intervention and preventive care. Early detection and preventive care, powered by AI tools, are at the forefront of transforming healthcare by identifying diseases at their nascent stages when they are most treatable. These AI systems excel in analyzing medical records, diagnostics, and even patterns within vast datasets to uncover early signs of diseases, paving the way for timely intervention and significantly enhancing the efficacy of preventive care measures. By sifting through medical histories, lab results, and imaging studies, AI can identify subtle changes and patterns that may indicate the early development of conditions such as cancer, cardiovascular diseases, and diabetes. This capability enables healthcare providers to act swiftly, often before the patient experiences any symptoms, thereby improving the chances of successful treatment and, in some cases, even preventing the disease from developing further. For example, AI algorithms can analyze mammograms with greater accuracy and speed than traditional methods, detecting early signs of breast cancer that may be missed by the human eye. Similarly, in the field of ophthalmology, AI tools can screen retinal images for early indicators of diabetic retinopathy, allowing for interventions that can prevent vision loss.

In addition to disease detection, AI's predictive capabilities are instrumental in preventive care. By analyzing patient data, including genetic information, lifestyle factors, and environmental exposures, AI can predict an individual's risk of developing certain conditions. This allows healthcare providers to recommend personalized preventive measures, such as lifestyle modifications, screenings, and vaccinations, tailored to each patient's risk profile. AI also supports the monitoring of chronic conditions, alerting patients and healthcare providers to potential exacerbations before they occur. For patients with heart disease, AI-enabled devices can monitor heart rhythms and detect early signs of atrial fibrillation, enabling prompt treatment to prevent stroke and other complications. Moreover, AI-driven platforms can encourage patient engagement in their health and wellness, offering tailored advice on diet, exercise, and wellness practices that can reduce the risk of disease. These platforms can act as virtual health coaches, providing continuous support and motivation for individuals to maintain healthy lifestyles. The integration of AI into early detection and preventive care is not only enhancing the accuracy and timeliness of diagnoses but also shifting the healthcare paradigm towards a more proactive and preventive approach. This shift promises to significantly reduce the burden of diseases on individuals and healthcare systems alike, highlighting the transformative potential of AI in promoting health and well-being.

Integration with Wearable Health Devices

AI can analyze data from wearable health devices (like smartwatches) to monitor patients' health in real time and alert healthcare providers in case of abnormalities. The integration of AI with wearable health devices, such as smartwatches and fitness trackers, marks a significant advancement in real-time health monitoring, offering a more dynamic and responsive approach to patient care. This fusion allows for the continuous tracking of health metrics and behaviors, with AI algorithms analyzing the data to detect deviations from normal patterns, signaling potential health issues or emergencies. Wearable devices collect a wealth of data, including heart rate, activity levels, sleep patterns, and more. AI leverages this data to provide insights into the wearer's health status, offering a detailed picture of their physiological and activity-related metrics over time. For instance, by monitoring heart rate variability and other cardiac markers, AI can identify early signs of stress, atrial fibrillation, or heart conditions that may require medical attention.

The real-time nature of this monitoring means that individuals can receive immediate feedback on their health status. AI algorithms can detect abnormalities in the data and send alerts to both the wearer and their healthcare provider. This capability is particularly valuable for patients with chronic conditions, such as diabetes, where real-time glucose monitoring can alert patients to potentially dangerous blood sugar levels, enabling prompt action to prevent severe complications. Moreover, AI's analysis of data from wearable devices can contribute to personalized healthcare. By understanding an individual's unique health patterns, AI can tailor recommendations for lifestyle adjustments, exercise, and diet that are specifically suited to the wearer's health goals and conditions. This personalized advice supports individuals in making informed decisions about their health, encouraging proactive management of their wellbeing. The integration also facilitates a more collaborative approach to healthcare, where patients and providers share insights derived from wearable device data. Healthcare providers can access a more comprehensive view of their patients' health, beyond what is typically observable during infrequent clinical visits. This ongoing stream of data enriches patient records, providing a basis for more informed clinical decisions and personalized care plans.

Furthermore, AI-driven analysis of wearable device data can enhance preventive health measures by identifying risk factors and early signs of disease, supporting early intervention strategies that can significantly improve health outcomes. For example, AI algorithms can analyze trends in physical activity and sleep quality to identify risk factors for conditions like cardiovascular disease, enabling preventive interventions that may reduce the risk of developing these conditions. The integration of AI with wearable health devices represents a forward leap in healthcare, moving towards a model that emphasizes continuous monitoring, early intervention, and personalized care. By harnessing the power of real-time data and AI analytics, healthcare can become more responsive, predictive, and tailored to the individual needs of each patient, promising significant improvements in health outcomes and patient engagement in their health management.

Streamlining Administrative Tasks

AI can handle various administrative tasks like billing, claims processing, and record maintenance, allowing healthcare staff to focus more on patient care. Streamlining administrative tasks through AI is revolutionizing the healthcare sector by automating processes such as billing, claims processing, and record maintenance. This technological intervention allows healthcare staff to dedicate more of their time and resources to patient care, enhancing the overall efficiency and effectiveness of healthcare services. AI systems are particularly adept at managing the complex and often tedious tasks of billing and claims processing. They can quickly analyze and process vast amounts of data, ensuring accuracy in billing codes, reducing errors, and speeding up the reimbursement process. This not only improves the financial operations of healthcare facilities but also enhances patient satisfaction by minimizing billing discrepancies and delays in claims processing. Record maintenance, another critical yet time-consuming administrative task, is vastly improved through AI. AI algorithms can organize, update, and maintain patient records with high efficiency, ensuring that healthcare providers have easy access to accurate and up-to-date patient information. This streamlined access supports better clinical decision-making and patient care planning, reducing administrative burdens and allowing healthcare professionals to focus on their primary role of delivering care.

Moreover, AI can automate appointment scheduling, optimizing the process to reduce waiting times and improve patient flow. By analyzing patterns in appointment no-shows and cancellations, AI can adjust scheduling dynamically, ensuring that healthcare providers' time is utilized efficiently and patients receive timely care. In the realm of compliance and regulation, AI tools can assist healthcare organizations in navigating the complex landscape of healthcare laws and regulations. By continuously monitoring regulatory updates and analyzing the implications for practice, AI can help ensure that healthcare providers remain compliant, reducing the risk of penalties and enhancing the quality of patient care. The impact of AI in streamlining administrative tasks extends to the enhancement of communication within healthcare settings. AI-powered systems can facilitate effective communication between different departments, ensuring that critical information is shared promptly and accurately. This improved communication supports coordinated care efforts and enhances the overall functioning of healthcare facilities. The adoption of AI in handling administrative tasks represents a significant step towards a more efficient healthcare system, where the focus can shift more towards patient-centered care. By reducing the administrative load on healthcare professionals, AI allows them to concentrate more on what matters most—providing high-quality care to patients. This shift not only improves patient outcomes but also contributes to the job satisfaction of healthcare staff, fostering a more positive and productive healthcare environment.

Telemedicine and Remote Monitoring

AI improves telemedicine by providing sophisticated diagnostic tools and advanced patient monitoring capabilities, hence increasing the accessibility of healthcare, particularly in rural regions. The utilization of telemedicine and remote monitoring, enhanced by AI, is greatly extending the scope and efficiency of healthcare services, hence enhancing accessibility, especially in distant and underserved regions. AI is transforming telemedicine by improving the accuracy of diagnoses and the monitoring of patients, hence increasing the availability of healthcare services, particularly in rural regions (Patel et al., 2023). It is enhancing patient experiences, facilitating expedited and more precise diagnosis, and diminishing the necessity for face-to-face appointments (Patel et al., 2023). AI-enabled remote patient monitoring is enhancing the accessibility of healthcare services and enhancing clinical results (Opon and Henry, 2020). AI is also impacting telehealth in the United States by facilitating immediate, data-based decision-making and customized healthcare (Amjad et al., 2023). The integration of AI and telemedicine is propelling advancements in the healthcare industry, specifically in the areas of patient monitoring, healthcare information technology (IT), diagnostics, and information analysis (Amjad et al., 2023). AI technologies such as ML and DL are revolutionizing the fields of diagnostics, patient monitoring, and drug development (Iqbal et al., 2023). The integration of AI with electronic health (eHealth) technology is facilitating the provision of dependable and cost-effective healthcare services in distant areas (Amjad et al., 2023). In underdeveloped nations, AI is being used to automate the process of remote monitoring and information therapy, hence overcoming obstacles to the deployment of telemedicine (Puustjärvi and Puustjärvi, 2011).

The shift is facilitated by the enhanced diagnostics and patient monitoring capabilities of AI, which provide patients with high-quality treatment in the convenience of their own homes. AI-driven telemedicine solutions have the capability to analyze medical data, perform initial evaluations, and aid healthcare providers in identifying illnesses with enhanced precision and efficiency. For example, AI systems have the ability to evaluate imaging data, detect patterns in electronic health records, and even assess verbal cues during patient consultations in order to assist physicians in making more knowledgeable judgments. This degree of support is extremely valuable, particularly in regions where specialized treatment is limited. AI-powered remote monitoring allows for constant surveillance of patients' health condition, notifying healthcare professionals of potential problems before they escalate. Wearable devices and home monitoring equipment have the capability to monitor vital signs, physical activity, and other health parameters. The data collected is then analyzed in real-time using AI algorithms. This strategy not only facilitates early intervention but also enables patients to actively participate in controlling their health.

AI-enhanced telemedicine and remote monitoring have revolutionized chronic disease management. Individuals suffering from ailments such as diabetes, cardiovascular disease, and respiratory diseases can obtain personalized recommendations based on their health data, thereby minimizing the necessity for repeated visits to the hospital. AI has the capability to forecast the worsening of medical conditions, propose modifications to treatment strategies, and offer tailored suggestions for lifestyle changes. This leads to enhanced disease outcomes and an improved quality of life for patients. Telemedicine, aided by AI, can offer prompt access to therapeutic resources and crisis intervention in the field of mental healthcare, thereby eliminating obstacles to receiving treatment. AI systems have the capability to examine both spoken and written language to detect indications of emotional suffering, thereby assisting therapists in monitoring the advancement of their patients and intervening when required. The immediate feedback loop is especially crucial for patients residing in distant regions, where access to mental health treatments may be restricted. Telemedicine and remote monitoring improve healthcare efficiency by alleviating the burden on healthcare systems. Hospitals and clinics can optimize resource allocation for acute and critical care requirements by effectively managing a substantial amount of care delivery remotely. This not only enhances the results for patients but also leads to a more sustainable healthcare system. The incorporation of AI into telemedicine and remote monitoring is generating a healthcare environment that is more interconnected, easily accessible, and optimized in terms of efficiency. AI expands the reach of high-quality treatment by providing enhanced diagnostic and monitoring capabilities, allowing patients to receive medical attention regardless of their location. This technological innovation is enhancing the inclusivity, personalization, and responsiveness of healthcare to cater to the different demands of patient populations worldwide.

Conclusion

The integration of AI into patient management and scheduling represents a significant advancement in healthcare administration. Through detailed analyses and real-world applications, it is evident that AI can substantially improve the efficiency and effectiveness of healthcare services. Predictive analytics optimize scheduling and resource management, while personalized treatment plans tailored by AI algorithms enhance patient care. However, the successful implementation of such technologies requires careful consideration of ethical issues, data privacy, and the continuous adaptation of healthcare policies. As AI technology continues to evolve, it will be crucial for healthcare providers and administrators to embrace these changes to maximize the benefits of patient care and operational efficiency. This chapter highlights the critical role AI plays in modernizing healthcare systems and sets a foundation for future research and development in this dynamic field.

References

Ala, A. and Chen, F. (2022). Appointment scheduling problem in complexity systems of the healthcare services: A comprehensive review. *Journal of Healthcare Engineering, 2022*(2), 1–16.

Allam, H., Elsheikh, M.S., Elwahidy, A., Monir, R., Medhat, A., Ziada, Y. M., ... and Hamdy, G. (2024). Post-COVID-19 syndrome and its sequelae: a cross-sectional study. The Egyptian Journal of Bronchology, *18*(1), 29.

Alowais, S.A., Alghamdi, S.S., Alsuhebany, N., Alqahtani, T., Alshaya, A.I., Almohareb, S.N., ... and Albekairy, A.M. (2023). Revolutionizing healthcare: The role of artificial intelligence in clinical practice. *BMC Medical Education, 23*(1), 689.

Amjad, A., Kordel, P. and Fernandes, G. (2023). A review on innovation in healthcare sector (telehealth) through artificial intelligence. *Sustainability, 15*(8), 6655.

Bahalkeh, K., Abedi, M., Dianati Tilaki, G.A. and Michalet, R. (2021). Fire slightly decreases the competitive effects of a thorny cushion shrub in a semi-arid mountain steppe in the short term. Applied Vegetation Science, *24*(2), e12575.

Baker, C.E. (2001). Media, markets, and democracy. Cambridge University Press.

Borglum, S.J. (2014). Understanding Elm Coulee Bakken production variability with discrete fracture networks. Montana Tech of The University of Montana.

Borglum, S.J. (2014). Understanding Elm Coulee Bakken production variability with discrete fracture networks. Montana Tech of The University of Montana.

Boufford, J.I. (1991). Managing the unmanageable: Public hospital systems. The International Journal of Health Planning and Management, *6*(2), 143–54.

Braaksma, B., Zeelenberg, K. and De Broe, S. (2020). Big data in official statistics: a perspective from Statistics Netherlands. Big Data Meets Survey Science: A Collection of Innovative Methods, 303–38.

Cayirli, T., Yang, K.K. and Quek, S.A. (2012). A universal appointment rule in the presence of no-shows and walkins. Production and Operations Management, *21*(4), 682–97.

Collins, H.M. (1990). Artificial experts. Social knowledge and intelligent machines.

Cubillas, J.J., Ramos, M.I., Feito, F.R. and Ureña, T. (2014). An improvement in the appointment scheduling in primary health care centers using data mining. Journal of medical systems, 38, 1–10.

Ed-Driouch, C., Mars, F., Gourraud, P.A. and Dumas, C. (2022). Addressing the challenges and barriers to the integration of machine learning into clinical practice: An innovative method to hybrid human–machine intelligence. Sensors, *22*(21), 8313.

Gartner, R. and Gartner, R. (2016). Metadata. Springer.

Gifari, M.K., Lhaksmana, K.M. and Dwifebri, P.M. (2021, October). Sentiment analysis on movie review using ensemble stacking model. In 2021 International Conference Advancement in Data Science, E-learning and Information Systems (ICADEIS) (pp. 1–5). IEEE.

Gingrass, J. (2015). Changing the channel: strategies for expanding patient access: the changing healthcare marketplace requires organizations to examine access to care in new ways and to find strategies that can increase opportunities for patients to receive their services. Healthcare Financial Management, *69*(4), 64–69.

Green, L.V. (2008). Using Operations Research to reduce delays for healthcare. In State-of-the-Art Decision-Making Tools in the Information-Intensive Age (pp. 1-16). INFORMS.

Gupta, B.M. and Dhawan, S.M. (2018). Artificial Intelligence Research in India: A Scientometric Assessment of Publications Output during 2007-16. DESIDOC Journal of Library & Information Technology, *38*(6).

Hall, C.M. (2012). Sustainable mega-events: Beyond the myth of balanced approaches to mega-event sustainability. Event Management, *16*(2), 119–31.

Huang, M.H. and Rust, R.T. (2018). Artificial intelligence in service. Journal of service research, *21*(2), 155–72.

Hunter, C. (1997). Sustainable tourism as an adaptive paradigm. Annals of tourism research, *24*(4), 850–67.

Ivanovic, M., Autexier, S. and Kokkonidis, M. (2022, August). AI approaches in processing and using data in personalized medicine. In European Conference on Advances in Databases and Information Systems (pp. 11-24). Cham: Springer International Publishing.

Iqbal, E., Bray, J.O., Sutton, T., Akhter, M., Orenstein, S.B. and Nikolian, V.C. (2023). Perioperative Telemedicine utilization among geriatric patients being evaluated for Abdominal Wall Reconstruction and Hernia Repair. *Telemedicine and e-Health, 29*(6), 927–35.

Jeddi, Z. and Bohr, A. (2020). Remote patient monitoring using artificial intelligence. *In: Artificial Intelligence in Healthcare* (pp. 203–34). Academic Press.

Kane, B.P. (2024). Schema-Based Dialogue Management: From Friendly Peer to Virtual Standardized Cancer Patient (Doctoral dissertation, University of Rochester).

Kerridge, R.K. (2006). Perioperative patient management. Best Practice & Research Clinical Obstetrics & Gynaecology, 20(1), 23–40.

Klotz, L.C. and Blanken, R.L. (1981). A practical method for calculating evolutionary trees from sequence data. Journal of Theoretical Biology, 91(2), 261–72.

Knights, D., Piliouras, A., Schwenk, J., Hariharan, J. and Russoniello, C. (2023). Seasonal and morphological controls on nitrate retention in Arctic deltas. Geophysical Research Letters, 50(7), e2022GL102201.

Knight, D., Aakre, C.A., Anstine, C.V., Munipalli, B., Biazar, P., Mitri, G., ... and Halamka, J.D. (2023). Artificial Intelligence for Patient Scheduling in the Real-World Health Care Setting: A Metanarrative Review. *Health Policy and Technology*, 100824.

Leigh, J.P. (1986). Correlates of absence from work due to illness. Human Relations, 39(1), 81–100.

Lella, L. (2021). Predictive clustering learning algorithms for stroke patients discharge planning. In Proceedings of the Future Technologies Conference (FTC) 2020, Volume 1 (pp. 435-442). Springer International Publishing.

Leonard, B.E. (2007). Inflammation, depression and dementia: are they connected?. Neurochemical research, 32(10), 1749–56.

Li, L., Diouf, F. and Gorkhali, A. (2022). Managing outpatient flow via an artificial intelligence enabled solution. *Systems Research and Behavioral Science*, 39(3), 415–27.

Mhlanga, D. (2021). Artificial intelligence in the industry 4.0, and its impact on poverty, innovation, infrastructure development, and the sustainable development goals: Lessons from emerging economies? *Sustainability*, 13(11), 5788.

Mageshwari, K. and Sathyamoorthy, R. (2012). Studies on photocatalytic performance of MgO nanoparticles prepared by wet chemical method. Transactions of the Indian Institute of Metals, 65, 49–55.

Matulis, C.A., Chen, J., Gonzalez-Suarez, A.D., Behnia, R. and Clark, D.A. (2020). Heterogeneous temporal contrast adaptation in Drosophila direction-selective circuits. Current Biology, 30(2), 222–36.

Maxwell, J.C. (2010). Everyone communicates, few connect: What the most effective people do differently. HarperCollins Leadership.

Mehra, M.R., Desai, S.S., Kuy, S., Henry, T.D. and Patel, A.N. (2020). Cardiovascular disease, drug therapy, and mortality in COVID-19. New England Journal of Medicine, 382(25), e102.

Mhlanga, D. (2022). Human-centered artificial intelligence: The superlative approach to achieve sustainable development goals in the fourth industrial revolution. *Sustainability*, 14(13), 7804.

Mhlanga, D. (2023a). Artificial Intelligence (AI) Solutions for Financial Inclusion of the Excluded: What are the Challenges? *In: Economic Inclusion in Post-Independence Africa: An Inclusive Approach to Economic Development* (pp. 257–72). Cham: Springer Nature Switzerland.

Mhlanga, D. (2023b). Financial Technology, Artificial Intelligence, and the Health Sector, Lessons We are Learning on Good Health and Well-Being. *In: FinTech and Artificial Intelligence for Sustainable Development*. Sustainable Development Goals Series. Cham: Palgrave Macmillan. https://doi.org/10.1007/978-3-031-37776-1_7.

Mhlanga, D. (2023c). Artificial Intelligence in Elderly Care: Navigating Ethical and Responsible AI Adoption for Seniors. *SSRN*, 4675564.

Mhlanga, D. (2023d). Artificial Intelligence and Machine Learning for Sustainable Development Case Studies in Emerging Markets. *In: FinTech and Artificial Intelligence for Sustainable Development*. Sustainable Development Goals Series. Cham: Palgrave Macmillan. https://doi.org/10.1007/978-3-031-37776-1_16.

Montague, N.S. (1997). Critical components for dual language programs. Bilingual Research Journal, 21(4), 409–417.

Ndhlovu, E. and Mhlanga, D. (2024). African Agency in Medical Innovation and Practices: From Antiquity to the Present. *African Renaissance, 21*(1), 323–40.

Nov, E. and Moisseiev, E. (2020). The top 100 most-cited papers on intravitreal injections: a bibliographic perspective. Clinical Ophthalmology, 2757–72.

Opon, J. and Henry, M. (2020). A multicriteria analytical framework for sustainability evaluation under methodological uncertainties. Environmental Impact Assessment Review, 83, 106403.

Parikh, P.P., Kanabar, M.G. and Sidhu, T.S. (2010, July). Opportunities and challenges of wireless communication technologies for smart grid applications. *In: IEEE PES General Meeting* (pp. 1–7). IEEE.

Patel, H., Hassell, A., Keniston, A. and Davis, C. (2023). Impact of remote patient monitoring on length of stay for patients with COVID-19. *Telemedicine and e-Health, 29*(2), 298–303.

Patil, S. and Shankar, H. (2023). Transforming healthcare: Harnessing the power of AI in the modern era. *International Journal of Multidisciplinary Sciences and Arts, 2*(1), 60–70.

Phillips-Harris, C. (1996). The integration of primary care and case management in chronic disease. Quality Management in Healthcare, 5(1), 1–6.

Puustjärvi, J. and Puustjärvi, L. (2011, May). Automating remote monitoring and information therapy: An opportunity to practice telemedicine in developing countries. *In: 2011 IST-Africa Conference Proceedings* (pp. 1–9). IEEE.

Ross, L.F. (1998). Children, families, and health care decision making. Oxford University Press.

Safdar, S., Khan, S.A. and Shaukat, A. (2021). A Novel Data-Driven Adaptive Technique to Generate a Physician Visiting Schedule for Better Patient Experience. IEEE Access, 10, 3935–48.

Salazar, L., Leithardt, V.R.Q., Parreira, W.D., Fernandes, A.M., Barbosa, J.L.V. and Correia, S.D. (2021). Predicting Patient No-Show Using Machine Learning Techniques in the Healthcare Sector.

Shakhabov, I.V., Melnikov, Y.Y. and Smyshlyaev, A.V. (2020). Analysis of doctors of different specialties staffing in the Russian Federation and abroad. Siberian Medical Review, 5(125), 96–101.

Shin, D. (2018). Empathy and embodied experience in virtual environment: To what extent can virtual reality stimulate empathy and embodied experience?. Computers in human behavior, 78, 64–73.

Todd, R.E., Rudnick, D.L., Mazloff, M.R., Cornuelle, B.D. and Davis, R.E. (2012). Thermohaline structure in the California Current System: Observations and modeling of spice variance. Journal of Geophysical Research: Oceans, 117(C2).

Wang, S.P., Hsieh, Y.K., Zhuang, Z.Y. and Ou, N.C. (2014). Solving an outpatient nurse scheduling problem by binary goal programming. Journal of Industrial and Production Engineering, 31(1), 41–50.

Wahl, B., Cossy-Gantner, A., Germann, S. and Schwalbe, N.R. (2018). Artificial intelligence (AI) and global health: How can AI contribute to health in resource-poor settings? *BMJ Global Health, 3*(4), e000798.

Wijewickrama, A. and Takakuwa, S. (2005, December). Simulation analysis of appointment scheduling in an outpatient department of internal medicine. In Proceedings of the Winter Simulation Conference, 2005. (pp. 10-pp). IEEE.

Woods, R. (2011). The effectiveness of reminder phone calls on reducing no-show rates in ambulatory care. *Nursing Economics, 29*(5), 278.

Xue, L., Li, Y., Wang, Z., Chung, S.H. and Wen, X. (2024). Distributed appointment assignment and scheduling under uncertainty. International Journal of Production Research, *62*(1-2), 318–35.

4 | The Synergy of AI and Electronic Health Records
Revolutionizing Data Management and Patient Care

This chapter explores the transformative synergy between Artificial Intelligence (AI) and Electronic Health Records (EHRs), focusing on their combined potential to revolutionize healthcare data management and improve patient outcomes. By integrating AI with EHRs, healthcare systems can enhance data processing efficiency, boost diagnostic accuracy, and facilitate personalized treatment plans. This integration not only optimizes healthcare delivery but also increases the accessibility and equity of medical services. Through a detailed examination of AI-driven innovations and case studies, this chapter illustrates how AI and EHRs collaboratively drive advancements in healthcare technology, highlighting both opportunities and challenges within this dynamic field.

Introduction

In the modern era, the fusion of Artificial Intelligence (AI) and Electronic Health Records (EHRs) stands at the forefront of a transformative wave in healthcare data management and patient care. The core ambition behind the deployment of EHR systems, as highlighted by Kawamoto and colleagues in 2021, was to harness the data-rich nature of clinical medicine to optimize health outcomes and healthcare delivery. EHRs were envisioned as a panacea for a slew of pressing issues, including the reduction of patient fatalities due to preventable medical mistakes, the enhancement of patient care with evidence-based recommendations, and the curtailment of surging medical costs. In pursuit of these lofty goals, significant global investments were made towards adoption of EHRs, with the United States alone channeling over $30 billion into achieving near-universal EHR implementation. Despite these substantial investments, the anticipated revolution in healthcare through EHRs has encountered notable hurdles. Customization and training enhancements notwithstanding, healthcare professionals find themselves embroiled in a daunting digital labyrinth—spending excessive hours on EHRs, navigating thousands of clicks, and facing the early onset of physiological fatigue during their shifts. This stark reality is exacerbated by reports of widespread dissatisfaction with EHR usability, which has been implicated in contributing to professional burnout without corresponding improvements in outpatient care quality.

Janssen et al. (2022) advocate for the potential of EHRs as a comprehensive repository of patient data capable of reshaping healthcare practices through improved clinical decision-making and patient outcomes. The integration of cloud technology with EHRs introduces novel opportunities for enhanced data management and interoperability, albeit with the challenge of safeguarding data privacy and security. Moreover, the rich tapestry of data contained within EHRs, encompassing everything from patient demographics to detailed medical histories, presents a fertile ground for transformative insights. Kim, et al. (2016) have underscored the power of large-scale, standardized EHR data in understanding disease progression, evaluating treatment efficacy, and gauging the impact of care processes on health outcomes. Indeed, some studies, like that of the Mayo Clinic in 2018, have demonstrated the utility of EHR data in significantly reducing health complications, such as surgical site infections. Nonetheless, challenges in interoperability and data sharing persist, highlighting the complexities of fully realizing the potential of EHRs. This chapter delves into the intricate synergy between AI and EHR systems, exploring both the ground-breaking advancements they promise in healthcare data management and patient care, and the myriad challenges that have so far prevented their full potential from being realized.

Electronic Health Records (EHRs)

EHRs are digital versions of patients' paper charts, offering a more comprehensive and accessible view of a patient's medical history (Kavitha, et al. 2016; Nielson, et al. 2015). They are designed to be shared information systems, allowing authorized users instant access to evidence-based tools that providers can use to make decisions about a patient's care (Seymour, 2012; Ndhlovu and Mhlanga, 2024). EHRs have been shown to improve clinical documentation, quality, healthcare utilization tracking, billing and coding, and making health records portable (Seymour, 2012; Mhlanga, 2023). However, challenges such as costly software packages, system security, patient confidentiality, and unknown future government regulations need to be addressed (Seymour, 2012; Mhlanga and Ndhlovu, 2021). Despite these challenges, EHRs offer significant benefits, including improved patient care, reduced healthcare costs, and expedited information transfer (Buell, et al. 2009; Mehta, 2007; Mhlanga and Ndhlovu, 2023). They contain information from all the clinicians involved in a patient's care and can include a wide range of data, including demographics, medical history, medication and allergies, immunization status, laboratory test results, radiology images, vital signs, personal statistics like age and weight, and billing information. The goals of EHRs extend beyond simply digitizing a patient's medical chart. They aim to:

- *Improve Patient Care*: EHRs can provide healthcare providers with quick access to patient records from anywhere, improving the quality of care through more coordinated and efficient delivery.
- *Enhance Coordination*: They facilitate better communication and coordination among the members of a healthcare team and across healthcare facilities, which is particularly important for patients with complex conditions requiring care from multiple providers.

- *Increase Accuracy Digitizing Health Records*: EHRs reduce the risks associated with manual errors in patient data management and record-keeping.
- *Secure Sharing of Information*: EHRs enable secure sharing of patient information among healthcare providers, leading to more informed decision-making and avoiding duplication of tests and procedures.
- *Improve Patient and Provider Convenience*: Patients can have easier access to their records, and providers can easily integrate decision support tools into care routines.
- *Enhance Privacy and Security*: EHRs are subject to strict privacy and security standards to protect sensitive health information.

Despite their potential benefits, the adoption and effective use of EHRs come with challenges. These include high initial costs, ongoing maintenance, changes to the workflow that require training and adjustment, concerns about data security and privacy, and issues of interoperability meaning the ability of different EHR systems to work together within and across organizational boundaries. To address some of these challenges, various countries have enacted regulations and provided incentives to encourage the adoption and meaningful use of EHRs. For example, the United States passed the Health Information Technology for Economic and Clinical Health (HITECH) Act, which promotes the adoption and meaningful use of health information technology, notably EHRs. In conclusion, EHRs represent a significant step forward in the digital transformation of healthcare. When effectively implemented and utilized, they can contribute to more informed and efficient patient care, improved health outcomes, and a more seamless healthcare experience for patients and providers alike. However, realizing the full potential of EHRs requires overcoming substantial technological, financial, and organizational challenges.

Literature Review

In the current scholarly discourse, the expansive realm of AI within healthcare has been extensively scrutinized, highlighting its crucial influence on advancing medical research, clinical procedures, and the healthcare infrastructure at large. This exploration delves into the synergistic relationship between AI and EHRs, showcasing their collective potential to transform data management practices and significantly improve the quality of patient care. Pablo et al. (2021) highlight how big data facilitates and improves everyday tasks within these domains, focusing on the necessity of adept data organization and analysis to enhance healthcare delivery in terms of cost-effectiveness, quality of life, and patient outcomes. This review aims to shed light on the cutting-edge developments in big data, particularly its integration with blockchain and AI technologies, while also proposing the exploration of its applications in medical education and digital anatomy as potentially fruitful areas of research. Parker and Parker (2023) delve into the transformative impact of EHRs on healthcare, identifying key challenges such as interoperability, data silos, and privacy concerns. They underscore the importance of optimizing EHR systems to leverage their full potential in revolutionizing healthcare.

Tailor et al. (2023) discuss technology's undeniable impact on nursing, citing enhancements in data management, patient engagement, and care accessibility due to EHRs, telehealth, and wearable technologies. They advocate for maintaining the essential balance between technological advancements and the intrinsic human touch of nursing. Kawamoto et al. (2021) describe the initiative by the University of Utah Health to improve healthcare through interoperable EHR innovations, emphasizing the importance of a supportive infrastructure and the significant impacts of EHR-integrated digital innovations on enhancing patient care and provider efficiency. Chang (2023) explores the advancements in clinical medicine and healthcare driven by AI over the past decade, highlighting the role of digital medicine and health technologies in improving care quality and responsiveness to health situations. Stanfill and Marc (2019) examine AI's implications on healthcare data management, stressing the evolving roles of Health Information Management (HIM) professionals in managing healthcare data in an AI-enabled world. Haddad et al. (2022) discuss the integration of blockchain technology with EHRs, presenting blockchain as a solution to the limitations faced by EHR management in terms of privacy, security, and data integrity. They also propose the synergy between AI and blockchain technology to enhance the performance of AI algorithms through secure and reliable data sources. This literature review encapsulates a comprehensive analysis of the synergistic relationship between AI and EHRs, showcasing their collective potential to transform data management practices and significantly improve the quality of patient care.

The Integration of Artificial Intelligence (AI) with Electronic Health Records (EHRs)

The integration of AI with EHRs is revolutionizing the field of healthcare. This synergy is enhancing data management and patient care in several significant ways as shown in Figure 1.

Improved Data Management

AI algorithms can efficiently process and analyze large volumes of data stored in EHRs. This capability allows for the organization and management of patient information more effectively, leading to quicker and easier access for healthcare providers. Integrating AI with EHRs represents a significant leap forward in the management and utilization of healthcare data. AI algorithms have the potential to revolutionize healthcare data management, as they can efficiently process and analyze large volumes of data stored in EHRs (Palmer, 1991; Kejriwal, 2022). This capability allows for quicker and easier access to patient information, leading to more effective organization and management (Sardjono, et al. 2021). AI can also play a key role in population health by analyzing large patient datasets

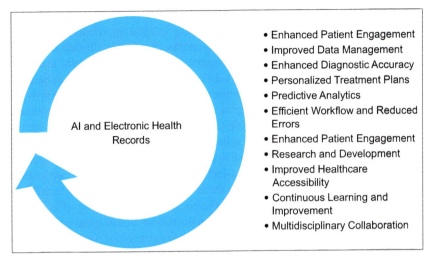

Fig. 1 Integration of AI and EHRs in enhancing data management and patient care.

(Lewis, et al. 2021). However, the integration of AI into healthcare also raises concerns about risk management and litigation issues (Keris, 2020). Despite these challenges, the use of AI in healthcare is expected to increase, with the potential to improve the care delivery process (Lin, 2021; Mlambo et al., 2023). This powerful synergy promises to transform the landscape of healthcare, making patient data more accessible, and the insights derived from it more actionable. At the heart of this transformation is AI's unparalleled capability to process, analyze, and interpret the vast amounts of data contained within EHRs. Unlike traditional data management methods, which often struggle to keep pace with the complexity and volume of healthcare data, AI algorithms thrive in this environment, offering new ways to organize and access patient information efficiently. The impact of AI on EHRs extends across several dimensions of healthcare data management. For starters, AI excels in sifting through and organizing large datasets, automating the categorization and indexing of patient records. This not only enhances the efficiency of data management processes but also reduces the likelihood of errors, ensuring that healthcare providers have quick and reliable access to the information they need. Moreover, AI-powered EHR systems come equipped with advanced search capabilities, thanks to natural language processing (NLP) and other AI technologies. These systems can understand queries in plain language, allowing healthcare professionals to find specific patient information more quickly and easily than ever before.

Beyond improving access to data, AI also introduces the potential for predictive analytics in healthcare. By analyzing patterns in historical patient data, AI algorithms can forecast future health events or conditions, offering insights that can inform preventive care strategies and personalized treatment plans. This aspect of AI not only enhances the quality of patient care but also supports a more proactive approach to healthcare. AI's contribution to decision support systems further exemplifies its value to healthcare. By integrating AI-driven insights directly into the clinical workflow, these systems can alert healthcare providers to potential issues, suggest possible diagnoses based on patient data, and even recommend treatment options. This level of support is instrumental in enhancing diagnostic accuracy, optimizing treatment efficacy, and ultimately, improving patient outcomes. However, the integration of AI into healthcare data management is not without its challenges. Ensuring the privacy and security of patient data is paramount, as is the accuracy and reliability of the AI algorithms themselves. Additionally, ethical considerations such as transparency in AI's decision-making processes and equitable access to AI-enhanced healthcare services are critical issues that must be addressed. Despite these challenges, the potential benefits of combining AI with EHRs—improved efficiency, enhanced quality of care, and more personalized treatment approaches—make this an area of great promise and ongoing innovation. As we forge ahead with the integration of AI and EHRs, it's clear that this technology holds the key to unlocking a new era of healthcare. One where data management is not just about storing information but about making that information work in service of better health outcomes. With careful attention to the challenges and ethical considerations involved, the future of healthcare looks increasingly intelligent, interconnected, and patient focused.

Enhanced Diagnostic Accuracy

AI can assist in diagnosing diseases by analyzing patient data from EHRs and identifying patterns that human eyes might miss. This can lead to earlier and more accurate diagnoses. The advent of AI in healthcare brings a new dimension to diagnostic processes, particularly through its integration with EHRs. By leveraging the rich repositories of patient data contained within EHRs, AI algorithms can identify complex patterns and correlations that may elude even the most experienced human practitioners. This capability is transforming the landscape of diagnostics, enabling earlier detection of diseases, and increasing the accuracy of diagnoses. One of the most profound impacts of AI on diagnostics is its ability to comb through vast amounts of data quickly and efficiently. In the context of EHRs, this means that AI can analyze a patient's medical history, lab results, imaging studies, and other relevant data points, all within a fraction of the time it would take a human. Moreover, AI is not subject to the same fatigue and cognitive biases that can affect human judgment, allowing for a consistent and objective analysis of patient information.

The power of AI in diagnostics lies not only in its speed and efficiency but also in its ability to discern subtle patterns and anomalies that might go unnoticed by humans. For instance, AI algorithms can detect nuanced changes in imaging studies or slight variations in lab results that could indicate the early stages of a disease. This level of detail and precision can significantly enhance the accuracy of diagnoses, leading to more effective and timely interventions. Furthermore,

AI's predictive capabilities can be harnessed to forecast the likelihood of a patient developing certain conditions, based on their medical history and current health data. This predictive analysis can alert healthcare providers to potential health risks before they become manifest, enabling preventive measures that can avert the onset of disease or mitigate its impact. Despite the promising advantages of AI in enhancing diagnostic accuracy, it's important to approach its integration with care. The reliance on AI must be balanced with clinical expertise, ensuring that the technology serves as a support tool rather than a replacement for human judgment. Additionally, ethical considerations, such as ensuring patient data privacy and addressing potential biases in AI algorithms, must be carefully managed. In conclusion, the role of AI in diagnosing diseases by analyzing patient data from EHRs represents a significant leap forward in medical science. By uncovering patterns that human eyes might miss, AI is setting the stage for earlier, more accurate diagnoses. This advancement not only has the potential to improve patient outcomes significantly but also to revolutionize the diagnostic process itself, making it more efficient, objective, and data-driven. As we continue to explore the capabilities of AI in healthcare, the promise of enhanced diagnostic accuracy offers a glimpse into a future where technology and medicine converge to better serve patients worldwide.

Personalized Treatment Plans

AI can help in creating personalized treatment plans for patients by analyzing their unique health data stored in EHRs. This ensures that each patient receives a treatment plan that is specifically tailored to their individual health needs. The integration of AI with EHRs is paving the way for a more personalized approach to healthcare, especially in the development of treatment plans. Through the analytical prowess of AI, healthcare providers can now sift through a patient's unique health data contained within EHRs, enabling the crafting of treatment strategies that are specifically tailored to the individual's health needs and conditions. This marks a significant departure from the one-size-fits-all approach that has traditionally dominated medical treatment planning, moving towards a more patient-centric model of care. AI's role in creating personalized treatment plans stems from its ability to process and analyze vast amounts of data quickly and accurately. By examining a patient's medical history, genetic information, lifestyle factors, and current health status, AI algorithms can identify the most effective treatment options for that individual. This level of analysis considers the nuances of each patient's condition, including potential risks and the likelihood of positive outcomes, ensuring that the recommended treatment plans are as effective and safe as possible.

Moreover, AI can continually update and adjust these personalized treatment plans based on new data. As additional information from ongoing treatment, new research findings, or changes in a patient's health status become available, AI algorithms can reassess and modify the treatment plan accordingly. This dynamic approach ensures that the treatment remains aligned with the patient's evolving health needs, maximizing the effectiveness of the care provided. The use of AI in developing personalized treatment plans also extends to predicting how patients will respond to certain medications or therapies. By analyzing patterns in the data, AI can identify which treatments are likely to be most beneficial for a patient, reducing the trial-and-error process often associated with finding the right medication or therapy. This not only accelerates the path to effective treatment but also minimizes the risk of adverse reactions, contributing to better patient outcomes.

However, the application of AI in personalized treatment planning is not without challenges. Ensuring the accuracy of the data within EHRs, protecting patient privacy, and addressing the ethical implications of AI-driven decisions are critical considerations that must be navigated carefully. Furthermore, the integration of AI into clinical practice requires a collaborative approach, where technology complements the expertise of healthcare professionals rather than replacing it. In essence, the capability of AI to analyze individual health data stored in EHRs for creating personalized treatment plans heralds a new era in healthcare delivery. This approach not only enhances the efficacy of treatments but also places the patient's unique health needs at the center of care planning. As AI technologies continue to evolve and integrate more deeply into healthcare systems, the potential for further personalizing medical treatment—and thereby improving patient outcomes—becomes increasingly tangible. This shift towards individualized care represents a significant step forward in realizing the full promise of modern medicine, offering a future where each patient receives care that is as unique as their health journey.

Predictive Analytics

AI can use the data in EHRs for predictive analytics, identifying patients at risk of certain conditions before they manifest. This can lead to preventive measures and early interventions, improving patient outcomes. The advent of AI in the realm of healthcare has opened up unprecedented avenues for predictive analytics, especially through its application to EHRs. By harnessing the detailed and comprehensive data contained within EHRs, AI algorithms can forecast the likelihood of patients developing specific conditions even before any symptoms appear. This foresight enables healthcare providers to implement preventive measures and early interventions, potentially averting the onset of diseases or mitigating their impact, thereby significantly improving patient outcomes. AI's ability to perform predictive analytics is grounded in its sophisticated data analysis techniques, which can sift through vast amounts of patient information—ranging from medical histories and genetic data to lifestyle choices and environmental factors. By identifying patterns and correlations within this data, AI models can pinpoint individuals who are at increased risk for certain diseases or health conditions. This predictive capability is a game-changer, shifting the healthcare paradigm from reactive treatment to proactive and preventive care. For instance, AI can analyze a patient's EHR to predict the risk of developing chronic conditions such as diabetes, heart disease, or certain types of cancer. With these predictions, healthcare providers can advise at-risk patients on lifestyle adjustments, prescribe preventive medications, or recommend more frequent monitoring to catch any signs of the condition early. Similarly, AI-powered predictive analytics can be instrumental in identifying patients who are more likely to experience complications or readmissions following surgery, allowing for targeted follow-up care and interventions to prevent such outcomes.

Moreover, predictive analytics can play a crucial role in managing infectious diseases, where AI models can forecast outbreaks or the spread of infections within communities, guiding public health responses and individual patient care strategies alike. This aspect of AI is particularly valuable in anticipating healthcare needs and allocating resources effectively to address potential health crises. The implementation of AI-driven predictive analytics in healthcare, however, must be approached with caution. Ensuring the accuracy and reliability of the predictions, safeguarding patient privacy, and ethically using predictive insights are paramount. Additionally, these AI tools must be used to supplement, not replace, the clinical judgment and expertise of healthcare professionals. The human element remains essential in interpreting AI predictions, making informed decisions, and providing compassionate care. In essence, the use of AI for predictive analytics in healthcare, particularly through the analysis of EHR data, represents a significant leap forward in our ability to foresee and pre-emptively address patient health issues. This shift towards anticipatory care not only has the potential to drastically improve patient outcomes but also to optimize the overall efficiency and effectiveness of the healthcare system. As AI technologies continue to evolve and become more integrated into healthcare practices, the future of medicine looks increasingly proactive, personalized, and patient-centered, marking a new chapter in our approach to health and wellness.

Efficient Workflow and Reduced Errors

AI can automate routine tasks such as data entry, appointment scheduling, and prescription management, reducing the workload on healthcare professionals and minimizing the risk of human error. The integration of AI into healthcare systems is revolutionizing the way medical establishments operate, significantly streamlining workflows and reducing the incidence of errors. By automating routine tasks such as data entry, appointment scheduling, and prescription management, AI is not only alleviating the workload on healthcare professionals but also enhancing the precision of these operations, thereby minimizing the risk of human error. Routine administrative tasks, while essential, can be time-consuming and prone to mistakes when performed manually. AI, with its capacity for rapid data processing and automation, can undertake these tasks with unmatched efficiency and accuracy. For instance, AI algorithms can quickly sift through patient information to update records, schedule appointments based on patient and provider availability, and manage prescription orders, ensuring that the right medication is prescribed and refilled on time. This automation extends to more complex tasks as well, such as analyzing test results and flagging anomalies for further review, supporting healthcare professionals in making more informed decisions.

The impact of AI on improving workflow efficiency and reducing errors is profound. Healthcare providers can redirect the time and resources typically spent on administrative duties to more critical aspects of patient care. This shift not only improves the quality of care provided but also enhances patient satisfaction by ensuring more timely and personalized interactions with healthcare professionals. Moreover, the reduction in manual errors contributes to safer healthcare delivery. Mistakes in medication prescriptions, patient records, and appointment scheduling can have serious consequences for patient health. By minimizing these errors, AI significantly mitigates the risks associated with healthcare delivery. Furthermore, the automation of routine tasks by AI introduces a level of consistency and reliability that is challenging to achieve through human effort alone. This reliability is crucial in maintaining the integrity of patient records and ensuring the smooth operation of healthcare services. Additionally, the data generated through AI's automated processes can provide valuable insights into operational efficiencies, patient flow, and resource allocation, informing strategic decisions that can further improve healthcare delivery.

While the benefits of AI in automating routine tasks and reducing errors are clear, it is essential to approach its implementation thoughtfully. Ensuring the interoperability of AI systems with existing healthcare technologies, protecting patient privacy, and maintaining a human touch in patient care are key considerations. Moreover, training healthcare professionals to work effectively with AI tools is crucial for maximizing the benefits of this technology. The role of AI in automating routine healthcare tasks and minimizing errors is a significant advancement in medical practice. By enhancing workflow efficiency and reducing the risk of human error, AI is setting a new standard in healthcare efficiency and safety. As AI technologies continue to evolve and become more integrated into the healthcare sector, they promise to further transform healthcare operations, making them more efficient, accurate, and patient-centered. This evolution not only benefits healthcare providers by easing their workloads but also significantly contributes to improved patient care and safety.

Enhanced Patient Engagement

With AI-driven tools integrated into EHRs, patients can have better access to their health information, empowering them to take an active role in managing their health. The integration of AI into EHRs marks a pivotal shift in patient care, significantly enhancing patient engagement by providing individuals with better access to their health information. This empowerment allows patients to take a more active role in managing their health, fostering a collaborative approach to healthcare that aligns with modern expectations of personalized and accessible care. AI-driven tools embedded within EHR systems can simplify the presentation of health data, making it easier for patients to understand their health status, treatment plans, and any other health-related information. By demystifying medical jargon and presenting information in a user-friendly format, these tools ensure that patients are not just passive recipients of healthcare services but are well-informed participants in their health journey. This enhanced access and understanding pave the way for patients to engage more meaningfully with their healthcare providers, ask informed questions, and make decisions that align with their health goals and values. Moreover, AI can personalize the healthcare experience by sending tailored health reminders, alerts, and educational content directly to patients through EHR platforms. These personalized communications can remind patients of upcoming appointments, medication schedules, or necessary health screenings, encouraging adherence to treatment plans and proactive health management. Furthermore, AI-driven predictive analytics can help identify patients at risk of chronic diseases or those who may benefit from specific health interventions, enabling targeted outreach that can motivate patients to engage in preventive health measures.

The use of AI in enhancing patient engagement also extends to digital health tools such as mobile health apps and wearable devices, which can be integrated with EHRs. Through these integrations, patients can track their health metrics in real-time, share this data with their healthcare providers, and receive instant feedback or adjustments to their treatment plans. This continuous loop of information and feedback fosters a sense of ownership over one's health and encourages active participation in health management. However, to fully realize the benefits of AI in enhancing patient engagement, it is crucial to address potential challenges such as ensuring the privacy and security of patient data and making these technologies accessible to all patients, including those with limited tech-savviness or access to digital tools. Additionally, there is a need for ongoing education for both patients and healthcare providers on how to effectively use these AI-driven tools within EHRs to foster a productive partnership in healthcare. In conclusion, the integration of AI-driven tools into EHRs represents a significant advancement in patient engagement, offering patients unparalleled access to their health information and empowering them to take an active role in their healthcare. This shift towards more engaged and informed patients not only enhances the quality of care but also contributes to better health outcomes by fostering a collaborative and proactive approach to health management. As we continue to navigate the evolving landscape of healthcare technology, the promise of AI in enhancing patient engagement offers a glimpse into a future where healthcare is more personalized, accessible, and patient-centered.

Research and Development

The combination of AI and EHRs can significantly contribute to medical research by providing a vast amount of data for analysis. The combination of AI and EHRs has the potential to revolutionize medical research by providing a wealth of data for analysis (Dilsizian and Siegel, 2014). EHRs, as a source of real-world data, can be used to develop clinical algorithms and predictive models using machine learning and deep learning techniques (Knevel and Liao, 2023 Caroprese et al., 2018). The application of AI to healthcare claims data can help identify complex patterns and improve insurance claim processing (Thesmar et al., 2019). EHRs can also be used for observational studies, comparative effectiveness trials, and participatory research (Pearson et al., 2011). However, challenges such as data ownership, access, and privacy need to be addressed (Nordo et al., 2019; Lee et al., 2021). Despite these challenges, the use of EHRs for predictive modeling and clinical decision support holds promise for bridging the gap between research and practice (Bennett, 2012). This can accelerate the development of new treatments and medical technologies. The amalgamation of AI with EHRs is set to redefine the landscape of medical research and development. By tapping into the wealth of data contained within EHRs, AI has the potential to accelerate the discovery and development of new treatments and medical technologies, marking a significant leap forward in the quest for advanced healthcare solutions. EHRs encompass a vast repository of patient health information, including medical histories, treatment outcomes, and responses to various interventions. This data, when analyzed through AI algorithms, can uncover patterns, trends, and correlations that might not be evident to human researchers. AI's ability to process and analyze data at an unprecedented scale and speed enables researchers to glean insights more quickly and accurately, thereby shortening the timeline for medical discoveries. The application of AI in analyzing EHR data can significantly enhance the efficiency of clinical trials. By identifying suitable candidates for clinical trials based on specific health profiles and predicting potential outcomes, AI can help streamline participant selection and optimize trial designs. This not only accelerates the research process but also increases the likelihood of success by ensuring that trials are more targeted and effective.

Furthermore, the insights derived from AI-driven analysis of EHR data can lead to the development of personalized medicine. By understanding the intricate ways in which different patients respond to treatments, researchers can design therapies that are tailored to individual genetic profiles and health conditions. This precision in treatment development has the potential to drastically improve patient outcomes and minimize side effects, pushing the boundaries of what is currently possible in medical treatment. AI's contribution to medical research also extends to the identification of emerging health trends and potential epidemics. By analyzing population health data, AI can predict outbreaks and inform public health strategies, contributing to the global effort to combat infectious diseases and prevent health crises.

Despite these promising advancements, the integration of AI and EHRs in medical research presents challenges that need to be addressed. Ensuring the privacy and security of patient data is paramount, as is the need for robust algorithms that can provide reliable and unbiased insights. Moreover, the success of this integration relies on the collaboration between technologists, healthcare professionals, and researchers, necessitating a multidisciplinary approach to harness the full potential of AI in medical research. In essence, the synergy between AI and EHRs offers a transformative potential for medical research and development. By providing a rich source of data for analysis, AI can accelerate the pace of discoveries, making the development of new treatments and medical technologies more efficient and effective. As we continue to explore and expand the capabilities of AI in healthcare, the promise of faster, more personalized, and more effective medical solutions become increasingly attainable, heralding a new era in healthcare innovation.

Improved Healthcare Accessibility

AI can help in identifying underserved areas and patient populations by analyzing EHR data, leading to improved healthcare accessibility and equity. The integration of AI with EHRs is emerging as a powerful tool for enhancing healthcare accessibility and equity. By analyzing EHR data, AI algorithms can identify underserved areas and patient populations, shedding light on disparities in healthcare access and enabling targeted interventions to bridge these gaps. This application of AI not only promises to improve the reach of healthcare services but also to foster a more equitable healthcare system. AI's ability to process and analyze vast amounts of data from EHRs allows for a detailed understanding of healthcare utilization patterns across different demographics and regions. This includes identifying geographical areas with limited access to medical facilities, populations that may be at higher risk for certain health conditions but are receiving inadequate care, and barriers to healthcare access such as socioeconomic factors or lack of transportation. With these insights, healthcare providers and policymakers can develop strategies aimed at improving healthcare delivery in underserved areas, such as establishing new healthcare centers, mobile clinics, or telemedicine services tailored to meet the specific needs of these communities.

Moreover, AI-driven analysis of EHR data can highlight disparities in health outcomes, guiding efforts to address the root causes of these inequities. By pinpointing populations that are disproportionately affected by certain conditions, healthcare systems can allocate resources more effectively, design community-specific health programs, and tailor interventions to address the unique challenges faced by these groups. The predictive capabilities of AI also play a crucial role in improving healthcare accessibility. By forecasting future healthcare needs within communities, AI can help in planning and implementing preventive health measures, reducing the burden on healthcare systems, and ensuring that resources are available where and when they are needed most. This proactive approach can significantly mitigate the impact of health crises and ensure that all populations have access to the care they need. Additionally, AI can enhance healthcare equity by personalizing patient care. Through the analysis of EHR data, AI can help healthcare providers understand the specific health needs and preferences of individual patients, including those from underserved populations, ensuring that treatment plans are not only effective but also culturally sensitive and aligned with patients' circumstances.

However, leveraging AI to improve healthcare accessibility and equity requires careful consideration of data privacy and security, as well as the potential for biases in AI algorithms that could exacerbate existing disparities. Ensuring that AI models are transparent, accountable, and inclusive is essential to realizing their potential to make healthcare more accessible and equitable. In conclusion, AI's potential to analyze EHR data and identify areas of need represents a significant step forward in making healthcare more accessible and equitable. By uncovering and addressing disparities in healthcare access and outcomes, AI can help to ensure that all individuals, regardless of their location or background, have the opportunity to achieve optimal health. This shift towards a more data-driven and targeted approach to healthcare delivery holds the promise of a future where healthcare equity is a reality, not just an aspiration.

Continuous Learning and Improvement

AI systems integrated with EHRs can continuously learn and improve from new data. This means that healthcare delivery can become more refined and effective over time, adapting to changing health trends and new medical knowledge. The integration of AI systems with EHRs has the potential to significantly improve healthcare delivery by continuously learning and adapting to new data. This integration can enhance privacy and security in EHRs (Alruwaili, 2020), generate predictive algorithms for individual patient treatment responses (Bennett, 2012), and mine EHR data for AI healthcare applications (Lin et al., 2019). It can also support the development of AI for new drug development and personalized treatments (Lee et al., 2021), improve efficiency in e-Health (Kulkarni, 2021), and provide actionable insights into healthcare (Callahan and Shah, 2017). The combination of AI and blockchain technology can further enhance the security and privacy of EHRs (Shahriar et al., 2022). The fusion of AI with EHRs embodies a dynamic and evolutionary approach to healthcare, where continuous learning and improvement are at the core. AI systems, through their integration with EHRs, possess the remarkable ability to learn from new data continuously. This characteristic ensures that healthcare delivery does not just remain static but evolves to become more refined and effective over time, seamlessly adapting to emerging health trends and expanding medical knowledge. AI's capacity for continuous learning stems from machine learning algorithms that adjust and improve their performance as they are exposed to more data. In the context of EHRs, this means every patient interaction, treatment outcome, and piece of new health information contributes to the AI's understanding, enabling it to make more accurate predictions and recommendations. This process of ongoing learning allows healthcare systems to not only keep pace with the latest in medical research and treatments but also to personalize care to the unique and changing needs of individual patients.

Furthermore, AI's ability to continuously incorporate new data and insights can lead to the discovery of previously unrecognized patterns or correlations in patient health data. This could result in the identification of new risk factors for diseases, more effective treatment combinations, or innovative approaches to patient care. As AI systems integrate these findings, healthcare delivery can become increasingly proactive and preventive, focusing on early intervention and tailored treatment strategies to improve health outcomes. The adaptive nature of AI also means that healthcare delivery can quickly respond to changing health trends. For example, in the face of a new infectious disease outbreak, AI can analyze real-time data to provide insights into effective containment and treatment strategies, adjusting to new information as the situation evolves. Similarly, as societal health challenges shift—such as rising chronic disease rates or ageing populations, AI systems can help healthcare providers adjust their approaches to meet these changing needs effectively.

Moreover, continuous learning through AI enhances the capacity of healthcare systems to implement and benefit from evidence-based practice. As new medical research and clinical guidelines emerge, AI systems can update their algorithms to reflect these advances, ensuring that patient care is always aligned with the best available evidence. However, realizing the full potential of AI's continuous learning capabilities requires careful attention to the quality of the data fed into these systems, the avoidance of biases that could skew outcomes, and the maintenance of stringent privacy and security measures to protect patient information. Additionally, the human aspect of healthcare—the insights, judgments, and empathy of healthcare professionals remain indispensable, with AI serving as a powerful tool to augment their ability to provide high-quality care. In conclusion, the integration of AI with EHRs offers a transformative approach to healthcare, characterized by its ability to continuously learn and improve. This dynamic process ensures that healthcare delivery becomes more effective, personalized, and responsive over time, better serving the needs of patients and adapting to the ever-evolving landscape of medical knowledge and health trends. As we navigate this exciting frontier, the promise of AI in fostering a more agile and informed healthcare system is both immense and inspiring, heralding a future where continuous improvement in healthcare is not just possible but inherent.

Multidisciplinary Collaboration

The integration of AI with EHRs encourages collaboration between technology experts, healthcare professionals, and researchers. The integration of AI with EHRs has the potential to enhance collaboration between technology experts, healthcare professionals, and researchers. AI technologies, such as machine learning algorithms, can be used to predict postoperative mortality, improve EHRs, and facilitate disease diagnosis and decision-making (Choi et al., 2020; Katiyar et al., 2022). The use of AI in EHRs can also improve patient care outcomes and reduce costs (Wan et al., 2020). However, the actualization of EHRs' collaborative affordances requires coordinated use by health professionals, which necessitates organizational, technical, and behavioral adaptations (Vos et al., 2020). The integration of AI and blockchain in EHR management can further enhance performance and security (Rao et al., 2022). Despite these potential benefits, challenges such as biases in clinical decision-making, lack of trust in AI, and adoption issues need to be addressed. This multidisciplinary approach is vital for developing AI applications that are clinically relevant and user-friendly for healthcare providers. The fusion of AI with EHRs not only enhances current healthcare practices but also opens new avenues for innovation and improvement. This synergy promises a future where healthcare is more proactive, personalized, and accessible, ultimately leading to better health outcomes and a more efficient healthcare system. The seamless integration of AI with EHRs is fostering a unique environment of multidisciplinary collaboration, bringing together technology experts, healthcare professionals, and researchers. This collaborative approach is crucial, ensuring the development of AI applications that are not only clinically relevant but also intuitive and user-friendly for those on the front lines of healthcare delivery. Such partnerships are the bedrock of an evolving healthcare system that aims to be more proactive, customized, and reachable.

By blending the expertise of technologists who design and refine AI algorithms with the practical insights of healthcare professionals who interact with patients and EHRs daily, solutions can be tailored to meet the real-world needs of both providers and patients. Researchers contribute to this synergy by evaluating the efficacy of AI applications in clinical settings, ensuring they are grounded in evidence-based medicine. This confluence of perspectives ensures that AI tools are both technically sound and practically applicable, maximizing their utility and acceptance in healthcare environments. The impact of this multidisciplinary collaboration extends beyond the refinement of tools and workflows. It acts as a catalyst for innovation, unlocking new possibilities for enhancing patient care and healthcare operations. For example, through collaborative efforts, AI can be leveraged to predict disease outbreaks, personalize treatment plans based on genetic markers, and automate routine tasks, thereby freeing healthcare professionals to focus more on patient care. This collaborative innovation pathway ensures that technological advancements in AI are aligned with healthcare goals, such as improving patient outcomes and streamlining healthcare delivery.

Moreover, the integration of AI with EHRs through multidisciplinary collaboration ensures that the development of AI applications keeps pace with the evolving landscape of healthcare needs and challenges. As health trends shift and new medical knowledge emerges, this collaborative approach enables the swift adaptation and refinement of AI tools to address these changes effectively. It also facilitates a continuous feedback loop, where insights gained from clinical use of AI can inform further technological improvements, creating a virtuous cycle of innovation and enhancement. However, realizing the full potential of this multidisciplinary collaboration requires overcoming barriers such as siloed knowledge bases, language and cultural differences between fields, and the need for ongoing education and training to keep pace with rapid technological advancements. Encouraging open communication, mutual respect, and shared goals are essential strategies for fostering effective collaboration across disciplines.

In conclusion, the integration of AI with EHRs is not just a technical endeavor but a collaborative journey that brings together diverse expertise to enhance and innovate healthcare delivery. This multidisciplinary approach is key to developing AI applications that are clinically relevant, user-friendly, and capable of addressing the complex needs of the healthcare sector. It promises a future where healthcare is more responsive, efficient, and tailored to individual needs, ultimately contributing to better health outcomes and a more effective healthcare system. As we move forward, the continued collaboration across technology, healthcare, and research domains will be vital in harnessing the full potential of AI to transform healthcare for the better.

Conclusion

Throughout this chapter, we have examined the profound impact of integrating AI with EHRs on healthcare. This synergy not only enhances data management and patient care but also propels healthcare towards more predictive, personalized, and preventive practices. Despite the challenges of data privacy, interoperability, and the need for a balanced human-machine interaction, the potential benefits include improved diagnostic accuracy, efficient workflows, and greater healthcare accessibility. The ongoing evolution in AI technologies and their integration into healthcare practices promises to further revolutionize patient care, making it more efficient and tailored to individual needs. As we look to the future, the partnership between AI and EHRs will continue to be a cornerstone of innovative healthcare solutions, fostering a healthcare environment that is more responsive, effective, and patient-centered.

References

Alruwaili, F.F. (2020). Artificial intelligence and multi-agent-based distributed ledger system for better privacy and security of electronic healthcare records. *Peer J. Computer Science, 6*, e323.

Bennett, C.C. (2012). Utilizing RxNorm to support practical computing applications: Capturing medication history in live electronic health records. *Journal of Biomedical Informatics, 45*(4), 634–41.

Buell, J.F., Cherqui, D., Geller, D.A., O'rourke, N., Iannitti, D., Dagher, I., ... and Chari, R.S. (2009). The international position on laparoscopic liver surgery: The Louisville Statement, 2008. Annals of surgery, *250*(5), 825–830.

Callahan, A. and Shah, N.H. (2017). Machine learning in healthcare. *In: Key Advances in Clinical Informatics* (pp. 279–91). Academic Press.

Caroprese, L., Veltri, P., Vocaturo, E. and Zumpano, E. (2018, July). Deep learning techniques for electronic health record analysis. *In: 2018 9th International Conference on Information, Intelligence, Systems, and Applications (IISA)*, (pp. 1–4). IEEE.

Chang, A. (2023). The role of artificial intelligence in digital health. *In: Digital Health Entrepreneurship* (pp. 75–85). Cham: Springer International Publishing.

Choi, E., Xu, Z., Li, Y., Dusenberry, M., Flores, G., Xue, E. and Dai, A. (2020, April). Learning the graphical structure of electronic health records with graph convolutional transformer. *In: Proceedings of the AAAI Conference on Artificial Intelligence, 34*, (01), 606–613.

Dilsizian, S.E. and Siegel, E.L. (2014). Artificial intelligence in medicine and cardiac imaging: Harnessing big data and advanced computing to provide personalized medical diagnosis and treatment. *Current Cardiology Reports, 16*, 1–8.

Haddad, A., Habaebi, M.H., Islam, M.R., Hasbullah, N.F. and Zabidi, S.A. (2022). Systematic review on AI-blockchain-based e-healthcare records management systems. *IEEE Access, 10*, 94583–94615.

Janssen, A., Kay, J., Talic, S., Pusic, M., Birnbaum, R.J., Cavalcanti, R., ... and Shaw, T. (2022). Electronic health records that support health professional reflective practice: A missed opportunity in digital health. Journal of Healthcare Informatics Research, *6*(4), 375–84.

Katiyar, K. (2022). AI-based predictive analytics for patients' psychological disorder. *In: Predictive Analytics of Psychological Disorders in Healthcare: Data Analytics on Psychological Disorders* (pp. 37–53). Singapore: Springer Nature Singapore.

Kavitha, O.R., Shanthi, V.M., Arulraj, G.P. and Sivakumar, V.R. (2016). Microstructural studies on eco-friendly and durable Self-compacting concrete blended with metakaolin. Applied Clay Science, 124, 143–49.

Kawamoto, K., Kukhareva, P.V., Weir, C., Flynn, M.C., Nanjo, C.J., Martin, D.K., Warner, P.B., Shields, D.E., Bradshaw, R.L., Cornia, R.C., Reese, T.J., Kramer, H.S., Taft, T., Curran, R.L., Morgan, K.L., Borbolla, D., Hightower, M., Turnbull, W.J., Strong, M. B., ... Del Fiol, G. (2021). Establishing a multidisciplinary initiative for interoperable electronic health record innovations at an academic medical center. *JAMIA Open, 4*(3). https://doi.org/10.1093/jamiaopen/ooab041.

Kejriwal, R. (2022, November). Artificial intelligence (AI) in medicine and modern healthcare systems. In 2022 International Conference on Augmented Intelligence and Sustainable Systems (ICAISS) (pp. 25–31). IEEE.

Kim, H., Doan, S., Lin, K. W., Conway, M., Hsieh, A., Garland, A., ... and Ohno-Machado, L. Phenotype Discovery in NHLBI Genomic Studies.

Knevel, R. and Liao, K. P. (2023). From real-world electronic health record data to real-world results using artificial intelligence. *Annals of the Rheumatic Diseases, 82*(3), 306–311.

Kulkarni, S. (2021). Hypertension management in 2030: A kaleidoscopic view. *Journal of Human Hypertension, 35*(9), 812–817.

Lee, R.Y., Brumback, L.C., Lober, W.B., Sibley, J., Nielsen, E.L., Treece, P.D., ... and Curtis, J.R. (2021). Identifying goals of care conversations in the electronic health record using natural language processing and machine learning. *Journal of Pain and Symptom Management, 61*(1), 136–42.

Lin, Y.K., Lin, M. and Chen, H. (2019). Do electronic health records affect quality of care? Evidence from the HITECH Act. *Information Systems Research, 30*(1), 306–318.

Mhlanga, D. (2023). Digital Transformation in the Healthcare Sector: The Role of Artificial Intelligence for Inclusive Long-Term Care around the World, Lessons for Africa. *In: Economic Inclusion in Post-Independence Africa: An Inclusive Approach to Economic Development* (pp. 347–62). Cham: Springer Nature Switzerland.

Mhlanga, D. and Ndhlovu, E. (2021). Explaining the demand for private healthcare in South Africa. *Interdisciplinary Journal of Economics and Business Law, 10*(2), 98–118.

Mhlanga, D. and Ndhlovu, E. (2023). Economic Inclusion: Transforming the Lives of the Poor and How to Make Economic Inclusion Work in Africa. *In: Economic Inclusion in Post-Independence Africa: An Inclusive Approach to Economic Development* (pp. 21–43). Cham: Springer Nature Switzerland.

Mlambo, F., Chironda, C., George, J. and Mhlanga, D. (2023). The Role of Machine Learning and Artificial Intelligence in Improving Health Outcomes in Africa During and After the Pandemic: What are We Learning on the Attainment of Sustainable Development Goals? *In: The Fourth Industrial Revolution in Africa: Exploring the Development Implications of Smart Technologies in Africa* (pp. 117–49). Cham: Springer Nature Switzerland.

Ndhlovu, E. and Mhlanga, D. (2024). African Agency in Medical Innovation and Practices: From Antiquity to the Present. *African Renaissance* (1744–2532), *21*(1), 323–40.

Nielson, J.L., Paquette, J., Liu, A.W., Guandique, C.F., Tovar, C.A., Inoue, T., ... and Ferguson, A.R. (2015). Topological data analysis for discovery in preclinical spinal cord injury and traumatic brain injury. Nature communications, 6(1), 8581.

Nordo, A.H., Levaux, H.P., Becnel, L.B., Galvez, J., Rao, P., Stem, K., ... and Kush, R.D. (2019). Use of EHRs data for clinical research: Historical progress and current applications. *Learning Health Systems*, 3(1), e10076.

Pablo, R. G.J., Roberto, D.P., Victor, S.U., Isabel, G.R., Paul, C. and Elizabeth, O.R. (2021). Big data in the healthcare system: A synergy with artificial intelligence and blockchain technology. *Journal of Integrative Bioinformatics*, 19(1), 20200035.

Palmer, R.A. (1991). The hospital library is crucial to quality healthcare. Hospital Topics, 69(3), 20–25.

Parker, P.D. and Parker, C. (2023). Future of Electronic Health Records: A Challenge to Maximize Their Utility. *SSRN*, 4457214.

Pearson, J.F., Brownstein, C.A. and Brownstein, J.S. (2011). Potential for electronic health records and online social networking to redefine medical research. *Clinical Chemistry*, 57(2), 196–204.

Qian Wan, Jie Liu, Luona Wei and Bin Ji. A self-attention based neural architecture for Chinese medical named entity recognition[J]. *Mathematical Biosciences and Engineering*, 2020, 17(4): 3498–3511. doi: 10.3934/mbe.2020197

Rao, S., Mamouei, M., Salimi-Khorshidi, G., Li, Y., Ramakrishnan, R., Hassaine, A., ... and Rahimi, K. (2022). Targeted-BEHRT: Deep learning for observational causal inference on longitudinal electronic health records. *IEEE Transactions on Neural Networks and Learning Systems*, 2024 April, 35(4), 5027–38.

Sardjono, W., Retnowardhani, A., Emil Kaburuan, R. and Rahmasari, A. (2021, December). Artificial intelligence and big data analysis implementation in electronic medical records. In Proceedings of the 2021 9th International Conference on Information Technology: IoT and Smart City (pp. 231–237).

Sardjono, W., Retnowardhani, A., Emil Kaburuan, R. and Rahmasari, A. (2021, December). Artificial intelligence and big data analysis implementation in electronic medical records. In Proceedings of the 2021 9th International Conference on Information Technology: IoT and Smart City (pp. 231–237).

Seymour, W. (2012). Remaking the body: Rehabilitation and change. Routledge.

Shahriar, H., Haddad, H.M. and Farhadi, M. (2022). Assessing HIPAA compliance of open source electronic health record applications. *In: Research Anthology on Securing Medical Systems and Records* (pp. 995–1011). IGI Global.

Stanfill, M.H. and Marc, D.T. (2019). Health information management: Implications of artificial intelligence on healthcare data and information management. *Yearbook of Medical Informatics*, 28(01), 56–64.

Tailor, P.K., Rukumani, J., Bhutia, H.L. and Surin, J.N. (2023). Nursing in the Digital Age: Technology's Impact on Healthcare. *Tuijin Jishu/Journal of Propulsion Technology*, 44(2).

Thesmar, D., Sraer, D., Pinheiro, L., Dadson, N., Veliche, R. and Greenberg, P. (2019). Combining the power of artificial intelligence with the richness of healthcare claims data: Opportunities and challenges. *Pharmaco Economics*, 37, 745–52.

Vos, J.F., Boonstra, A., Kooistra, A., Seelen, M. and Van Offenbeek, M. (2020). The influence of electronic health record use on collaboration among medical specialties. *BMC health Services Research*, 20, 1–11.

5 | Medical Imaging and Diagnostics
The Fundamentals of Medical Imaging and AI

The chapter delves into the complex connection between medical imaging and artificial intelligence (AI) in the field of healthcare. This chapter explores the core principles that form the basis of medical imaging techniques and the transformative impact of AI in improving the accuracy, efficiency, and quality of diagnosis and patient treatment. The chapter commences by clarifying the many modalities of medical imaging, including X-ray, computed tomography (CT), magnetic resonance imaging (MRI), ultrasound, and positron emission tomography (PET). This text presents a summary of the fundamental physical concepts and technical progress that make each modality possible, highlighting their distinct advantages and constraints. An overview of medical imaging technologies, including X-ray, MRI, CT, and others is discussed. The role of AI in improving medical imaging analysis and interpretation and utilizing AI to enhance diagnostic accuracy and efficiency is provided.

Introduction

The use of artificial intelligence (AI) into medical imaging represents a notable frontier in health innovation, with transformative possibilities in multiple facets of radiology. Pesapane et al. (2018) state that AI applications have a wide range of uses, including image collecting, aided reporting, follow-up planning, data storage, and data mining, among other fields. The wide array of uses demonstrates a significant change in the day-to-day tasks and duties of radiologists. Nevertheless, the advancement and widespread use of AI technologies in medical imaging pose a significant issue: the need to effectively incorporate these advanced technologies into current healthcare systems without causing disruptions to the workflow and ensuring that they enhance rather than replace the nuanced expertise of medical professionals (Pesapane et al., 2018; Mhlanga, 2023a, b, 2022a).

This introduction provides a foundation for a comprehensive examination of the several modalities of medical imaging technologies, which are crucial for identifying and treating a wide range of health disorders. From conventional X-rays, which uncover the concealed structures of bones and organs, to the intricate imagery produced by computed tomography (CT) and magnetic resonance imaging (MRI), each modality represents remarkable technological progress and is based on fundamental physical principles (Mhlanga, 2022b, 2023c). Gaining comprehension of these concepts offers a deeper understanding of the functioning of each technique, as well as their distinct talents and constraints. The conversation moves from the technical issues of medical imaging to the transformative impact of AI in this domain. The remarkable capacity of AI in recognizing patterns and analyzing data has positioned it as an essential tool in understanding intricate medical imaging and converting extensive databases into practical insights. The combination of AI and imaging technology improves the precision and effectiveness of diagnostic procedures, going beyond theoretical applications to actively transform both diagnostic accuracy and operational efficiency in real-time clinical environments. The integration of AI in healthcare enables the detection of subtle anomalies and facilitates predictive analytics, which can foresee the evolution of diseases and the response to therapy. This integration brings about major advances in individualized patient care. The chapter provides as an instructional guide to the breakthroughs in medical imaging and AI, highlighting their joint impact on improving healthcare outcomes. Through comprehension of this mutually beneficial association, readers acquire a thorough perspective on how technology and intelligent systems are transforming the domain of medicine, guaranteeing that breakthroughs in AI are both ground-breaking and ethically included into clinical practice.

Medical Imaging and Diagnostics

Medical imaging and diagnostics involve a wide range of techniques and technology used to create visual representations of the human body or its many parts. These photos are used for clinical purposes, such as identifying and monitoring illnesses. These approaches provide essential insights that are sometimes inaccessible through physical examinations alone, allowing healthcare professionals to understand the underlying workings of the human body without needing intrusive procedures. Advancements in AI and technology have brought about substantial changes in the field of medical imaging and diagnostics. These developments have led to improved accuracy, effectiveness, and accessibility of healthcare solutions (Pesapane et al., 2018). The field of medicine has seen a considerable transformation due to the introduction of medical imaging technologies. These technologies have provided clinicians with the ability to observe the inside structures of the human body with amazing accuracy. Technological innovations such as X-ray, MRI, CT, and other comparable methods have become essential tools in the fields of medical diagnosis, treatment planning, and illness monitoring. This chapter provides a thorough analysis of the basic imaging techniques, including their underlying principles, practical applications, and the current advancements that have a substantial impact on modern healthcare.

X-Ray Imaging

X-ray imaging, usually referred to as radiography, is one of the oldest and widely used diagnostic techniques in medical imaging. This method utilizes the penetrating ability of X-ray radiation to observe the inside structures of the body, offering significant information on different anatomical and clinical disorders. X-rays, a type of high-energy electromagnetic radiation analogous to visible light, have the ability to penetrate through the tissues of the body. During this process, the absorption of the substances varies based on the density and content of each type of tissue. The fundamental idea underlying X-ray imaging is simple, yet potent. When X-rays are aimed at the body, materials with high density such as bones absorb a greater amount of radiation and are depicted as white in the ensuing image. On the other hand, softer tissues that absorb less energy are seen in various colors of grey. This disparity in absorption generates a distinction that is recorded on an X-ray film or, more frequently in contemporary uses, on a digital detector. The resultant images offer a stationary depiction of the internal structures of the body, enabling the evaluation of fractures, dislocations, infections, and diverse disorders.

Technological advancements have greatly improved the quality and safety of X-ray imaging. Modern digital X-ray systems provide higher resolution images while using lower levels of radiation in comparison to conventional film-based systems. In addition, there are certain variations of X-ray imaging, such as fluoroscopy, which offer immediate and dynamic images that are valuable for directing specific diagnostic and therapeutic operations. CT is an advanced technique that uses several X-ray scans collected from different angles to create comprehensive cross-sectional views of the body, providing enhanced information. Although X-ray imaging is highly useful, it does entail exposure to ionizing radiation, which might potentially have adverse effects on health. Hence, medical practitioners exercise caution in justifying its utilization by weighing the potential diagnostic or therapeutic advantages against the associated hazards. In addition, they use the ALARA principle, which stands for "As Low As Reasonably Achievable", to reduce radiation exposure while maintaining image quality. Therefore, although X-ray imaging is an essential tool in contemporary medicine, its utilization is regulated by strict safety protocols to safeguard patient well-being.

Magnetic Resonance Imaging (MRI)

MRI uses powerful magnets and radio waves to generate detailed images of organs and tissues within the body. Unlike X-rays, MRI does not use ionizing radiation. The technique is based on the principles of nuclear magnetic resonance, where hydrogen atoms in the body align with a magnetic field and emit signals when exposed to radio waves. These signals are then converted into detailed images by a computer.

Computed Tomography (CT)

CT scans, also known as CAT scans, combine multiple X-ray images taken from different angles to produce cross-sectional views of areas inside the body. The use of computer processing brings a greater level of detail and clarity compared to traditional X-rays, particularly for soft tissues and blood vessels. CT is highly valuable for diagnosing diseases, injuries, or abnormalities within the body.

Ultrasound Imaging

Ultrasound imaging uses high-frequency sound waves to produce images of structures within the body. These sound waves are emitted by a transducer and echo back when they hit tissues. The returning echoes are then converted into an image. Ultrasound is widely used for monitoring fetal development, diagnosing conditions in organs like the heart and liver, and guiding needle placement during biopsies.

Nuclear Medicine Imaging

This form of imaging involves the administration of radioactive substances, called radiotracers, which accumulate in specific organs or lesions. Gamma cameras detect the radiation emitted by these tracers, creating images that show the function and structure of internal organs. Nuclear medicine is particularly useful in diagnosing and treating certain types of cancer, heart disease, and other abnormalities.

Digital and 3D Imaging

Advancements in digital technology have led to improved image quality, the ability to manipulate images for better diagnosis, and the development of 3D imaging techniques. 3D imaging, such as in 3D mammography, provides a more comprehensive view of the anatomy, enhancing the detection and treatment of diseases.

Positron Emission Tomography (PET)

A type of nuclear medicine imaging that uses small amounts of radioactive materials to help visualize and measure changes in metabolic processes and other physiological activities.

Empirical Literature

Integrating AI into medical imaging and diagnostics is a ground-breaking progress in healthcare technology, with significant implications for clinical practice. The growing body of research on the convergence of AI, machine learning (ML), and medical imaging demonstrates a comprehensive understanding of how these technologies are revolutionizing diagnostic processes. Tadiboina (2022) highlights the vast potential of AI and ML in various medical fields, particularly in cardiology and diagnostic imaging. The study classifies the developmental stages of AI as 'weak' and 'strong' AI, with a particular emphasis on the present applications of weak AI in predictive modeling and enhancing medical outcomes. These applications utilize both supervised and unsupervised learning methodologies. This perspective highlights both the versatility of the technology and its nascent level of advancement in the healthcare domain. Supporting this perspective, Pesapane et al. (2018) present a thorough analysis of the significant growth in publications related to AI and its dominance in the field of radiology. More than 50% of the latest studies specifically concentrate on MRI and CT scans, as noted by the researchers. The inquiry reveals a transformation in the field of radiology, where it has evolved from relying mostly on human vision to becoming a more definitive science. This movement has been driven by the ability of AI to detect small details that go beyond the capabilities of human perception. Furthermore, they support the crucial role of radiologists, suggesting that AI would improve rather than replace human expertise, particularly in integrating diagnostic observations with patient-centered healthcare.

Lee et al. (2017) chronicle the evolution of Artificial Neural Networks (ANNs), a vital component of deep learning, from its inception in the 1950s to its recent revival fueled by the accessibility of extensive datasets and high-performance computing resources. The resurgence of ANNs is credited to their ability to surpass human performance in some diagnostic tasks, indicating a promising future for AI in the domain of medical imaging. Najjar (2023) provides additional insights on the integration of AI in the field of radiology. The author analyzes the possibility of substantial transformations as well as the challenges that emerge, such as apprehensions regarding the accuracy of data and the inscrutable nature of AI systems. Najjar's work emphasizes the necessity of ongoing research and collaboration to properly tackle these challenges.

Liu et al. (2019) performed a comprehensive examination and statistical analysis to assess the precision of deep learning models in contrast to healthcare professionals. According to their research, deep learning has the capacity to attain or exceed human diagnostic accuracy in terms of sensitivity and specificity. Nevertheless, they underscore the necessity for enhanced reporting standards to guarantee the reliability of these investigations. Sasikala et al. (2021) differentiate deep learning from standard ML by emphasizing its ability to autonomously address problems without requiring direct human intervention. Deep learning is a highly sophisticated form of automation that falls under the umbrella of AI. The literature review offers a comprehensive and inclusive description of the increasing involvement of artificial intelligence in the domain of medical imaging. The collective body of research suggests that the integration of AI and ML has the capacity to profoundly revolutionize diagnostic techniques and enhance patient outcomes. Nevertheless, this procedure requires a careful evaluation of moral principles, human oversight, and continuous adaptation to technology advancements. It is imperative to integrate human expertise with AI in the digital era to effectively harness the possibilities of AI and enhance patient care.

The Role of Artificial Intelligence (AI) in Enhancing Medical Imaging Analysis and Interpretation

The role of AI in enhancing medical imaging analysis and interpretation is increasingly significant and transformative. AI and its subsets, like ML and deep learning, are revolutionizing how medical images are analyzed, interpreted, and used in clinical decision-making (Figure 1). AI technologies are integrated into various imaging techniques, including X-rays, CT scans, and MRIs, to enhance the accuracy and efficiency of diagnostic processes. These systems leverage complex algorithms and large datasets to train models that can identify patterns, anomalies, and features that may not be easily detectable by human clinicians.

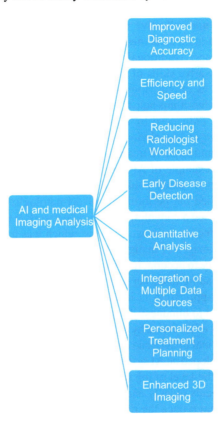

Fig. 1 The role of Artificial Intelligence (AI) in enhancing medical imaging analysis and interpretation.

Improved Diagnostic Accuracy

Improved diagnostic accuracy is one of the most promising benefits of integrating AI, particularly deep learning algorithms, into medical imaging. These advanced AI systems are adept at analyzing complex medical images, such as X-rays, CT scans, and MRIs. The prowess of AI in this field stems from its ability to process and learn from vast datasets which encapsulate a wide range of imaging examples and health conditions. This capability enables AI to recognize subtle patterns and abnormalities that may escape even the trained human eye. AI algorithms in medical imaging are typically trained using large datasets of annotated images. These datasets include a diverse array of conditions, from common to rare, each meticulously labeled by medical experts. This training process involves feeding these labeled images into deep learning models, which gradually learn to identify various features and anomalies in the images. By processing thousands, sometimes millions of examples, the AI models develop the ability to discern nuances in medical images that are indicative of specific health conditions. The primary advantage of using AI in medical imaging is its potential to enhance the accuracy and speed of diagnoses. Traditional diagnostic processes rely heavily on the expertise and interpretative skills of radiologists who, while highly skilled, can face challenges such as fatigue, high caseloads, and the inherent variability in human judgment. AI algorithms help mitigate these issues by providing consistent readings that are not influenced by human factors. Moreover, AI can assist in identifying early-stage or less obvious conditions that are difficult to diagnose, thus enabling timely and targeted treatments.

One compelling example of AI's impact on diagnostics is in the detection of skin cancer. A notable study published in the journal *Nature* highlighted an AI system that matched the performance of dermatologists in identifying skin cancers. The system used a convolutional neural network, a type of deep learning model particularly effective in image analysis, which was trained on a dataset of tens of thousands of images of malignant melanomas and benign moles. The AI demonstrated an ability to accurately differentiate between benign and malignant lesions, potentially leading to earlier and more accurate diagnoses of melanoma. Another significant application is in the diagnosis of diabetic retinopathy, a condition that can lead to blindness if untreated. Traditionally, diagnosis relies on detailed examinations of the retina by experienced ophthalmologists. However, AI systems trained on retinal images can detect this condition with high accuracy. For instance, Google developed an AI system that analyzes retinal photos and has been shown to perform at the level of top retinal specialists. The AI's ability to screen large volumes of patients quickly and accurately can lead to better management of diabetic patients and reduce the risk of vision loss. The implications of these advancements extend beyond individual diagnostic tasks. AI can also contribute to personalized medicine approaches by integrating individual patient data from various sources, including genetic information and electronic health records, to tailor treatments to individual needs. Furthermore, as AI technology advances and more data becomes available, these systems are likely to become even more sophisticated and integrated into regular clinical practice. However, the integration of AI into clinical settings also raises challenges, including ethical considerations such as patient privacy, data security, and the need for transparency in AI decision-making processes. As these technologies evolve, continuous monitoring, regulation, and training will be essential to maximize their benefits while minimizing potential risks. The future of medical diagnostics will likely see a collaboration between AI tools and healthcare professionals, enhancing diagnostic accuracy and improving patient outcomes.

Efficiency and Speed

The integration of AI into the field of medical imaging brings a significant increase in both efficiency and speed, which are crucial attributes, especially in emergency medical situations. AI's capability to process and analyze medical images far exceeds the pace at which human radiologists can work, drastically reducing the time it takes to move from imaging to diagnosis. In traditional settings, radiologists face a high volume of cases daily, each requiring attention to detail and meticulous analysis. This process can be time-consuming and is often subject to the limitations of human endurance and efficiency, particularly under pressing circumstances. AI, on the other hand, operates with an unmatched speed, analyzing data and images within fractions of a second. This rapid processing ability of AI systems is due to their design, which allows them to simultaneously assess multiple aspects of an image and identify patterns that may indicate a disease. The value of this speed becomes particularly evident in emergency medical scenarios. For instance, in cases of stroke, where the timely restoration of blood flow is essential to minimize brain damage, AI can quickly interpret CT scans or MRIs and identify signs of a stroke, such as blood clots or bleeding. This rapid diagnosis allows for quicker decision-making regarding treatment options, such as thrombolytic therapies, which are most effective within a narrow time frame after the stroke's onset.

Furthermore, AI's capacity to expedite diagnostic processes is not only beneficial in life-threatening conditions but also enhances overall medical practice. By reducing the waiting time for diagnosis, patients can receive earlier interventions, which can improve outcomes and reduce hospital stays and associated healthcare costs. This efficiency also alleviates the workload on overburdened radiologists, allowing them to focus more on complex cases where human expertise is indispensable. Moreover, AI's integration into medical imaging is continually evolving, with systems becoming increasingly sophisticated at interpreting images with high accuracy and at speeds that no human can achieve. For example, AI applications are now being developed that can perform comprehensive analyses of diagnostic images, highlight areas of concern, and even suggest potential diagnoses. These tools not only speed up the diagnostic process but also enhance diagnostic accuracy, contributing to more precise and personalized medical care. However, the rapid deployment of AI in medical imaging also raises important considerations regarding its implementation. Ensuring the accuracy of AI predictions, validating its effectiveness across diverse populations, and integrating it seamlessly with existing medical workflows are critical challenges that need to be addressed. Moreover, the reliance on AI for rapid diagnostics must be balanced with safeguards to prevent over-dependence on technology without sufficient human oversight. As AI technology continues to mature and integrate more deeply into healthcare systems, its potential to revolutionize medical diagnostics by combining speed, accuracy, and efficiency promises to enhance patient care significantly. By reducing diagnostic times, AI helps to streamline medical processes, enabling healthcare providers to offer timely and effective treatments, ultimately saving lives and improving patient outcomes.

Reducing Radiologist Workload

The integration of AI into the field of radiology is revolutionizing how radiologists manage their workload, particularly through the automation of routine and straightforward cases. This technological advancement allows radiologists to prioritize their expertise and attention on more complex and nuanced cases, significantly enhancing workflow efficiency and reducing the potential for burnout. Radiologists typically handle a high volume of imaging data every day, with many cases involving straightforward scans such as chest X-rays or mammograms that show clear signs of common conditions or no pathology at all. AI is particularly useful in these scenarios because it can quickly and accurately analyze large sets of imaging data, identifying normal and abnormal patterns with a precision that matches, and sometimes surpasses human capabilities. For instance, AI systems developed to screen for pulmonary conditions can sift through hundreds of chest X-rays, flagging only those with indications of abnormalities such as pneumonia for further human review. This automation helps clear the bulk of a radiologist's workload, allowing them to concentrate on more critical cases that AI alone cannot definitively diagnose.

The real value of AI in radiology lies in its ability to free up time for radiologists to engage with complex cases that demand a high level of diagnostic acumen. These cases often involve subtle imaging signs that are difficult to interpret or rare diseases that are not frequently encountered. While AI can pre-screen these scans and highlight potential areas of concern, the nuanced judgment required to differentiate between benign and malignant cases, for instance, still rests with the radiologist. This focused approach not only improves the accuracy of diagnoses but also enhances patient outcomes by ensuring that complex cases receive the detailed attention they require. Furthermore, the use of AI in routine screenings has practical applications that have already begun to show results in clinical settings. At a leading hospital, the implementation of AI to review incoming chest X-rays demonstrated a substantial decrease in the time radiologists spent on each scan. By automatically categorizing scans into 'normal' and 'review needed' groups, the system effectively reduced the average analysis time per X-ray, allowing radiologists to devote more time to scrutinizing cases that the AI system flagged as needing further investigation. Additionally, the reduction in routine task load through AI significantly alleviates the risk of burnout among radiologists. Burnout in the medical profession is a serious issue, often caused by the repetitive nature of tasks and the high-pressure environment of healthcare. With AI taking over the more monotonous parts of the job, radiologists experience less mental fatigue, which contributes to better mental health and higher job satisfaction. Moreover, engaging more frequently with challenging cases provides a sense of professional fulfilment that routine work often lacks. In conclusion, AI's role in radiology is a transformative force, not only in enhancing diagnostic precision and efficiency but also in improving the quality of work life for radiologists. By shouldering the burden of routine image analysis, AI enables radiologists to focus on areas where their expertise is most critically needed, thus fostering a more efficient, satisfying, and sustainable practice. As AI technology continues to evolve, its impact on healthcare is expected to grow, further enhancing the capacity for high-quality medical care.

Early Disease Detection

The application of AI in the field of medical imaging is revolutionizing early disease detection, significantly enhancing the ability to identify the initial stages of serious conditions such as cancer and degenerative neurological diseases. AI's capacity to discern subtle changes in imaging scans that might elude even the most trained eyes offers a profound advantage in diagnosing diseases at a stage where they are most treatable, thereby improving patient outcomes. AI systems are equipped with sophisticated algorithms trained on vast datasets of medical images, allowing them to recognize minute abnormalities that signal the onset of disease. These systems analyze imaging data with a level of detail and consistency that surpasses human capability, particularly in high-volume settings where fatigue might affect human performance. For instance, in the detection of early-stage cancers, AI can pinpoint tiny tumors in breast mammograms or subtle lesions in lung CT scans that might not be immediately apparent to a radiologist. This early detection is crucial because it often allows for interventions that can halt disease progression, potentially saving lives. Moreover, AI's impact extends beyond cancer to include other critical areas such as neurological conditions, where early detection is equally vital. Diseases like Alzheimer's and Parkinson's can begin to affect the brain long before symptoms become apparent to the patient or doctors. AI tools can analyze brain scans to identify early signs of these diseases, such as slight structural changes or abnormal protein accumulations, that may not be detected through standard diagnostic procedures. By identifying these conditions early, treatment strategies can be implemented sooner, which may slow the progression of the disease and offer a better quality of life over time.

The effectiveness of AI in early disease detection is not only a testament to its precision but also its scalability. Traditional diagnostic methods can be time-consuming and resource-intensive, limiting their availability in underserved regions or overburdened healthcare systems. AI, on the other hand, can process large quantities of data quickly and with fewer resources, making high-quality diagnostic capabilities more accessible to a broader population. This scalability is particularly important in global health contexts, where access to skilled radiologists and advanced diagnostic tools might be limited. The integration of AI into medical diagnostics also opens up new avenues for personalized medicine. By detecting diseases early and with high accuracy, AI enables more tailored treatment plans based on individual risk profiles and disease characteristics. This personalized approach not only enhances the effectiveness of treatments but also minimizes unnecessary interventions, reducing the physical, emotional, and financial burden on patients. The role of AI in early disease detection represents a significant leap forward in medical technology. Its ability to identify subtle changes in imaging that signify early disease stages offers a critical advantage in the fight against some of the most challenging health conditions. As AI technology continues to advance and become more integrated into healthcare systems, it promises to significantly enhance patient outcomes and revolutionize the approach to disease management and treatment.

Quantitative Analysis

AI has transformed the landscape of medical imaging by enabling not just qualitative but also quantitative analyses. This shift allows for a more detailed and objective assessment of various health conditions by providing precise measurements that are crucial for clinical decision-making. AI's ability to quantify aspects of medical images such as tumor size, bone density, or brain volume—marks a significant advancement in medical diagnostics, offering a more systematic approach to treatment planning and monitoring of diseases. Quantitative analysis in medical imaging is essential because it allows clinicians to track minute changes in a patient's condition that might not be visible through qualitative assessment alone. For instance, in oncology, the exact measurement of a tumor's size and its response to treatment over time is critical. AI excels in this area by using advanced algorithms to analyze scan images and accurately measure tumor dimensions. These measurements can be compared over successive scans to objectively determine whether a tumour is responding to treatment, growing, or receding. This precision helps oncologists tailor their therapeutic approaches more effectively, choosing to intensify, modify, or cease treatment based on quantifiable data rather than solely on symptomatic analysis.

Similarly, in conditions like osteoporosis, AI's capacity to precisely measure bone density from imaging scans enables endocrinologists and other specialists to assess the severity of bone loss more accurately. Traditional methods might only provide qualitative indications of bone density loss, but AI algorithms can calculate exact density measurements, helping in the early diagnosis and treatment of osteoporosis. These measurements provide a clear, numerical baseline against which treatment efficacy can be measured, enhancing patient management and care. Furthermore, in neurology, quantitative analysis by AI of brain volume and other structural metrics from MRI scans plays a pivotal role in diagnosing and monitoring degenerative brain diseases such as Alzheimer's and Parkinson's disease. Early changes in brain structure, particularly in specific regions that may shrink or change due to the disease, can be meticulously quantified by AI. This capability is invaluable, as it allows for early intervention and more targeted neuroprotective treatments, potentially slowing the progression of such debilitating conditions.

The introduction of AI-driven quantitative analysis also brings standardization to the diagnostic process. Different radiologists may have varying interpretations of the same scan, leading to subjective differences in diagnosis and treatment planning. AI helps mitigate these variations by providing consistent, repeatable, and objective data that can be universally understood and utilized, thus supporting more standardized care pathways. Moreover, AI's ability to deliver quantitative data rapidly and accurately helps streamline the diagnostic workflow in medical facilities. By automating the measurement process, AI reduces the time clinicians and technicians need to spend on manual measurements, allowing them to focus more on patient care and less on the technicalities of data extraction. In conclusion, AI's contribution to quantitative analysis in medical imaging represents a paradigm shift from traditional, often subjective, diagnostic methods to a more precise, data-driven approach. This not only enhances the accuracy of diagnoses and the effectiveness of treatments but also improves the overall efficiency of medical processes. As AI technology continues to evolve, its integration into healthcare systems is likely to expand, further revolutionizing the way medical professionals approach diagnosis and treatment planning.

Integration of Multiple Data Sources

The integration of AI in medicine has profoundly expanded the capability to synthesize information from multiple data sources, enhancing the comprehensive understanding of a patient's health status. By leveraging AI, healthcare professionals can now merge data from various imaging modalities such as PET, MRI, and CT scans with other critical medical data like electronic health records (EHRs). This synthesis provides a holistic view of a patient's health, facilitating more informed clinical decision-making and personalized treatment planning. AI's ability to integrate and analyze data from different sources addresses one of the significant challenges in healthcare: the fragmentation of patient information across various platforms and systems. Each imaging modality—PET, MRI, and CT—offers unique insights into the body's structure and function. For instance, PET scans are crucial for showing metabolic processes and are often used in cancer diagnosis, while MRIs provide detailed images of soft tissues, beneficial for diagnosing brain disorders, and CT scans offer a fast and detailed overview of body structures, including bones and blood vessels. Traditionally, correlating findings from these diverse sources could be time-consuming and prone to errors, depending on the clinician's ability to manually integrate and interpret disparate datasets.

AI streamlines this process by automatically compiling and correlating data from these different imaging technologies. Advanced algorithms can detect patterns and anomalies across the datasets, identifying correlations that might not be evident through manual analysis. For example, AI can combine imaging results with historical data from a patient's EHR, including past medical diagnoses, laboratory results, and treatment histories, to provide a nuanced perspective on the patient's current condition. This capability is particularly valuable in complex clinical scenarios where multiple factors influence health outcomes, such as in cases of chronic diseases or when multiple conditions coexist. Moreover, the integration of AI in handling diverse data types extends beyond diagnosis to include monitoring and prognosis. In cancer treatment, for instance, AI can analyze changes in tumor size from imaging scans over time, interpret laboratory test trends from the EHR, and monitor patient-reported symptoms to gauge treatment effectiveness, and adjust protocols accordingly. This approach not only enhances the precision of treatments but also personalizes the care based on the patient's unique medical journey.

The use of AI to integrate multiple data sources also significantly improves the efficiency of the healthcare system. It reduces the cognitive load on clinicians who would otherwise need to review and interpret vast amounts of data manually. With AI, data integration is not only faster but also more accurate, reducing the risk of human error and ensuring that critical information is considered in the decision-making process. In conclusion, AI's role in integrating various imaging modalities and other medical data is transforming patient care by providing a more comprehensive and accurate view of health conditions. This integration enables a deeper understanding of complex medical cases, supports personalized treatment plans, and improves the overall quality of healthcare delivery. As AI technology continues to advance, its potential to further enhance the integration and utilization of medical data in clinical practice is immense, promising even greater improvements in healthcare outcomes.

Personalized Treatment Planning

AI is playing a transformative role in personalized treatment planning, especially in fields like oncology where precision and customization are paramount. The ability of AI to analyze complex datasets allows for highly individualized treatment strategies that can significantly improve patient outcomes. This is particularly evident in the planning of radiation therapy, where AI algorithms enhance the accuracy and effectiveness of treatments by ensuring that radiation is precisely targeted to tumors, thereby minimizing exposure to surrounding healthy tissues. In traditional radiation therapy planning, the process of delineating tumors and adjacent healthy tissues involves a substantial degree of manual input, which can be subject to variability and potential inaccuracies. Clinicians must carefully balance the intensity and angle of radiation beams to maximize tumor eradication while sparing healthy tissues as much as possible—a process that is both time-consuming and complex.

AI revolutionizes this process by employing sophisticated algorithms capable of processing vast amounts of imaging data with extreme precision. These algorithms analyze multiple layers of data, including high-resolution scans from various modalities such as CT, MRI, and PET. They can delineate the exact contours of tumors with an accuracy that matches, and often exceeds, human capabilities. Furthermore, AI systems can integrate past treatment data and outcomes to refine their algorithms, continuously improving their precision. For instance, in the treatment of brain tumors, AI can analyze MRI scans to identify not just the tumor itself but also the subtle variations in tissue density around it. This analysis helps in formulating a radiation plan that maximizes the dose to the tumor while avoiding critical structures such as the optic nerves or other sensitive areas. AI-driven systems can simulate multiple radiation treatment plans in a fraction of the time it would take human planners, allowing oncologists to choose the optimal plan that offers the best chance for success with the least risk of side effects.

Moreover, AI's contribution to personalized treatment planning extends beyond cancer care. In cardiovascular disease management, AI algorithms can predict the progression of diseases such as atherosclerosis by analyzing imaging data alongside genetic and lifestyle information. This enables cardiologists to tailor interventions more effectively, possibly preventing severe outcomes like heart attacks or strokes. The use of AI in treatment planning also offers the potential for dynamic adjustments. As patients respond to treatment, AI systems can quickly recalibrate plans based on new imaging data and clinical results, allowing for ongoing optimization of the therapy. This dynamic planning is crucial in scenarios where the disease's response to treatment can vary widely among individuals. In conclusion, AI's advanced data analysis capabilities significantly enhance personalized treatment planning across multiple medical specialties, particularly in oncology. By enabling more precise targeting of treatments and allowing for ongoing adjustment based on patient response, AI not only improves the efficacy of interventions but also significantly reduces the potential for adverse effects. As AI technology continues to evolve and become more integrated into clinical settings, its impact on personalized medicine is poised to grow, heralding a new era in healthcare where treatments are tailored to the specific needs of each patient.

Training and Education

AI is significantly enhancing the training and education of medical professionals by serving as an advanced training tool that offers interactive case studies and simulates various clinical scenarios. This technology is reshaping how medical knowledge is conveyed and practiced, providing a dynamic learning environment that is both engaging and highly informative. AI-driven simulations and case studies are particularly effective in medical training because they allow healthcare professionals to gain practical experience and decision-making skills without the risk of harming actual patients. The use of AI in medical training involves creating detailed simulations based on real patient data, which helps trainees understand complex medical conditions and learn diagnostic and treatment strategies. For instance, AI can simulate cardiovascular emergencies or complex surgical procedures by integrating patient imaging data, historical outcome data, and current medical best practices to create realistic scenarios. These simulations can be programmed to present various outcomes based on the interventions chosen by the trainee, thereby providing immediate feedback on the decision-making process and clinical skills.

Moreover, AI systems can adapt to the skill level of the user, offering more complex cases or alternative scenarios as the trainee's competence grows. This personalized learning approach ensures that medical professionals can progress at their own pace, gradually increasing their confidence and competence in handling complex medical situations. Interactive AI-based case studies are another critical aspect of training. These case studies often use anonymized real patient data, allowing trainees to work through actual cases, including making diagnosis and treatment decisions. Trainees can interact with the AI by asking questions, exploring different diagnostic paths, and proposing treatments to see how different choices could lead to different outcomes. This method not only enhances critical thinking and analytical skills but also helps in understanding the subtleties of patient care, such as managing comorbidities and recognizing rare symptoms.

Additionally, AI-driven tools in medical education can continually update and include the latest research findings and clinical guidelines, ensuring that trainees are learning the most current information. This is essential in fields like oncology or infectious diseases, where treatment protocols frequently evolve. AI also facilitates greater accessibility to high-quality training resources, particularly beneficial for medical professionals in remote or underserved areas. Trainees in these locations can access the same high-quality simulations and case studies as those in well-resourced urban centers, helping to reduce disparities in medical education and raise the overall standard of healthcare. AI's role as a training tool in medicine represents a substantial forward leap in medical education. By providing realistic, interactive, and adaptable learning experiences based on actual patient data, AI helps medical professionals develop their skills in a safe, controlled environment. This training not only improves their clinical abilities but also prepares them to handle real-life situations with greater competence and confidence, ultimately leading to better patient outcomes. As AI technology continues to evolve, its integration into medical training programs is likely to become even more extensive, further transforming the educational landscape in healthcare.

Enhancement of Image Quality

AI is revolutionizing the field of medical imaging by enhancing the quality of images, which plays a critical role in diagnosis and treatment planning. AI algorithms are capable of improving the clarity and resolution of medical images, as well as reconstructing suboptimal images that may have been compromised by factors like patient movement or technical issues. This capability significantly aids in the accurate interpretation of medical images, ensuring that healthcare professionals can make informed decisions based on the clearest and most accurate information available. AI-driven image enhancement involves several advanced techniques. One common method is the use of deep learning models that have been trained on thousands of high-quality medical images. These models learn to recognize the structures and patterns typical of these images, allowing them to enhance details that are not as clear in poorer-quality images. For instance, in situations where a patient's involuntary movement during an MRI scan results in blurred images, AI can effectively sharpen the image, bringing into focus critical details that are essential for accurate diagnosis.

Moreover, AI algorithms can increase the resolution of images, allowing finer details to become more apparent and easily analyzed. This is particularly useful in fields like neurology, where the detailed observation of brain structures can help diagnose conditions such as tumors or vascular abnormalities. High-resolution images that highlight these structures can lead to earlier and more precise interventions, improving patient outcomes. AI is also adept at reconstructing images when original scans are not optimal due to technical limitations of imaging equipment or challenging patient scenarios, such as in pediatric care where young patients may find it difficult to remain still. AI can compensate for these factors by reconstructing images to reduce noise and enhance structural integrity, making the diagnostic process faster and more reliable.

The benefits of AI in enhancing image quality extend beyond improving existing images. AI also contributes to reducing the need for repeat scans, thereby minimizing patients' exposure to radiation and reducing the overall cost and time spent in imaging procedures. This is particularly beneficial in settings with limited access to advanced imaging technology or where the cost of multiple imaging sessions can be prohibitive. In emergency medical situations, the speed and quality of imaging can be crucial. Here, AI's ability to quickly enhance image quality plays a vital role in the rapid assessment and management of emergency conditions, such as strokes or internal injuries, where every minute counts. In conclusion, the enhancement of image quality by AI algorithms represents a significant advance in medical imaging technology. By improving clarity, increasing resolution, and reconstructing suboptimal images, AI not only enhances the accuracy of diagnoses but also optimizes the efficiency of medical imaging processes. As AI technology continues to evolve, its impact on the quality of medical imaging is expected to grow, further transforming the capabilities of healthcare providers in diagnosing and treating a wide range of medical conditions.

Predictive Analytics

AI extends its utility in the medical field beyond just diagnosis to predictive analytics, offering profound insights into the likely progression of diseases. This predictive capability is particularly transformative in managing long-term conditions, where understanding disease trajectories can significantly impact prognosis and care planning. By analyzing patterns in imaging data over time, AI algorithms can forecast disease progression, enabling healthcare professionals to make more informed decisions about treatment strategies and patient management. Predictive analytics in medicine leverages AI to process and interpret vast arrays of data collected from patient imaging across multiple time points. This approach allows AI systems to identify subtle changes in disease states that may not be apparent to even the most trained human eyes. For example, in patients with chronic illnesses such as multiple sclerosis or cancer, periodic imaging is a critical component of ongoing care. AI can analyze these images to detect minute alterations in the structure or size of tumors or lesions, predicting their growth or reduction in response to treatment. This ongoing monitoring aids in adjusting treatments promptly, potentially improving outcomes by adapting therapy plans more dynamically and responsively.

AI's predictive power is also crucial in conditions that require careful monitoring over years, such as cardiovascular disease or chronic pulmonary conditions. By analyzing trends in heart or lung imaging, AI can predict worsening signs or improvement, advising on preventive measures or the need for more aggressive interventions before the patient's condition reaches a critical stage. This proactive approach in managing chronic diseases can lead to better patient outcomes and reduced healthcare costs by preventing disease escalation that would require more intensive treatment. Furthermore, predictive analytics facilitated by AI is invaluable in the realm of personalized medicine. It allows for the tailoring of treatment plans to the individual patient based on predicted disease courses. This individualized approach ensures that patients receive the most appropriate treatments at optimal times, enhancing the effectiveness of medical interventions and reducing unnecessary procedures.

AI-driven predictive analytics also supports healthcare systems in resource allocation. By providing forecasts about disease progression in populations, healthcare providers can better prepare and allocate resources such as medications, hospital beds, and specialized staff to meet anticipated needs, enhancing the overall efficiency of healthcare delivery. In addition to clinical applications, AI's predictive analytics contribute to research by identifying potential trends and outcomes for diseases that are not well understood. Researchers can use AI models to simulate disease progressions under various scenarios, helping to uncover potential new treatment pathways and therapeutic targets. In conclusion, AI's role in predictive analytics marks a significant advancement in the management of health conditions, particularly those requiring long-term care. By analyzing imaging data and other health metrics over time, AI helps forecast disease progression, supporting proactive treatment adjustments and better resource management. This not only improves individual patient care but also enhances the operational efficiency of healthcare systems, ultimately leading to more sustained health outcomes and optimized healthcare delivery. As AI technologies continue to advance, their impact on predictive healthcare analytics is expected to deepen, further revolutionizing the approach to disease management and care planning.

Remote Diagnostics

AI is significantly advancing the capabilities of remote diagnostics, a development that is particularly beneficial in underserved or rural areas where access to expert radiologists and other medical specialists is limited. By enabling the diagnosis of medical conditions from afar, AI helps bridge the gap in healthcare accessibility, ensuring that individuals in remote locations receive timely and accurate medical evaluations. Remote diagnostics powered by AI involves the use of sophisticated algorithms that can analyze medical images and other diagnostic data remotely.

These AI systems are trained on extensive datasets, allowing them to recognize a wide range of conditions from standard imaging results like X-rays, CT scans, and MRI images. For instance, an AI model might analyze chest X-rays to identify signs of pneumonia or tuberculosis without the need for a radiologist's immediate presence. This capability is invaluable in rural clinics where the nearest radiology expert might be several hours away or in regions where medical resources are stretched thin. AI enhances the effectiveness of remote diagnostics by providing high-quality, consistent interpretations of medical images. This reliability is crucial for maintaining the standard of care in remote settings, where healthcare providers might otherwise rely on less definitive diagnostic methods due to the unavailability of specialists. Furthermore, AI-driven diagnostics are typically faster, reducing the time from imaging to diagnosis, which is critical for conditions that require immediate intervention.

Additionally, the integration of AI into remote diagnostics facilitates a continuous learning and improvement cycle. AI algorithms can be updated remotely with new data and findings, enhancing their accuracy and adaptability over time. This means that as more data becomes available, the AI system's diagnostic capabilities can continually improve, benefiting even the most remote healthcare settings. Remote diagnostics with AI also extends to the monitoring of chronic conditions, where consistent and regular data analysis is needed. For chronic diseases like diabetes or heart disease, AI can analyze data transmitted remotely from patient monitoring devices, providing regular updates to healthcare professionals and alerting them to potential complications before they become severe. This proactive approach can prevent hospitalizations and reduce the burden on healthcare systems, especially in areas where medical resources are limited. In the context of global health emergencies, such as pandemics, the role of AI in remote diagnostics becomes even more crucial. AI can help manage the large volumes of diagnostic data required during such crises, providing rapid assessments that are essential for containing outbreaks. This was evident during the COVID-19 pandemic, where AI tools were used to quickly analyze chest images and assist in diagnosing the virus, significantly aiding efforts where medical imaging specialists were not readily available. In conclusion, AI's role in enabling remote diagnostics represents a transformative shift in how healthcare is delivered, particularly in underserved and rural areas. By providing reliable, accurate, and timely medical diagnoses, AI helps mitigate the challenges posed by the scarcity of local medical expertise, ensuring that high-quality healthcare extends to all corners of the globe. As AI technology continues to evolve and its adoption becomes more widespread, its impact on improving global health equity is expected to be profound, offering a more inclusive approach to medical care for everyone, regardless of their geographical location.

Standardization of Interpretations

AI is increasingly vital in the realm of medical imaging, particularly for standardizing image interpretations. This capability significantly reduces the variability and subjectivity often associated with different radiologists' readings, which can vary due to individual experience, fatigue, or even differing educational backgrounds. The integration of AI into this process not only promises enhanced healthcare delivery and improved patient outcomes but also heralds a new horizon in medical diagnostics and treatment planning. AI achieves standardization by applying consistent algorithms to interpret medical images. These algorithms are designed and trained using large datasets of annotated images that encapsulate a wide range of conditions, ensuring that the AI systems develop a comprehensive understanding of various pathologies. Once deployed, these AI models provide uniform analyses, offering the same high-quality interpretation regardless of where or when the analysis is performed. This level of consistency is particularly crucial in complex cases where slight discrepancies in interpretation can lead to significantly different treatment decisions. The benefit of this standardization is profound. In traditional settings, a diagnosis might differ depending on the radiologist's level of expertise or current workload. AI eliminates such discrepancies, ensuring that every patient's imaging studies are evaluated with the same meticulous detail, thereby reducing the risk of misdiagnosis and ensuring that all patients receive care based on the same high standards.

Furthermore, the use of AI in medical imaging facilitates a feedback loop where the algorithms continually learn and improve from each new case they analyze. This process not only refines the accuracy of AI over time but also contributes to the ongoing education of medical professionals. Radiologists can compare their analyses with those suggested by AI, potentially highlighting aspects of images they might have overlooked or confirming their assessments, thus enhancing their diagnostic skills. Additionally, AI's ability to standardize image interpretations has significant implications for healthcare systems globally. In regions with limited access to highly trained specialists, AI can provide diagnostic support that matches the level of top-tier medical facilities, democratizing access to quality medical care. This standardization ensures that regardless of geographical location, patients receive a reliable and accurate diagnosis, bridging the gap between developed and developing healthcare systems. The integration of AI into medical imaging also enhances efficiency in healthcare delivery. With AI handling routine and clear-cut cases, radiologists are free to focus on more complex and nuanced cases, optimizing the use of their expertise where it is most needed. This not only speeds up the diagnostic process but also improves the overall workflow within medical facilities, leading to faster treatment initiation and potentially better outcomes for patients.

In conclusion, the role of AI in standardizing image interpretations represents a significant advance in medical technology, offering a more uniform, accurate, and efficient approach to diagnosing diseases. As AI continues to evolve and become more integrated into medical imaging, it promises to transform healthcare delivery, ensuring that all patients, regardless of where they are treated, benefit from the highest standards of diagnostic accuracy and care. This move towards standardized interpretations is not just a technical improvement but a fundamental shift towards more equitable healthcare.

Results Summary

The incorporation of AI into medical imaging is a notable progress that surpasses conventional diagnostic techniques, providing substantial enhancements in precision and productivity. This technology represents a paradigm shift in medicine, rather than just improving current processes. The advancement of AI is leading to the expansion of its use in healthcare. This is enabling the development of new and creative methods in personalized medicine, where therapies are customized to match the unique characteristics of each patient. As a result, patient care and outcomes are being enhanced. The capacity of AI to establish uniform picture interpretations tackles a significant obstacle in medical diagnosis, which is the inconsistency and subjectivity observed across different practitioners. AI improves the quality of diagnostics in various locations and institutions by offering consistent and dependable readings. This ensures that all patients receive a uniform and excellent level of care. Standardization is essential for ensuring fair healthcare provision, particularly in impoverished regions where there may be limited availability of experienced radiologists. Moreover, the capacity of AI to effectively handle and examine extensive quantities of data not only accelerates the diagnosis procedure but also diminishes the probability of human fallibility. This talent is extremely important in high-stress situations where quick decision-making is crucial to the results for patients. Moreover, the involvement of AI in predictive analytics provides a preview of the future of healthcare, wherein data-based observations might anticipate the advancement of diseases and enable the implementation of early intervention tactics. With the increasing advancement of AI technology and its growing integration into healthcare systems, the entire medical industry is on the verge of entering a new era. The use of AI-enhanced diagnostics signifies a transition towards a healthcare approach that relies on data-driven analysis and precision, and prioritizes the needs of the patient. It not only enhances the effectiveness of healthcare systems but also establishes a basis for future advancements in medical treatment and administration. Ultimately, the ongoing progress and integration of AI in medical imaging is anticipated to have a profound effect, revolutionizing medical diagnostics and creating opportunities for improved patient care on a global scale. The future of healthcare appears auspicious, as AI takes the forefront in developing increasingly advanced, easily accessible, and tailored medical treatments.

Conclusion

In conclusion, the chapter provides a comprehensive examination of the intricate relationship between medical imaging and AI in healthcare. By exploring the foundational principles underpinning various medical imaging techniques, the chapter elucidates the significant impact of AI on enhancing diagnostic accuracy, efficiency, and overall patient care. The discussion begins with a detailed overview of medical imaging modalities such as X-ray, CT, MRI, ultrasound, and PET, summarizing the essential physical concepts and technical advancements that enable each technique, while also highlighting their unique advantages and limitations. The chapter further emphasizes the transformative role of AI in medical imaging analysis and interpretation, underscoring how AI advancements are pivotal in improving diagnostic accuracy and efficiency, ultimately leading to better patient outcomes.

References

Lee, J.G., Jun, S., Cho, Y.W., Lee, H., Kim, G.B., Seo, J.B. and Kim, N. (2017). Deep learning in medical imaging: General overview. *Korean Journal of Radiology*, *18*(4), 570–84.

Liu, X., Faes, L., Kale, A.U., Wagner, S.K., Fu, D.J., Bruynseels, A., ... and Denniston, A.K. (2019). A comparison of deep learning performance against healthcare professionals in detecting diseases from medical imaging: A systematic review and meta-analysis. *The Lancet Digital Health*, *1*(6), e271–e297.

Mhlanga, D. (2021). A dynamic analysis of the demand for healthcare in post-apartheid South Africa. *Nursing Reports*, *11*(02), 484–94.

Mhlanga, D. (2022b). Stakeholder Capitalism, the Fourth Industrial Revolution (4IR), and Sustainable Development: Issues to be Resolved. *Sustainability* (Switzerland), *14* (7).

Mhlanga, D. (2022b). The role of financial inclusion and FinTech in addressing climate-related challenges in the industry 4.0: Lessons for sustainable development goals. *Frontiers in Climate*, *4*, 949178.

Mhlanga, D. (2023a). Digital Transformation in the Healthcare Sector: The Role of Artificial Intelligence for Inclusive Long-term Care around the World, Lessons for Africa. *In: Economic Inclusion in Post-Independence Africa: An Inclusive Approach to Economic Development* (pp. 347–62). Cham: Springer Nature Switzerland.

Mhlanga, D. (2023b). Financial Technology, Artificial Intelligence, and the Health Sector, Lessons We are Learning on Good Health and Well-Being. *In: FinTech and Artificial Intelligence for Sustainable Development*. Sustainable Development Goals Series. Cham: Palgrave Macmillan. https://doi.org/10.1007/978-3-031-37776-1_7.

Mhlanga, D. (2023c). Artificial Intelligence in Elderly Care: Navigating Ethical and Responsible AI Adoption for Seniors. *SSRN*, 4675564. https://ssrn.com/abstract=4675564 or http://dx.doi.org/10.2139/ssrn.4675564.

Najjar, R. (2023). Redefining radiology: A review of artificial intelligence integration in medical imaging. *Diagnostics*, *13*(17), 2760.

Pesapane, F., Codari, M. and Sardanelli, F. (2018). Artificial intelligence in medical imaging: Threat or opportunity? Radiologists again at the forefront of innovation in medicine. *European Radiology Experimental*, *2*, 1–10.

Sasikala, S., Subhashini, S.J., Alli, P. and Angelina, J.J.R. (2021). Deep Learning Applications in Medical Imaging: Artificial Intelligence, Machine Learning, and Deep Learning. *In: Deep Learning Applications in Medical Imaging* (pp. 178–208). IGI Global.

Tadiboina, S.N. (2022). The use of AI in advanced medical imaging. *Journal of Positive School Psychology*, *6*(11), 1939–46.

6 | AI and Predictive Analytics and Risk Assessment in Healthcare

This chapter explores the integration of Artificial Intelligence (AI) and predictive analytics in healthcare to improve risk assessment practices. It delves into the potential benefits, challenges, and ethical considerations associated with leveraging AI technologies in healthcare settings. By harnessing the power of AI and predictive analytics, healthcare professionals can make more informed decisions, enhance patient care, and mitigate potential risks. The chapter also discusses various applications of AI and predictive analytics, such as early disease detection, treatment optimization, and proactive intervention strategies, highlighting their potential to revolutionize healthcare delivery.

Introduction

Artificial Intelligence (AI) has significantly transformed various sectors, with healthcare being a prime example where AI's impact on patient care and quality of life is profound. This chapter explores the integration of AI and predictive analytics in healthcare, specifically in the domain of risk assessment. By leveraging AI, healthcare providers can enhance disease diagnosis, treatment selection, and clinical testing, thus surpassing traditional methods in terms of accuracy, efficiency, and cost-effectiveness. This technology not only minimizes human errors but also catalyzes advancements in personalized medicine, population health management, and patient-physician relationships, as highlighted by Alowais et al. (2023). Despite the substantial benefits of AI in healthcare, several challenges persist. The management of extensive datasets—which are essential for AI operations—poses significant ethical and privacy concerns. The integration of AI in clinical settings necessitates stringent oversight to mitigate issues related to data privacy, algorithmic bias, and the indispensable role of human judgment in decision-making processes. Moreover, the existing risk assessment models, which often focus on singular health outcomes, fall short of addressing the multifaceted nature of patient risks, especially in chronic disease management. There is a pressing need for predictive models that can evaluate multiple risk factors concurrently and provide comprehensive risk profiles that enhance preventive care and patient management strategies.

This chapter will examine how methodologies such as Bayesian multitask learning, as proposed by Lin et al. (2017), can revolutionize healthcare by enabling the simultaneous assessment of various health risks, thereby improving predictive accuracy and clinical outcomes. Additionally, it will address the regulatory and ethical challenges in implementing AI in healthcare, particularly focusing on the gaps in data governance and legal frameworks in regions like Bangladesh, as discussed by Hassan et al. (2021). The insights from Kilic (2020) on the use of AI and machine learning in cardiovascular healthcare will also be incorporated to underline the specific applications and potential of these technologies in a critical subdomain of healthcare. This chapter aims to provide a comprehensive overview of the current state and future prospects of AI and predictive analytics in healthcare risk assessment. By integrating the findings and perspectives from Alowais et al. (2023), Lin et al. (2017), Kilic (2020), and Hassan et al. (2021), the discussion will encompass the technological advancements, practical applications, challenges, and regulatory considerations associated with AI in healthcare. The goal is to offer actionable insights and forward-looking recommendations that can help healthcare providers, policymakers, and regulators harness the benefits of AI while ensuring ethical practices and patient safety. By examining these aspects, the chapter seeks to contribute to a better understanding of AI's role in healthcare and to facilitate its responsible integration into clinical practice, ultimately enhancing patient outcomes and the efficacy of healthcare systems globally.

Predictive Analytics

Predictive analytics, a field rooted in statistics, machine learning, and database techniques, uses historical data to predict future outcomes (Kumar, 2018; Sharmila, 2022). It is particularly useful in identifying risks and opportunities in various industries (Kumari, 2022). The central element of predictive analytics is the predictor, which is used to forecast future probabilities (Mishra, 2012). This field has seen significant growth, especially in the context of social networks and tailored services (Mathew, 2016). However, it also faces challenges, such as dealing with continuous and discontinuous changes (Mishra, 2012). The goal is to go beyond knowing what has happened to provide the best assessment of what will happen in the future. This method is widely used across industries for a variety of purposes, such as risk assessment, marketing forecasts, healthcare prognosis, and much more. In practice, predictive analytics involves collecting data, developing a statistical model, and then applying predictive analytics techniques to make predictions. For instance, in business settings, companies use predictive analytics to anticipate customer behaviors, optimize marketing campaigns, and manage risks. In healthcare, it can be used to predict patient outcomes and tailor treatments accordingly.

Risk Assessment in Healthcare

Risk assessment in healthcare is a crucial process for ensuring patient safety and quality care (Apostoli, 1999). It involves identifying, evaluating, and managing potential risks (Guzys, 2017). This process is particularly important in home healthcare settings, where nurses often work alone and have little control over the environment (Guzys, 2017). Various techniques, such as Monte Carlo modeling and HAZOP analysis, can be used to assess and quantify these risks (Brown, 2014). The goal of risk assessment is to reduce the likelihood of undesirable incidents (Guzys, 2017). It is also a key component of risk management in healthcare, which is essential for patient safety (Santacruz-Varela, 2010). Risk assessment tools, such as clinical practice guidelines, can help identify and prioritize risks for further action (Yarmohammadian, 2015). The use of risk matrices can aid in the analysis and mitigation of these risks (Sutherland, 2022).

This process involves several critical steps aimed at identifying, evaluating, and managing potential risks that may arise in healthcare settings. It begins with the identification of hazards, which could be anything from biological pathogens to psychological stressors that might impact patients or staff. Following this, a thorough analysis of these risks is conducted to understand their potential impact and the likelihood of their occurrence. Once risks are analyzed, the next step involves evaluating them against predefined criteria to determine if they are acceptable or if they require intervention. Depending on the outcome of this evaluation, risk control measures are then implemented. These measures might include developing new protocols, enhancing training for healthcare providers, or introducing safety mechanisms within clinical settings. Finally, an ongoing monitoring and review process is crucial. This continuous evaluation helps to ensure that the risk management strategies are effective and allows for adjustments as new risks emerge or as the healthcare environment changes. This proactive approach is vital for adapting to the ever-evolving landscape of healthcare, where new technologies and treatments continuously reshape the potential risks and their management.

AI and Predictive Analytics and Risk Assessment in Healthcare

AI and predictive analytics are increasingly important tools in healthcare risk assessment, offering the potential to enhance decision-making processes, improve patient outcomes, and optimize resource allocation. There are so many ways in which AI is transforming this critical area.

Predictive Modeling

Predictive modeling in healthcare, powered by AI, is revolutionizing the industry by enabling proactive, personalized care. Machine learning algorithms, such as deep learning models, are being used to analyze patient data and predict future health outcomes (Shruti, 2023; Bhavya, 2021). These models are increasingly accurate, with AI techniques doubling the accuracy of traditional methods (Axelrod, 2003). However, the lack of explainability in some AI algorithms is a challenge, which is being addressed by the emerging field of explainable AI (Yang, 2022).

Despite the potential of these models, there is a need for further improvement to ensure their accuracy and dynamism (Alanazi, 2018). The application of AI in predicting clinical needs, such as disease development and survivability, is particularly promising (Houfani, 2022). Overall, the use of predictive modeling in healthcare is a rapidly evolving field with the potential to significantly improve patient care. By examining patient records, genetic information, and lifestyle factors, AI algorithms can anticipate outcomes such as disease risk, likelihood of hospital readmission, and potential complications. This ability to foresee health challenges enables healthcare providers to deploy early intervention strategies, craft personalized treatment plans, and focus on preventive healthcare measures, thereby optimizing both patient outcomes and resource allocation. The process of predictive modeling involves several interconnected stages, starting with the comprehensive collection of data. This data includes patient medical histories, genetic information, and real-time health monitoring inputs from wearable devices. Once collected, the data undergoes rigorous processing to ensure its accuracy and usability for analysis. The core of predictive modeling lies in the development phase, where machine learning algorithms are applied to the prepared datasets. Techniques such as logistic regression, decision trees, support vector machines, or more complex frameworks like deep learning are used depending on the specific health outcomes being targeted.

After a predictive model is developed, it must be validated and tested using separate datasets to assess its predictive power and reliability. This critical evaluation helps refine the model, enhancing its ability to accurately forecast health events. Upon successful validation, the model is implemented in clinical settings, providing healthcare professionals with powerful tools to anticipate patient needs. Continuous monitoring and updating of the model are essential, as this maintains its relevance by adjusting to new data and evolving health trends. An illustrative example of predictive modeling in action is its application in the management of asthma, a widespread chronic respiratory condition. Asthma's unpredictability in symptom occurrence and severity makes managing it particularly challenging. A predictive model designed for asthma management would integrate diverse data points from a patient's medical history, including previous asthma attacks, medication adherence rates, environmental triggers, and even local air quality reports. This model enables healthcare providers to identify patients at heightened risk of severe asthma attacks and tailor their treatment accordingly. For example, the model might predict a higher risk of an asthma attack during pollen season in specific patients, prompting pre-emptive adjustments in medication or lifestyle recommendations to mitigate risk.

The impact of such predictive modeling extends beyond individual patient care. It introduces a level of personalized medicine that significantly enhances treatment efficacy and patient quality of life. Furthermore, by enabling preventive care through early risk identification, predictive modeling helps avert the progression of diseases, potentially reducing the incidence of severe health episodes and associated costs. Efficient resource utilization also becomes more feasible as healthcare systems can allocate medical attention and treatments to individuals who are most in need, thus avoiding wasteful spending. In summary, predictive modeling represents a revolutionary advancement in healthcare, shifting the focus towards a more informed, efficient, and patient-centered approach. As technology evolves, the potential for even more sophisticated predictive tools grows, promising further improvements in healthcare outcomes and operational efficiencies. This evolution in healthcare technology not only supports better patient outcomes but also aligns with the broader goals of enhancing healthcare delivery and reducing costs on a systemic level.

Risk Stratification

Risk stratification is a crucial process in healthcare management, greatly enhanced by the integration of AI. AI algorithms analyze a wide range of data from patient records, including genetic markers, lifestyle habits, and previous health history, to categorize patients according to their risk of developing specific medical conditions. This method of stratifying patients allows healthcare providers to prioritize care and allocate resources more efficiently, focusing on individuals who are at a higher risk of serious health issues. The process begins with the collection of extensive patient data, which AI systems evaluate to identify patterns and risk factors associated with various diseases. By leveraging predictive analytics, these systems can accurately segment patients into different risk categories. This categorization is not only based on historical health data but also incorporates continuous updates from ongoing patient interactions and newer health data inputs, which help in refining the risk assessments over time.

Once the risk categories are defined, healthcare providers can tailor their interventions more effectively. High-risk patients might receive more frequent screenings, targeted preventive measures, and intensive management plans that could involve specialized medications or lifestyle modification programs. These proactive measures are vital as they can prevent the onset of disease or the escalation of an existing condition, thereby improving patient outcomes and enhancing quality of life. Moreover, risk stratification using AI also brings substantial economic benefits. By identifying those at higher risk and intervening early, healthcare systems can prevent the costly treatments required for advanced diseases. For instance, catching and managing diabetes early through lifestyle changes and medication can prevent expensive and debilitating complications such as kidney failure or heart disease. Similarly, in chronic conditions like heart failure, early intervention guided by risk stratification can prevent hospital readmissions, which are both distressing for patients and costly for healthcare systems. The effectiveness of AI in risk stratification is exemplified in its application to cardiovascular diseases. Patients can be assessed for risk factors like hypertension, cholesterol levels, smoking habits, and family history to predict their likelihood of heart attacks or strokes. An AI-driven system could analyze these data points in conjunction with real-time health monitoring, allowing for dynamic adjustments to treatment plans as patient conditions evolve. For example, if a patient's monitored data indicates rising blood pressure despite ongoing treatment, the AI system could alert healthcare providers to adjust medications or recommend additional preventive measures.

By automating the risk stratification process, AI not only saves significant time and resources but also enhances the precision with which health professionals can predict and manage health outcomes. It allows healthcare providers to focus their efforts where they are most needed, leading to better management of patient care and more judicious use of medical resources. This strategic focus ultimately leads to a reduction in healthcare costs and an improvement in the overall efficiency of healthcare delivery. AI-driven risk stratification is a powerful tool in modern healthcare, enabling more personalized, effective, and cost-efficient patient care. As AI technology continues to advance, its role in enhancing predictive accuracy and operational efficiency in healthcare promises to grow, offering significant benefits to both patients and healthcare providers by paving the way for more proactive and tailored healthcare solutions.

Clinical Decision Support (CDS) Systems

Clinical Decision Support (CDS) systems represent a significant advancement in healthcare technology, utilizing AI to enhance the decision-making processes of medical professionals. By integrating AI tools with electronic health records (EHRs), clinicians are provided with real-time insights and recommendations that aid in diagnosing complex cases, suggesting appropriate treatment options, and alerting them to potential issues before they escalate into serious problems. The effectiveness of CDS systems begins with their ability to access and analyze comprehensive EHRs that contain a patient's medical history, treatment records, and ongoing health data. These systems apply sophisticated algorithms to process and interpret this vast amount of data, comparing it against the latest medical research and existing clinical guidelines. The AI-driven analysis helps identify patterns and anomalies that might not be immediately obvious to human clinicians, thereby supporting more accurate and timely diagnoses. For instance, in the case of a patient presenting symptoms that could be indicative of multiple neurological disorders, a CDS system can quickly sift through similar cases, medical literature, and clinical outcomes to suggest the most likely diagnosis. This tool can also recommend the most effective treatment protocols based on the latest research and tailored to the patient's specific health profile, including potential drug interactions and preferences based on past treatments.

Moreover, these systems are incredibly valuable for preventative care. By continuously monitoring patient data, CDS tools can detect early signs of deterioration in a patient's condition and alert healthcare providers. This early warning system is crucial for managing chronic diseases where timely intervention can prevent severe complications. For example, in patients with heart disease, a CDS system can monitor vital signs and lab results to predict and prevent episodes of heart failure, suggesting interventions such as medication adjustments or emergency care before the patient's condition becomes critical. Additionally, CDS systems play a critical role in ensuring that treatments are consistent with the most current medical knowledge. As medical research advances rapidly, keeping up-to-date with the latest treatment guidelines can be challenging for healthcare providers. CDS systems alleviate this challenge by integrating new research findings into the clinical workflow, providing clinicians with evidence-based treatment options that are continually updated. The implementation of AI in clinical decision support also enhances the efficiency of healthcare delivery. By reducing the cognitive load on clinicians and minimizing the risks of human error, these systems allow healthcare professionals to focus more on patient care rather than administrative tasks or information synthesis. This shift not only improves patient outcomes but also optimizes the use of hospital resources, reducing unnecessary tests and procedures, and focusing efforts where they are most needed.

CDS systems embody the integration of AI with healthcare to create a more informed, efficient, and proactive medical environment. These tools empower clinicians with actionable insights, backed by comprehensive data analysis and the latest medical research, to make better-informed decisions that improve patient care. As AI technology continues to evolve, its potential to revolutionize healthcare practices through advanced decision-support tools is immense, promising even greater advances in medical diagnostics and patient management.

Resource Optimization

Resource optimization in healthcare is significantly enhanced by the use of predictive analytics, a branch of data science that utilizes historical data, statistical algorithms, and machine learning techniques to forecast future trends and demands. This predictive capability is particularly valuable in managing healthcare resources, as it allows hospitals and clinics to anticipate and respond to fluctuations in demand effectively. Predictive analytics operates by analyzing patterns in historical data to make educated guesses about future occurrences. In the context of healthcare, this might involve predicting spikes in infectious diseases, which can be seasonal or linked to emerging health crises. By identifying potential outbreaks before they occur, healthcare facilities can mobilize resources, staff, and equipment to handle an influx of patients efficiently. This pre-emptive planning is crucial for maintaining quality of care during periods of high demand. Another vital application of predictive analytics is in the management of medical supplies. For example, by forecasting the future needs for specific medications, personal protective equipment, or medical devices, hospitals can optimize their inventory levels, ensuring that they are neither overstocked, which can lead to wastage, nor understocked, which can compromise patient care. This kind of foresight allows healthcare administrators to make more informed purchasing decisions, leading to cost savings and improved operational efficiency.

The benefits of predictive analytics extend to staffing decisions as well. By predicting busier periods, healthcare providers can adjust staff schedules in advance, ensuring that enough clinicians are on hand to meet patient needs without incurring unnecessary overtime costs. This not only helps in managing human resources more effectively but also enhances staff satisfaction by providing more predictable work schedules. Moreover, predictive analytics can aid in long-term strategic planning. For instance, if data indicates a growing demand for certain types of medical care or procedures, a hospital might decide to invest in specialized training for its staff or in new medical technologies that will allow it to serve its patients better in the future. This proactive approach can give healthcare facilities a competitive edge, enabling them to offer cutting-edge treatments and attract more patients. In an example of predictive analytics in action, during the early stages of the COVID-19 pandemic, some healthcare systems used predictive models to estimate the number of cases and the subsequent needs for hospital beds, ventilators, and intensive care units. This foresight proved invaluable in managing the crisis, as hospitals could prepare adequately, ensuring they were not overwhelmed by sudden surges in patient numbers. Predictive analytics is a powerful tool that enables healthcare organizations to forecast future demands accurately and allocate resources efficiently. By anticipating future trends and needs, healthcare providers can maintain a high level of preparedness, optimize their operations, and ultimately deliver better patient care. As data analytics technology continues to advance, its role in healthcare resource optimization is expected to grow, further enhancing the ability of healthcare systems to respond to patient needs effectively and efficiently.

Improving Patient Monitoring

Improving patient monitoring through AI-driven devices and applications represents a significant advancement in healthcare technology. These tools continuously track patient vitals and health conditions, providing real-time data that can be critical for the management of chronic conditions and post-operative care. The capability of these devices to automatically detect anomalies and send alerts to healthcare providers ensures timely interventions, which can be crucial in preventing complications and improving patient outcomes. AI-driven monitoring devices range from wearable technology, like smartwatches that measure heart rate and oxygen saturation, to more specialized medical devices that monitor blood glucose levels or cardiac rhythms. These devices collect vast amounts of health data in real-time, which AI algorithms analyze to detect any deviations from normal parameters. If an anomaly is detected, the system can immediately alert both the patient and their healthcare providers, prompting rapid response that can prevent adverse events and stabilize the patient's condition.

For example, in the management of diabetes, continuous glucose monitors (CGMs) equipped with AI can predict and alert patients about potential episodes of hyperglycemia or hypoglycemia before they occur. This proactive monitoring allows patients to adjust their insulin doses or dietary choices accordingly, preventing severe complications associated with abnormal glucose levels. In postoperative care, AI-driven monitoring is equally critical. Patients recovering from surgery are at risk of complications such as infections, blood clots, or sudden drops in blood pressure. AI-equipped monitoring devices can continuously assess the patient's vitals, wound status, and overall recovery progress. Healthcare providers receive alerts if the recovery deviates from the expected course, enabling them to intervene promptly. This not only helps in addressing complications early but also reduces the length of hospital stays and improves overall recovery rates. Furthermore, AI-driven patient monitoring extends beyond physical health to include mental health management. Wearable devices that monitor physiological indicators of stress and mental health apps that use AI to track patterns in user-reported mood and behavior can alert healthcare providers to signs of depression or anxiety in patients. This aspect of monitoring is particularly useful for individuals with chronic conditions, where mental health often intersects with physical health outcomes.

The benefits of AI-driven patient monitoring are multifaceted. By providing continuous, accurate, and real-time data, these technologies allow for a more dynamic and responsive approach to healthcare. Patients receive more personalized and timely care, healthcare providers can manage conditions more effectively, and the overall system benefits from enhanced efficiency and reduced costs. For chronic conditions, this means better disease management with fewer hospital admissions and for post-operative care, quicker recovery times and lower rates of readmission. AI-driven monitoring devices are transforming patient care by enabling continuous and precise health monitoring. As these technologies evolve, their integration into healthcare systems is likely to deepen, offering even more robust tools for disease management and health maintenance. This ongoing evolution in patient monitoring promises to make healthcare more proactive, personalized, and preventive, contributing significantly to improved health outcomes and quality of life for patients.

Enhancing Research and Drug Development

Enhancing research and drug development through AI represents a revolutionary shift in how new medications and therapies are created and refined. AI tools are pivotal in analyzing clinical trial data, predicting molecular behavior, and simulating drug interactions, which considerably speeds up the process of bringing new treatments to market. Moreover, AI's ability to sift through vast datasets allows for the identification of potential new uses for existing drugs, adding an invaluable layer of efficiency and innovation to pharmaceutical research. The integration of AI in drug development begins with its ability to process and analyze large amounts of data from clinical trials quickly and accurately. Traditional methods of data analysis are often time-consuming and may overlook complex patterns that AI algorithms can detect. By using AI to evaluate clinical trial data, researchers can understand more rapidly the efficacy and safety profiles of new drugs, thereby accelerating the iterative process of drug development. This swift analysis is critical not only for speeding up the approval of new drugs but also for ensuring that they are safe and effective for patient use. AI's capabilities extend into the realm of molecular science as well. Through predictive modeling, AI can forecast how different molecules will behave and interact with each other in the body. This predictive power is particularly useful in the early stages of drug design, where AI models simulate millions of potential interactions to identify promising candidates for further development. These simulations can drastically reduce the need for physical experiments in the initial phases, saving both time and resources.

Furthermore, AI algorithms are instrumental in identifying potential new applications for existing drugs, a process known as drug repurposing or repositioning. By analyzing how drugs interact at the molecular level, AI can predict whether a medication approved for one condition might be effective against another. This approach was notably utilized during the COVID-19 pandemic, where AI tools helped to quickly identify existing drugs that could be repurposed to treat the virus, significantly speeding up the response to the health crisis. In addition to these applications, AI also enhances the personalization of therapy. By integrating genetic data from patients with drug interaction models, AI can help predict how individuals might respond to certain medications, leading to more personalized treatment plans and minimizing the risk of adverse reactions. This level of customization is especially important in fields like oncology, where personalized medicine is rapidly becoming the standard of care. AI's impact on drug development and research is profound. It not only accelerates the pace at which new therapies can be developed and brought to market but also enhances the precision with which these therapies are tailored to individual needs. As AI technology continues to advance, its role in pharmaceutical research is expected to expand further, promising to reshape the landscape of medical treatment and drug development. This ongoing evolution points towards a future where medical treatments are more effective, more rapidly available, and more closely aligned with the specific health needs of individual patients, ultimately leading to better health outcomes and more efficient healthcare delivery.

Reducing Human Error

Reducing human error in healthcare settings is a crucial benefit of integrating AI systems. AI's capacity to enhance patient safety is particularly evident in areas like medication management and the interpretation of patient data, where precision is essential. By minimizing errors, AI systems contribute significantly to improving overall patient outcomes and trust in healthcare services. Medication management is a complex area prone to errors, ranging from prescribing and dispensing to administering and monitoring drug use. AI systems can play a transformative role in this process by automating and overseeing the accuracy of each step. For example, AI can analyze prescriptions to ensure they do not contain potential drug-drug interactions or conflicts with a patient's existing conditions or allergies.

By cross-referencing vast databases of drug information and patient histories, AI systems can alert healthcare providers to potential issues before medications are administered, significantly reducing the risk of adverse drug events.

Another area where AI markedly reduces human error is in the interpretation of complex patient data. Medical professionals often have to make decisions based on large quantities of data, including laboratory results, imaging studies, and historical patient records. AI systems can assist by analyzing this data to highlight important trends and anomalies that might not be immediately obvious. For instance, AI-driven tools are used in radiology to enhance the accuracy of reading imaging results, such as X-rays or MRIs, by identifying subtle patterns that might indicate the early stages of disease. These AI tools serve as a second set of eyes, providing a safety net to ensure that critical information is not overlooked. Furthermore, AI can automate routine data entry tasks, which not only speeds up administrative processes but also reduces the likelihood of manual errors in patient records. Accurate record-keeping is essential for ensuring that all healthcare providers involved in a patient's care have access to the correct information, which directly impacts treatment effectiveness and patient safety. The implementation of AI in reducing human error not only leads to safer healthcare environments but also improves efficiency, allowing healthcare professionals to focus more on patient care rather than administrative duties. For example, AI-powered systems in pharmacies can oversee the dispensing process, ensuring that the correct medication and dosage are provided to patients, which mitigates risks associated with human fatigue and oversight.

The benefits of AI in reducing human error extend beyond individual patient interactions. By systematically reducing the incidence of errors across healthcare systems, AI contributes to a culture of safety and continuous improvement. This systemic enhancement is vital for advancing healthcare quality and patient satisfaction on a broad scale. AI systems significantly reduce human error in healthcare through precise medication management and detailed patient data interpretation. As AI technology continues to evolve and integrate more deeply into various aspects of healthcare, its role in enhancing patient safety and improving care quality becomes increasingly vital. This technological advancement promises a future where healthcare errors are significantly diminished, leading to safer, more efficient, and more effective patient care.

Enhancing Telemedicine

Enhancing telemedicine through the use of AI-powered tools is dramatically transforming healthcare, making it more accessible and efficient, particularly for populations in remote or underserved areas. These tools enable initial assessments of patient symptoms remotely, allowing for quicker and more convenient care without the need for patients to visit healthcare facilities in person. AI in telemedicine operates by using sophisticated algorithms to analyze the symptoms reported by patients via online platforms or telehealth applications. Patients can enter their symptoms into a system, and AI tools process this information to provide initial diagnostic impressions. This technology is especially beneficial for conditions that require quick intervention, as it can prioritize cases based on severity and direct patients to seek in-person care when necessary. For example, AI-powered chatbots and virtual health assistants are increasingly used to conduct preliminary assessments. These systems can ask patients a series of structured questions to gather more detailed information about their symptoms and health history. The AI evaluates this data against a vast repository of medical knowledge and current clinical guidelines to suggest potential diagnoses and advise on the next steps, whether that be self-care recommendations or a prompt to schedule a virtual consultation with a physician.

This application of AI not only speeds up the initial screening process but also enhances the reach of healthcare providers, allowing them to monitor and manage a larger number of patients more effectively. It is particularly valuable for managing chronic conditions, where regular monitoring and frequent interaction with healthcare systems are necessary. AI-driven telemedicine tools can remind patients to take medications, track their symptoms, and provide advice based on changes in their condition, all without needing to leave their homes. Moreover, AI-enhanced telemedicine improves healthcare accessibility for individuals who might otherwise face barriers to accessing care, such as those living in rural areas, elderly individuals, or those with mobility limitations. By providing reliable medical consultations remotely, these tools help reduce travel time and associated costs for patients, making healthcare more inclusive and equitable. The impact of AI on telemedicine also extends to the optimization of healthcare resources. By handling routine assessments and monitoring tasks, AI allows healthcare professionals to focus their efforts on more complex cases and direct interactions with patients, thereby increasing overall system efficiency. Additionally, these AI systems can collect and analyze data from numerous telemedicine interactions, providing valuable insights that can lead to improvements in service delivery and patient care strategies. AI-powered tools are essential in enhancing the capabilities of telemedicine. They provide crucial initial assessments, broaden healthcare accessibility, and improve the efficiency of medical services. As these technologies continue to advance and become more integrated into healthcare systems, their role in delivering timely, effective, and patient-centered care will only expand, further revolutionizing how healthcare is accessed and administered globally. These advancements are accompanied by considerations around data privacy, ethical use of AI, and the need for robust validation and regulatory oversight to ensure accuracy and fairness in AI-driven decisions. As technology evolves, it will be crucial to balance these innovations with safeguards that protect patient rights and promote equitable healthcare access.

Ethical and Privacy Considerations

The integration of AI in healthcare presents numerous benefits, including improved diagnosis and treatment, but also raises significant ethical and privacy concerns

(Upreti, 2023; Bartoletti, 2019). These concerns include patient privacy, biased results, patient safety, and human errors (Naik, 2022; Kooli, 2022; Mhlanga 2023b, Mhlanga 2023c). The legal and ethical challenges of AI in public health are further highlighted, emphasizing the need for algorithmic transparency, privacy, and cybersecurity (Al-hwsali, 2023). The use of AI in healthcare also challenges commonly held values and ethical principles, particularly in the areas of dynamic information and consent, transparency and ownership, and privacy and discrimination (Racine, 2021). Despite these challenges, AI has the potential to revolutionize healthcare, and a multifaceted approach involving policymakers, developers, healthcare providers, and patients is crucial to address these concerns (Prakash, 2022, Mlambo et al. 2023). The use of AI in healthcare raises important questions regarding data privacy and the potential for biases in decision-making algorithms, both of which have profound implications for patient trust and the fairness of medical treatment. Data privacy is a primary concern as AI systems often require access to vast amounts of personal health information to function effectively. This data includes sensitive information such as medical histories, genetic data, and even lifestyle information, which are integral for AI to provide personalized care. However, the collection, storage, and processing of this data must be handled with the highest levels of security to protect against breaches that could expose personal health information. Ensuring data privacy not only protects patients but also builds trust in healthcare systems using AI technology. Furthermore, the potential for bias in AI algorithms presents another critical ethical challenge. If the data used to train AI systems is not diverse or if it contains historical biases, the AI's decision-making may perpetuate these biases. For example, if an AI system is trained primarily on data from a particular demographic group, its diagnostic accuracy or treatment recommendations might not be as effective for people outside that group. This can lead to disparities in healthcare outcomes and could inadvertently worsen existing inequalities in medical treatment.

To address these issues, healthcare organizations and AI developers must adhere to strict ethical standards and regulatory requirements. This includes implementing robust data governance frameworks that ensure patient data is anonymized where possible and protected against unauthorized access. Additionally, continuous monitoring and updating of AI algorithms are necessary to identify and correct any biases that may exist. Transparency in how AI systems make decisions is also crucial, as it allows patients and healthcare providers to understand and trust AI-driven processes and outcomes. Moreover, engaging with diverse stakeholders during the development and deployment of AI in healthcare is essential to anticipate and mitigate ethical concerns. Involving ethicists, patient advocacy groups, and representatives from diverse populations can help ensure that AI systems are developed with a broad range of perspectives and are more likely to be equitable and respectful of all patient groups. Incorporating ethical considerations into AI applications in healthcare not only involves addressing privacy and bias concerns but also extends to broader questions of responsibility and accountability. Determining who is accountable when AI systems make errors or when they are involved in decisions leading to adverse outcomes is crucial. Establishing clear guidelines and protocols for accountability can help maintain trust in AI-enhanced healthcare services. While AI has the potential to transform healthcare significantly, ensuring these technologies are used responsibly and ethically is paramount. Addressing ethical and privacy considerations in AI applications is critical for maintaining patient trust and delivering fair and effective healthcare. As AI continues to evolve and permeate various aspects of healthcare, ongoing dialogue, rigorous ethical scrutiny, and adaptive regulatory frameworks will be essential in navigating these challenges and harnessing the full potential of AI in a manner that respects and protects individual rights and societal values.

Conclusion

In conclusion, the integration of AI and predictive analytics into healthcare risk assessment represents a transformative advancement with the potential to significantly enhance patient outcomes and optimize healthcare delivery. While the benefits are substantial—ranging from improved early disease detection to tailored treatment plans—there are also considerable challenges and ethical implications that must be addressed. Healthcare professionals must navigate these complexities responsibly to harness the full potential of AI technologies, ensuring that patient care is both effective and ethical. As this chapter has highlighted, by carefully balancing innovation with oversight, the future of AI and predictive analytics in healthcare promises not only to revolutionize how care is provided but also to ensure it is done with the highest standards of equity and respect for patient rights.

References

Alanazi, H.O., Abdullah, A.H., Qureshi, K.N. and Ismail, A.S. (2018). Accurate and dynamic predictive model for better prediction in medicine and healthcare. Irish Journal of Medical Science (1971), 187, 501–13.

Al-Hwsali, A., Alsaadi, B., Abdi, N., Khatab, S., Alzubaidi, M., Solaiman, B. and Househ, M. (2023). Scoping review: Legal and ethical principles of artificial intelligence in public health. Healthcare Transformation with Informatics and Artificial Intelligence, 640–43.

Alowais, S.A., Alghamdi, S.S., Alsuhebany, N., Alqahtani, T., Alshaya, A.I., Almohareb, S.N., ... and Albekairy, A.M. (2023). Revolutionizing healthcare: The role of artificial intelligence in clinical practice. *BMC Medical Education, 23*(1), 689.

Apostoli, P., Bartoli, D., Alessio, L. and Buchet, J.P. (1999). Biological monitoring of occupational exposure to inorganic arsenic. Occupational and environmental medicine, 56(12), 825–832.

Axelrod, R.C. and Vogel, D. (2003). Predictive modeling in health plans. Disease Management & Health Outcomes, 11, 779–87.

Bartoletti, I. (2019). AI in healthcare: Ethical and privacy challenges. In Artificial Intelligence in Medicine: 17th Conference on Artificial Intelligence in Medicine, AIME 2019, Poznan, Poland, June 26–29, 2019, Proceedings 17 (pp. 7-10). Springer International Publishing.

Bhavya, S. and Pillai, A.S. (2021). Prediction models in healthcare using deep learning. In Proceedings of the 11th International Conference on Soft Computing and Pattern Recognition (SoCPaR 2019) 11 (pp. 195-204). Springer International Publishing

Brown, E., Morales, M.A., Pierleoni, C. and Ceperley, D. (2014). Quantum Monte Carlo techniques and applications for warm dense matter. In Frontiers and Challenges in Warm Dense Matter (pp. 123-149). Springer International Publishing.

Guzys, D. (2017). Youth health nursing. An Introduction to Community and Primary Health Care, 263.

Hassan, S., Dhali, M., Zaman, F. and Tanveer, M. (2021). Big data and predictive analytics in healthcare in Bangladesh: regulatory challenges. *Heliyon, 7*(6).

Houfani, D., Slatnia, S., Kazar, O., Saouli, H. and Merizig, A. (2022). Artificial intelligence in healthcare: a review on predicting clinical needs. International Journal of Healthcare Management, *15*(3), 267–275.

Kilic, A. (2020). Artificial intelligence and machine learning in cardiovascular health- care. *The Annals of Thoracic Surgery, 109*(5), 1323–29.

Kooli, C. and Al Muftah, H. (2022). Artificial intelligence in healthcare: a comprehensive review of its ethical concerns. Technological Sustainability, *1*(2), 121–31.

Kumar, S., Stecher, G., Li, M., Knyaz, C. and Tamura, K. (2018). MEGA X: molecular evolutionary genetics analysis across computing platforms. Molecular biology and evolution, *35*(6), 1547–1549.

Kumari, M., Lu, R.M., Li, M.C., Huang, J.L., Hsu, F.F., Ko, S.H., ... and Wu, H.C. (2022). A critical overview of current progress for COVID-19: development of vaccines, antiviral drugs, and therapeutic antibodies. Journal of biomedical science, *29*(1), 68.

Lin, Y.K., Chen, H., Brown, R.A., Li, S. H. and Yang, H.J. (2017). Healthcare predictive analytics for risk profiling in chronic care. *Mis Quarterly, 41*(2), 473–96.

Mhlanga, D. (2022a). Human-centered artificial intelligence: The superlative approach to achieve sustainable development goals in the fourth industrial revolution. *Sustainability, 14*(13), 7804.

Mhlanga, D. (2022b). The role of artificial intelligence and machine learning amid the COVID-19 pandemic: What lessons are we learning on 4IR and the sustainable development goals. *International Journal of Environmental Research and Public Health, 19*(3), 1879.

Mhlanga, D. (2023a). The Role of FinTech and AI in Agriculture: Towards Eradicating Hunger and Ensuring Food Security. *In: FinTech and Artificial Intelligence for Sustainable Development.* Sustainable Development Goals Series. Cham: Palgrave Macmillan. https://doi.org/10.1007/978-3-031-37776-1_6.

Mhlanga, D. (2023b). Exploring the Evolution of Artificial Intelligence and the Fourth Industrial Revolution an Overview. *In: FinTech and Artificial Intelligence for Sustainable Development.* Sustainable Development Goals Series. Cham: Palgrave Macmillan. https://doi.org/10.1007/978-3-031-37776-1_2.

Mhlanga, D. (2023c). Block chain technology for digital financial inclusion in the industry 4.0, towards sustainable development? *Frontiers in Blockchain, 6*, 1035405.

Mishra, N. and Silakari, S. (2012). Predictive analytics: A survey, trends, applications, oppurtunities & challenges. International Journal of Computer Science and Information Technologies, 3(3), 4434–38.

Mlambo, F., Chironda, C., George, J., Mhlanga, D. (2023). The Role of Machine Learning and Artificial Intelligence in Improving Health Outcomes in Africa During and After the Pandemic: What are We Learning on the Attainment of Sustainable Development Goals? *In*: Mhlanga, D., Ndhlovu, E. (Eds.) *The Fourth Industrial Revolution in Africa. Advances in African Economic, Social, and Political Development.* Cham: Springer. https://doi.org/10.1007/978-3-031-28686-5_7.

Naik, N., Hameed, B.Z., Shetty, D.K., Swain, D., Shah, M., Paul, R., ... and Somani, B.K. (2022). Legal and ethical consideration in artificial intelligence in healthcare: who takes responsibility? Frontiers in surgery, 9, 862322.

Prakash, S., Balaji, J.N., Joshi, A. and Surapaneni, K.M. (2022). Ethical Conundrums in the application of artificial intelligence (AI) in healthcare—a scoping review of reviews. Journal of Personalized Medicine, *12*(11), 1914.

Racine, V. (2021). Can Blockchain solve the dilemma in the ethics of genomic biobanks?. Science and engineering ethics, *27*(3), 35.

Santacruz-Varela, J., Hernández-Torres, F. and Fajardo-Dolci, G. (2010). Evaluación del riesgo para la seguridad del paciente en establecimientos de salud. Cirugía y Cirujanos, *78*(6), 515–526.

Sharmila, B., Srinivasan, K., Devasena, D., Suresh, M., Panchal, H., Ashokkumar, R., ... and Shah, R. R. (2022). Modelling and performance analysis of electric vehicle. International Journal of Ambient Energy, *43*(1), 5034–40.

Shruti, J.R. and Malige, S.V. (2023). Survey of Big Data Analytics in IoT-Driven Healthcare Applications: A Comparative Approach. In RICE (pp. 79-84).

Sutherland, H., Recchia, G., Dryhurst, S. and Freeman, A.L. (2022). How people understand risk matrices, and how matrix design can improve their use: Findings from randomized controlled studies. Risk Analysis, *42*(5), 1023–1041.

Upreti, K., Haque, M., Vats, P., Mittal, S., Parashar, J. and Pawar, V. (2023, September). AI in Healthcare in India: Navigating the Ethical, Legal, and Social Implications. In World Conference on Information Systems for Business Management (pp. 55-67). Singapore: Springer Nature Singapore.

Yang, C.C. (2022). Explainable artificial intelligence for predictive modeling in healthcare. Journal of healthcare informatics research, *6*(2), 228–39.

Yarmohammadian, A. and Akhlaghi, A.K. (2015). The effectiveness of painting therapy on reducing aggressive behavior in boy students with mild to moderate mental retardation. Journal of Research in Rehabilitation Sciences, *10*(6), 833–44.

7 | Revolutionizing Resource Allocation and Optimization in Hospitals with AI

Effective resource allocation and optimization are crucial in hospital settings to ensure optimal patient care, streamline operations, and manage limited resources efficiently. The advent of Artificial Intelligence (AI) has brought forth new opportunities for hospitals to leverage advanced algorithms and data-driven decision-making to enhance resource allocation strategies. This article explores how AI is transforming resource allocation and optimization in hospitals, leading to improved patient outcomes, cost savings, and operational efficiency.

Introduction

The healthcare sector is undergoing a significant transformation, with artificial intelligence (AI) playing a pivotal role in reshaping resource management and allocation in hospitals (Sarkar, 2023; Austin-Morgan, 2021; Pawar, 2024; Jeyaraj and Narayanan AVSM, 2023; Poalelungi et al., 2023; Mohan et al., 2023; Bhattacharya, 2020; 2023). AI is being used to optimize administrative tasks, offer personalized medicine, improve diagnostics and treatment recommendations, and enhance patient care and healthcare delivery (Sarkar, 2023; Austin-Morgan, 2021; Pawar, 2024; Jeyaraj, 2023; Poalelungi, 2023; Mohan, 2023; Bhattacharya, 2020; Mhlanga, 2023a). It is also revolutionizing patient outcomes, healthcare delivery, and the way healthcare is practiced, leading to improved accessibility, affordability, and quality of care (Sarkar, 2023; Austin-Morgan, 2021; Pawar, 2024; Jeyaraj, 2023; Poalelungi, 2023; Mohan et al., 2023; Bhattacharya, 2020; Mhlanga, 2023b). The integration of AI into healthcare is expected to enhance the effectiveness, safety, and accessibility of healthcare services, ultimately achieving value-based care (Mohan et al., 2023; Shahrukh Irfan et al., 2023).

In an era where healthcare systems are burdened with rising patient demands, escalating costs, and the imperative for efficient resource management, the integration of AI offers a beacon of innovation and improvement. This chapter delves into the transformative role of AI in revolutionizing resource allocation and optimization in hospitals, a development that holds profound implications for the future of healthcare delivery. Traditionally, hospital resource allocation has been a complex, often manual process, influenced by historical data and human judgment. This conventional approach, while functional, has limitations in scalability, accuracy, and efficiency. In contrast, AI introduces a paradigm shift, offering sophisticated tools that transcend these limitations. The evolution from manual to AI-driven allocation is not just a technological leap but a fundamental change in approach, harnessing data-driven insights for decision-making.

AI's penetration into healthcare marks a significant milestone. It encompasses a spectrum of applications, from enhancing diagnostic accuracy to personalizing patient care. In resource allocation, AI's role is multifaceted, involving predictive analytics, operational efficiency, and strategic planning. By leveraging historical data, real-time inputs, and predictive modeling, AI empowers hospitals to anticipate and meet patient needs more effectively, optimize staff deployment, and manage inventory with unprecedented precision. The specific applications of AI in hospital resource allocation are diverse and impactful. Predictive analytics play a crucial role in anticipating patient inflows, enabling hospitals to prepare for varying demand levels. AI-driven scheduling systems optimize staff allocation, ensuring that the right personnel are available at the right time. In inventory management, AI algorithms predict usage patterns, minimizing waste, and ensuring the availability of essential supplies. Moreover, AI contributes to optimizing the use of hospital facilities, from operating rooms to patient beds, enhancing overall operational efficiency. Through exploring these developments, this chapter aims to highlight the transformative capabilities of AI, the challenges encountered in its integration, and the vast opportunities it presents for enhancing efficiency and effectiveness in healthcare resource management. As we examine detailed case studies and theoretical discussions, the narrative will unravel the complexities and innovative strides made possible by AI in the modern healthcare environment.

Historical Context and Evolution of Hospital Resource Allocation

The historical context and evolution of hospital resource allocation illustrate a significant transformation from traditional, manual methodologies to modern, AI-driven practices. Traditionally, hospitals have relied heavily on manual processes for allocating resources, such as scheduling staff, distributing medical supplies, and managing patient bed assignments. These tasks were often guided by historical data and the personal judgment of experienced staff members. For instance, a hospital administrator might use past admissions data to forecast staffing needs for the upcoming weeks, or a nurse manager might manually organize shift schedules based on known patient loads and staff availability. However, these conventional methods have inherent limitations. They are often time-consuming, subject to human error, and cannot scale effectively with the growing size and complexity of healthcare operations. Additionally, these manual processes can struggle with accuracy, as they depend on the assumption that future patterns will closely follow historical trends, which is not always the case.

In contrast, the advent of AI has introduced a paradigm shift in how resources are allocated within hospitals (Barrett et al., 2019; Sahu et al., 2022; Mhlanga, 2023c, d). AI technologies offer sophisticated tools that significantly improve scalability, accuracy, and efficiency. For example, AI-driven predictive analytics can process vast amounts of data from real-time hospital activity to broader epidemiological trends to make highly accurate predictions about future resource needs. This capability allows hospitals to anticipate patient inflows with greater precision, thus optimizing the deployment of nurses and doctors. Furthermore, AI can enhance decision-making processes by integrating various types of data, such as patient acuity levels, staff skill sets, and historical resource utilization rates, to generate more effective scheduling and resource allocation strategies. This transition from manual to AI-driven allocation represents not just a technological advancement but a fundamental shift towards data-driven management practices in healthcare (Majeed and Hwang, 2021; Mhlanga, 2022a, b). One illustrative example of AI in action is the use of machine learning algorithms to optimize bed allocation. These systems can analyze patterns in patients' admissions and discharges, predict peak times, and suggest optimal patient placement to reduce wait times and overcrowding. Another example is the implementation of AI for inventory management, where algorithms predict usage patterns of medical supplies, helping hospitals minimize waste and avoid shortages by automating orders when stocks reach critically low levels. These examples demonstrate how AI is not merely replacing old tools with new ones but is fundamentally changing the approach to decision-making in hospital resource allocation, leading to more efficient, responsive, and effective healthcare delivery. This evolution underscores a significant leap forward, promising a future where healthcare can be more adaptable and attuned to both the needs of patients and the capacities of medical facilities.

Specific Applications of AI in Hospital Resource Allocation

The specific applications of AI in hospital resource allocation are diverse and impactful. Predictive analytics play a crucial role in anticipating patient inflows, enabling hospitals to prepare for varying demand levels. AI-driven scheduling systems optimize staff allocation, ensuring that the right personnel are available at the right time. In inventory management, AI algorithms predict usage patterns, minimizing waste and ensuring the availability of essential supplies. Moreover, AI contributes to optimizing the use of hospital facilities, from operating rooms to patient beds, enhancing overall operational efficiency.

Case Studies and Success Stories

Real-world case studies underscore the transformative impact of AI in hospital resource management. Hospitals that have adopted AI-driven systems report significant improvements in efficiency, cost reduction, and patient satisfaction. These success stories serve as compelling evidence of AI's potential to overhaul traditional resource management practices in healthcare.

Mayo Clinic in the United States of America

Mayo Clinic, one of the leading healthcare institutions in the United States, has taken a significant step towards enhancing its operational efficiency and patient care quality by implementing a predictive analytics system for surgical scheduling. This advanced approach leverages data analytics to refine how the clinic schedules surgeries, aiming to optimize the use of operating rooms and improve patient outcomes. The predictive analytics system at Mayo Clinic is designed to analyze a vast array of data, including historical surgery durations and patient recovery times. By examining past surgical procedures, the system identifies patterns and trends that help forecast future surgical timelines more accurately. This capability is crucial, as traditional scheduling often relies on estimations that may not account for the variability in individual surgeries and patient responses. This system enables the clinic to plan its surgical schedules more effectively. For instance, if the data indicates that certain types of surgeries consistently take longer than scheduled, adjustments can be made to allocate more time for these procedures. Conversely, if surgeries are regularly completed quicker than anticipated, the system can schedule additional operations within the same timeframe. This dynamic scheduling greatly reduces the downtime of operating rooms and maximizes their utilization.

Moreover, by predicting recovery times more accurately, the clinic can better manage post-operative care. This ensures that beds are available when needed and helps in efficiently managing the flow of patients through recovery wards. This aspect of predictive analytics not only improves the allocation of hospital beds but also enhances the quality of care by ensuring that patients receive timely post-surgery attention. The impact of implementing predictive analytics in surgical scheduling at Mayo Clinic has been substantial. One of the most immediate benefits has been the reduction of delays. Surgical delays are not only frustrating for patients and staff but also costly for the hospital. By minimizing these delays, the clinic has been able to enhance patient throughput—essentially, the number of patients who can be treated within a given time frame—thus increasing the overall surgical volume. An increase in surgical volume directly translates to better resource utilization. Operating rooms are expensive to maintain, and every minute they lie unused represents a lost opportunity for the hospital. Predictive analytics ensures that these valuable resources are employed to their maximum potential, thereby increasing the return on investment for the clinic's infrastructure. Furthermore, the enhanced scheduling capability has significantly improved patient satisfaction. When surgeries go as planned without unnecessary delays, patient anxiety is reduced, and the overall hospital experience is improved. Satisfied patients are likely to have better health outcomes and are more inclined to trust their healthcare providers. In conclusion, Mayo Clinic's implementation of predictive analytics in surgical scheduling exemplifies how data-driven strategies can revolutionize hospital operations. This approach not only optimizes the use of critical resources like operating rooms but also significantly improves patient care and satisfaction. As healthcare continues to evolve, the integration of such technologies will likely become a standard, benefiting patients and healthcare providers alike by creating more efficient, responsive, and effective medical care environments.

Johns Hopkins Hospital in USA

Johns Hopkins Hospital, a renowned medical institution located in Baltimore, USA, has implemented a ground-breaking AI-driven tool named Sepsis Watch to combat one of the most challenging medical conditions sepsis. This innovative system uses advanced machine learning algorithms to detect early signs of sepsis in patients, a critical advancement in medical technology that enhances patient outcomes and optimizes hospital resource allocation. Sepsis, a life-threatening response to infection that can lead to tissue damage, organ failure, and death, requires rapid intervention to prevent severe outcomes and high mortality rates. The traditional approach to diagnosing sepsis involves monitoring for a range of symptoms and signs, which can be subjective and vary significantly among patients. This variability often leads to delays in diagnosis and treatment, exacerbating the patient's condition. "Sepsis Watch" addresses these challenges by continuously analyzing real-time data from patient monitoring systems. It incorporates various indicators such as vital signs, lab results, and clinical notes to assess the likelihood of sepsis. This AI system is trained on large datasets, allowing it to recognize patterns that might elude even the most experienced healthcare professionals. By identifying potential sepsis early, the tool triggers alerts to medical staff, facilitating immediate intervention.

The deployment of Sepsis Watch at Johns Hopkins Hospital has led to several significant improvements in patient care. Firstly, the system's ability to alert staff early in the onset of sepsis allows for quicker responses, which is crucial given the rapid progression of the condition. Early intervention typically involves the administration of antibiotics and fluids, which can be life-saving when delivered promptly. This rapid response capability has significantly improved patient outcomes. Statistics indicate that early detection and treatment of sepsis can dramatically reduce the mortality rate associated with the condition. Furthermore, because patients are treated more effectively at initial stages, the duration of their stays in intensive care units (ICUs) is reduced. Shorter ICU stays not only lower the risk of complications, such as hospital-acquired infections, but also free up critical care resources for other patients, enhancing the hospital's capacity to deliver care. Moreover, Sepsis Watch has had a profound impact on resource allocation within the hospital. ICUs are high-cost environments requiring extensive resources, including specialized staff and equipment. By reducing the length of ICU stays, Johns Hopkins can better manage these resources, allowing for the treatment of more patients without the need for additional expansions or expenditures. This optimization of resource allocation is especially crucial in times of high demand, such as during flu seasons or other health crises. In addition to improving medical outcomes and resource management, the introduction of "Sepsis Watch" also has broader implications for the standard of care in hospitals worldwide. As other institutions look to Johns Hopkins for best practices, similar AI-driven tools are likely to be adopted, potentially transforming how sepsis is managed on a global scale. In conclusion, Johns Hopkins Hospital's "Sepsis Watch" exemplifies the potential of AI and machine learning in revolutionizing healthcare practices. This system not only advances the fight against sepsis but also demonstrates how innovative technologies can enhance the efficiency of healthcare systems, improve patient outcomes, and optimize the use of vital medical resources. As such, "Sepsis Watch" serves as a model for future healthcare innovations.

Singapore's Tan Tock Seng Hospital

Singapore's Tan Tock Seng Hospital, one of the foremost healthcare institutions in the country, has harnessed the power of AI to create a sophisticated system for predicting outbreaks of infectious diseases. This innovative AI tool is a cornerstone of the hospital's strategy for managing public health crises, such as flu seasons and other outbreaks, by enabling effective resource allocation and preparedness measures. The primary goal of this AI-driven system is to anticipate the onset and severity of infectious disease outbreaks before they reach critical levels. This proactive approach is crucial, as early detection and preparedness can significantly mitigate the impact of such health crises on both the population and healthcare systems. By analyzing patterns from past outbreaks along with real-time data from various sources—including hospital admissions, laboratory results, and public health reports—the AI model can predict potential spikes in disease occurrences with considerable accuracy. This predictive capability allows Tan Tock Seng Hospital to prepare effectively for impending outbreaks. With advance notice, the hospital can strategically allocate medical resources, such as staffing, beds, medications, and vaccines, to areas where they are most needed. This preparation is vital during times like the flu season, where sudden surges in patient numbers can otherwise overwhelm healthcare facilities.

The system also enables the hospital to optimize its operational efficiency. By predicting high-demand periods, hospital management can adjust staffing levels, ensuring that sufficient healthcare professionals are available to handle an influx of patients without resorting to emergency hires or overtime, which are costly and can lead to staff burnout. Additionally, it facilitates better scheduling of elective procedures, which may be postponed during peak times to free up resources for more urgent cases. Moreover, the AI tool contributes to the hospital's ability to communicate more effectively with the public and other healthcare providers. By providing reliable forecasts of disease activity, the hospital can issue timely warnings to the public to take preventive measures, such as vaccination or avoiding crowded places. Similarly, it can alert other hospitals and clinics to prepare for increased patient loads, enhancing the collective response capability of the healthcare system. The success of Tan Tock Seng Hospital's AI system for outbreak prediction not only improves patient care during critical times but also offers a model that other institutions can emulate. This approach showcases how

AI can be a transformative tool in public health management, particularly in a densely populated urban setting like Singapore, where infectious diseases can spread rapidly. Tan Tock Seng Hospital's use of AI for predicting infectious disease outbreaks represents a significant advancement in medical technology and public health management. This system not only enhances the hospital's preparedness and response capabilities but also sets a benchmark for other healthcare facilities around the world. The ability to predict and thereby manage potential health crises more effectively ensures better patient outcomes, optimizes resource use, and strengthens the overall resilience of healthcare systems against infectious diseases.

Humber River Hospital, Toronto

Humber River Hospital in Toronto has embraced cutting-edge technology by integrating robotics and AI into its supply chain management. This strategic implementation involves the use of Automated Guided Vehicles (AGVs) that navigate throughout the hospital, delivering supplies efficiently. The deployment of robotics and AI in this capacity is designed to optimize the distribution of resources, ensuring that medical supplies reach where they are needed most, precisely when they are needed. The introduction of AGVs at Humber River Hospital is part of a broader initiative to enhance operational efficiency and reduce human error in supply chain management. These robotic vehicles are programmed to navigate hospital corridors autonomously, transporting everything from medications and linens to medical instruments and patient meals. Managed by advanced AI systems, AGVs are capable of planning and modifying their routes in real-time to avoid obstacles and ensure timely deliveries.

The AI system that oversees the AGVs is equipped with sophisticated algorithms that analyze hospital logistics and inventory needs. This system can predict and respond to the varying demands of different hospital departments, adjusting supply distribution schedules as required. For instance, if a particular unit experiences an unexpected increase inpatient admissions, the AI can immediately reroute vehicles to prioritize deliveries to that unit, ensuring that essential supplies and equipment are readily available. This automation of supply chain tasks offers several significant benefits. First, it increases efficiency by reducing the time staff spend on logistical tasks, allowing them to focus more on direct patient care. This is particularly crucial in a high-demand healthcare environment where time and accuracy are paramount. Additionally, the precision of AI and robotics minimizes the risks of supply shortages or surpluses, optimizing inventory levels and reducing waste. Moreover, the use of AGVs and AI in supply chain management contributes to enhanced safety and infection control—a critical consideration in hospital settings. By limiting the need for human handling of supplies, the system reduces the risk of cross-contamination and improves the overall hygiene within the hospital. This is especially important for preventing hospital-acquired infections and ensuring a safe environment for both patients and staff.

The impact of implementing these technologies at Humber River Hospital extends beyond internal operations. It also serves as a model for other healthcare institutions looking to innovate and improve efficiency. As hospitals worldwide face increasing pressures to manage costs and improve patient outcomes, the integration of robotics and AI into supply chain processes offers a viable solution for managing resources effectively while maintaining high standards of care. In conclusion, Humber River Hospital's use of robotics and AI in supply chain management exemplifies the potential of technology to transform healthcare operations. This system not only ensures the efficient and timely distribution of supplies but also enhances overall hospital efficiency, safety, and care quality. As technology continues to evolve, such innovations are likely to become more prevalent in healthcare settings, setting new standards for operational excellence and patient care. These case studies demonstrate the diverse applications and significant benefits of AI in healthcare, particularly in optimizing hospital resource allocation and management, ultimately leading to enhanced patient care and operational efficiency.

The Integration of Artificial Intelligence (AI) in Hospitals is Revolutionizing the Way Resources are Allocated and Optimized

Predictive Analytics for Patient Inflow

The implementation of predictive analytics in healthcare is revolutionizing hospital operations, particularly in managing patient inflow. Machine learning algorithms are being used to analyze patient data, predict outcomes, and optimize operations (Shruti and Trivedi, 2023). These algorithms, combined with electronic health records, can accurately predict patient flows, discharge destinations, and intensive care unit needs (Bertsimas et al., 2021). Predictive analytics is also being used to anticipate patient surges and manage hospital resources (Chan and Scheulen, 2017; Chan, 2017). However, concerns about patient data privacy and algorithmic bias need to be addressed (Shruti et al., 2023). Despite these challenges, predictive analytics has the potential to improve hospital management and patient care (Lopes et al., 2020). By utilizing AI algorithms to analyze historical data, healthcare facilities can predict daily or seasonal fluctuations in patient numbers, which in turn enables them to optimize staffing, bed allocation, and the management of emergency resources. Predictive analytics works by gathering and processing vast amounts of data related to past hospital admissions, including the times of year, week, or day when patient inflow peaks or drops. This data might include weather patterns, local events, or disease outbreaks that historically influence patient numbers. AI algorithms use this information to identify trends and patterns, enabling predictions about future demands on hospital services. These predictive capabilities allow hospital administrators to make informed decisions about resource allocation. For example, during flu season, when a higher number of patient admissions might be anticipated, hospitals can prepare by ensuring adequate staffing levels to handle the surge. This can involve scheduling more doctors, nurses, and support staff during predicted peak times, thereby maintaining high standards of patient care without overstraining resources. Similarly, predictive analytics helps in bed management—one of the most critical aspects of hospital logistics. Knowing potential patient inflow allows hospitals to optimize bed usage, ensuring that they have enough available beds during busy periods while avoiding the cost of empty beds during quieter times. This is particularly crucial for managing the flow in emergency departments, where the need for immediate bed availability is often unpredictable. Furthermore, predictive analytics plays a crucial role in managing emergency resources, such as blood supplies, medical equipment, and intensive care units. By accurately forecasting patient inflow, hospitals can ensure that essential resources are available when needed most. This not only improves the quality of care provided but also enhances the hospital's ability to respond to emergencies efficiently.

The benefits of using predictive analytics for managing patient inflow extend beyond operational efficiency. By enabling hospitals to anticipate and prepare for patient needs, they also significantly enhance patient satisfaction and safety. Patients benefit from reduced waiting times, better staff availability, and prompt access to necessary medical care, which can directly impact treatment outcomes. Moreover, predictive analytics also provides a strategic advantage in financial planning and management for healthcare facilities. By optimizing resource allocation, hospitals can reduce unnecessary expenditures on overtime pay or temporary staffing and can make better use of their physical and human resources. This fiscal responsibility is increasingly important as healthcare costs rise and as institutions are pressured to do more with less. In conclusion, predictive analytics is a transformative tool that allows hospitals to enhance their operational effectiveness, financial efficiency, and quality of care. By leveraging AI algorithms to predict patient inflow, healthcare institutions are better equipped to prepare for and manage the complex dynamics of patient care. This technology not only supports better healthcare delivery but also drives innovations that can adapt to future challenges in the healthcare industry.

Efficient Scheduling and Staff Allocation

The integration of AI systems into hospital operations to optimize scheduling and staff allocation represents a significant leap forward in healthcare management (Youn et al., 2022; Pillai, 2023). These advanced technologies enable hospitals to tailor staffing levels precisely according to predicted patient loads, thereby ensuring efficient and effective use of human resources. This approach not only enhances patient care but also maximizes staff satisfaction and operational cost-efficiency. AI-driven scheduling systems function by analyzing a variety of data sources, including historical admission rates, patient discharge times, and even external factors like local events or weather conditions that can influence patient influx.

This data is then processed using sophisticated algorithms that predict patient load with high accuracy. Based on these predictions, the AI system dynamically adjusts the schedules of doctors, nurses, and support staff to ensure that the hospital is adequately staffed to handle the expected demand. One of the primary benefits of such a system is its ability to maintain optimal staffing levels. This precision prevents scenarios where the hospital might be understaffed, risking patient care and overburdening staff, or overstaffed, leading to unnecessary payroll expenses. For example, on days with predicted lower patient volumes, the system might schedule fewer staff members, whereas more staff would be organized during anticipated peak times. This dynamic scheduling not only ensures that patients receive timely and effective care but also helps in managing staff workload, preventing burnout, and improving job satisfaction.

Moreover, the use of AI for scheduling and staff allocation can significantly improve emergency preparedness. In sudden high-demand situations, such as a mass casualty incident or a public health crisis, the system can quickly recalibrate to ensure that enough healthcare professionals are available to meet increased needs. This agility is crucial for maintaining service quality during unexpected events. AI systems also contribute to operational efficiency by reducing the administrative burden on hospital management. Traditional manual scheduling is a time-consuming and often error-prone process. AI automates these tasks, freeing up management to focus on more strategic initiatives that enhance patient care and hospital performance. Additionally, automated scheduling reduces the likelihood of human error, such as double-booking staff or failing to comply with work-hour regulations, thus ensuring legal and ethical adherence to staffing practices. The financial implications of AI-driven staff allocation are also significant. By optimizing staff schedules based on actual needs, hospitals can reduce overtime costs and the need for temporary staffing agencies, which are often more expensive than regular staff. Furthermore, efficient scheduling can lead to better resource management, allowing hospitals to allocate their budgets more effectively towards other critical areas such as patient care technologies, staff training, and facility improvements. The use of AI systems for efficient scheduling and staff allocation in hospitals offers numerous advantages. These systems ensure that healthcare facilities operate with the necessary staff levels to meet patient needs, enhance the quality of care, and maintain high levels of staff morale. Additionally, they optimize operational and financial efficiency, making them invaluable tools in the modern healthcare industry. As technology continues to evolve, AI-driven scheduling systems are likely to become a standard in healthcare, revolutionizing how hospitals manage their most valuable asset their people.

Supply Chain Management

Streamlining hospital supply chain management with AI offers transformative benefits, enhancing efficiency and ensuring the availability of medical supplies and equipment when needed. By utilizing predictive analytics, machine learning models, and real-time data analysis, AI optimizes inventory levels and manages the distribution of resources efficiently. AI-driven predictive analytics use historical data to forecast future demand for supplies. For instance, by analyzing past usage rates of surgical gloves along with upcoming surgery schedules, AI systems can predict future glove requirements accurately, thus preventing both surpluses, which consumes valuable storage space, and shortages, which risk surgical delays. Integration of real-time data from electronic health records (EHRs), procurement systems, and external supply chain databases allows hospitals to quickly adapt to changing circumstances. For example, during an outbreak of a disease, AI can adjust procurement dynamically by analyzing the increase in usage of specific medications or protective gear, ensuring that the hospital remains well-stocked. Furthermore, AI can automate the replenishment process. In California, a hospital deployed an AI-driven system that automatically places orders for IV fluids and syringes based on consumption rates and projected needs, significantly reducing the workload related to manual inventory management.

AI also enhances supplier relationship management by evaluating supplier performance based on delivery times, product quality, and contract compliance. This enables hospitals to make informed decisions about which suppliers are reliable. For example, AI analysis might reveal frequent late deliveries of surgical instruments from a certain supplier, prompting the hospital to renegotiate terms or switch to a more dependable supplier. Additionally, AI systems identify potential risks in the supply chain, such as geopolitical events or natural disasters that could disrupt supply routes. This information aids hospitals in developing contingency plans, like diversifying their supplier base or maintaining higher stock levels of critical supplies. During the COVID-19 pandemic, AI models predicted disruptions in the global supply of personal protective equipment (PPE), allowing hospitals to secure supplies before widespread shortages occurred. The proactive integration of AI in hospital supply chains not only ensures efficiency and cost-effectiveness but also significantly improves patient care by minimizing the risk of supply shortages. As technology continues to advance, the use of AI in hospital supply chain management is expected to become even more sophisticated, providing hospitals with the tools they need to predict, analyze, and respond effectively to the dynamic needs of healthcare facilities. This ensures that patient care is uninterrupted and maintains high quality, preparing hospitals for both routine operations and unexpected challenges.

Inventory Management

In the realm of healthcare, efficient inventory management is crucial for ensuring the availability of medical supplies while minimizing waste. The integration of AI into inventory management processes is transforming how hospitals handle everything from medications to surgical equipment. By tracking and predicting usage rates, AI enables healthcare facilities to maintain optimal inventory levels, ensuring that essential items are always available when needed without excessive overstocking.

AI systems in inventory management work by continuously analyzing usage data and patterns from hospital records. This data may include the frequency and quantities of items used for different types of procedures, the seasonal demand for certain medications, or the rate of turnover for perishable supplies. By processing this data, AI algorithms can accurately forecast future supply needs, enabling hospitals to adjust their inventory orders accordingly. This predictive capability significantly reduces the risk of both shortages and surplus inventory. For instance, running out of critical surgical equipment or essential medications can compromise patient care, leading to delayed or suboptimal treatments. Conversely, overstocking can lead to waste, especially with items that have limited shelf lives, such as certain drugs or sterilized supplies. AI helps avoid these issues by providing precise, data-driven guidance on what quantities of supplies should be ordered and when.

Moreover, AI-driven inventory management supports cost efficiency. By maintaining the right quantity of stock levels, hospitals can reduce the financial burden associated with excess inventory storage and spoilage. This is particularly important in the healthcare sector where the cost of supplies is continuously rising, and budgetary constraints are ever-present. Efficient inventory management ensures that funds are used judiciously, allocating more resources to direct patient care and other critical areas. AI also enhances operational efficiency by automating routine tasks associated with inventory management. Traditionally, these tasks required significant manual effort and were prone to human error, such as inaccuracies in tracking stock levels or failures in ordering supplies promptly. AI automates these processes, reducing errors and freeing up staff to focus on more strategic tasks that directly impact patient care and service quality.

The system's ability to integrate with other hospital management software further amplifies its benefits. For example, AI can be linked with EHRs and procurement systems, creating a cohesive network that automatically updates and orders stocks based on upcoming surgeries, patient admissions, and other relevant data. This level of integration ensures that the inventory management system is responsive to the dynamic needs of the hospital. The use of AI in inventory management within healthcare settings offers significant advantages by optimizing stock levels, reducing waste, and ensuring the availability of necessary medical supplies. This technology not only supports better financial and operational efficiency but also enhances the overall quality of patient care. As AI technology evolves and becomes more sophisticated, its role in transforming healthcare logistics and management will undoubtedly expand, making it an indispensable tool in modern healthcare administration.

Operating Room Optimization

Operating room optimization through AI significantly enhances the efficiency of surgical procedures by using detailed data analysis. AI systems analyze vast amounts of data, including surgery durations, recovery times, and room turnover rates, to improve the scheduling of surgeries and maximize the use of operating rooms. This process involves understanding patterns and predicting future trends to allocate resources more effectively. For example, AI can assess historical data on the length of different types of surgeries and factor in the associated recovery times to optimize the scheduling process. If the data indicates that certain surgeries frequently run longer than scheduled, AI can adjust future schedules to accommodate more realistic timeframes, thus reducing delays and improving patient flow. This data-driven approach ensures that surgeries start on time and that there is minimal downtime between operations. Moreover, AI can help manage room turnover, which is the process of preparing an operating room for the next surgery. By analyzing how long it typically takes to clean and set up rooms between procedures, AI can schedule surgeries in a way that overlaps with these turnover times, thus keeping the rooms in continuous use. This is particularly useful in busy hospitals where operating room availability is a critical bottleneck.

In practice, some hospitals are using AI systems to dynamically adjust surgery schedules in real-time based on ongoing day-to-day activities. For instance, if an emergency surgery comes in, AI can immediately recalibrate the schedule, prioritizing urgent cases while rescheduling less critical surgeries with minimal disruption. This flexibility is crucial for maintaining operational efficiency and patient care quality in dynamic clinical environments. AI also assists in the pre-operative and post-operative stages. It can predict which patients might require longer recovery times based on their medical histories and the type of surgery performed. This allows hospitals to plan post-operative care more effectively and allocate recovery beds in advance, reducing the time patients spend waiting for appropriate care after their surgeries. The benefits of AI in operating room optimization extend beyond scheduling and logistics. By ensuring that surgeries are planned according to precise, data-driven insights, hospitals can improve overall patient outcomes, reduce waiting times, and increase the satisfaction of both patients and medical staff. As AI technology evolves, its potential to transform operating room management continues to grow, offering even more sophisticated tools for hospitals to enhance their surgical services efficiently and effectively. This not only optimizes resource utilization but also fosters a more responsive and patient-centric healthcare environment.

Conclusion

In conclusion, the integration of AI into hospital resource allocation and optimization heralds a significant evolution in healthcare management. By harnessing the power of advanced algorithms and data analytics, hospitals can optimize their operations, leading to enhanced patient care, reduced costs, and improved operational efficiency. This article has highlighted the transformative potential of AI in reshaping how resources are allocated in healthcare settings. As AI continues to evolve, its role in facilitating more informed decision-making and efficient resource management becomes increasingly indispensable. Hospitals that adopt these AI-driven strategies are likely to see substantial improvements in patient outcomes and resource utilization, setting a new standard for excellence in healthcare services.

References

Austin-Morgan, T. (2021). How AI is Transforming the NHS. *New Electronics*.

Barrett, M., Boyne, J., Brandts, J., Brunner-La Rocca, H.P., De Maesschalck, L., De Wit, K., ... and Zippel-Schultz, B. (2019). Artificial intelligence supported patient self-care in chronic heart failure: A paradigm shift from reactive to predictive, preventive, and personalized care. *Epma Journal, 10*, 445–64.

Bertsimas, D., Pauphilet, J., Stevens, J.P. and Tandon, M. (2020). Predicting inpatient flow at a major hospital using interpretable analytics. *Manuf. Serv. Oper. Manag., 24*, 2809–24.

Bhattacharya, S. (2020). AI Set to Transform Healthcare. *New Electronics*.

Chan, C.W. and Scheulen, J.J. (2017). Administrators Leverage Predictive Analytics to Manage Capacity, Streamline Decision-making. *ED Management: The Monthly Update on Emergency Department Management, 29* (2), 19–23 .

Chan, M.P.S., Jones, C.R., Hall Jamieson, K. and Albarracín, D. (2017). Debunking: A meta-analysis of the psychological efficacy of messages countering misinformation. Psychological science, *28*(11), 1531–46.

Jeyaraj, B.D. and Narayanan AVSM, L.G. (2023). Role of Artificial Intelligence in Enhancing Healthcare Delivery. *International Journal of Innovative Science and Modern Engineering, 11*(12).

Lopes, J., Guimarães, T. and Santos, M.F. (2020, January). Predictive and Prescriptive Analytics in Healthcare: A Survey. *Procedia Computer Science, 170*, 1029–34.

Majeed, A. and Hwang, S.O. (2021). Data-driven analytics leveraging artificial intelligence in the era of COVID-19: An insightful review of recent developments. *Symmetry, 14*(1), 16.

Mhlanga, D. (2022a). The role of artificial intelligence and machine learning amid the COVID-19 pandemic: What lessons are we learning on 4IR and the sustainable development goals? *International Journal of Environmental Research and Public Health, 19*(3), 1879.

Mhlanga, D. (2022b). Human-centered artificial intelligence: The superlative approach to achieve sustainable development goals in the fourth industrial revolution. *Sustainability, 14*(13), 7804.

Mhlanga, D. (2023a). Artificial intelligence and machine learning for energy consumption and production in emerging markets: A review. *Energies, 16*(2), 745.

Mhlanga, D. (2023b). Financial Technology, Artificial Intelligence, and the Health Sector, Lessons We are Learning on Good Health and Well-Being. *In: FinTech and Artificial Intelligence for Sustainable Development: The Role of Smart Technologies in Achieving Development Goals* (pp. 145–170). Cham: Springer Nature Switzerland.

Mhlanga, D. (2023c). Artificial Intelligence in Elderly Care: Navigating Ethical and Responsible AI Adoption for Seniors. *SSRN*, 4675564.

Mhlanga, D. (2023d). Artificial Intelligence and Machine Learning in the Power Sector. *In: FinTech and Artificial Intelligence for Sustainable Development.* Sustainable Development Goals Series. Cham: Palgrave Macmillan. https://doi.org/10.1007/978-3-031-37776-1_11.

Mohan, D.A., Kumar, D.S., Annam, D.V., Yadav, M. and Prasanth, D.P. (2023). Role of AI (Artificial Intelligence) and Machine Learning in Transforming Operations in Healthcare Industry: An Empirical Study. *International Journal of Membrane Science and Technology, 10*(2), 2069–76.

Pawar, S. (2024, January). The Role of Artificial Intelligence in Revolutionizing Healthcare. *International Journal of Advanced Research in Science, Communication, and Technology*.

Pillai, A.S. (2023). AI-enabled Hospital Management Systems for Modern Healthcare: An Analysis of System Components and Interdependencies. *Journal of Advanced Analytics in Healthcare Management, 7*(1), 212–28.

Poalelungi, D.G., Muşat, C.L., Fulga, A., Neagu, M., Neagu, A., Piraianu, A.I. and Fulga, I. (2023). Advancing Patient Care: How Artificial Intelligence is Transforming Healthcare. *Journal of Personalized Medicine, 13*.

Sahu, M., Gupta, R., Ambasta, R.K. and Kumar, P. (2022). Artificial intelligence and machine learning in precision medicine: A paradigm shift in big data analysis. *Progress in Molecular Biology and Translational Science, 190*(1), 57–100.

Sarkar, A. (2023). The Impact and Potential of Artificial Intelligence in Healthcare: A Critical Review of Current Applications and Future Directions. *International Journal for Research in Applied Science and Engineering Technology, 11*(8), 2089–91.

Shahrukh Irfan, Prasanta Kumar Parida, Aakanksha B. and S.D. (2023). Advancing Healthcare through Artificial Intelligence: Innovations at the Intersection of AI and Medicine. *Tuijin Jishu/Journal of Propulsion Technology, 44*(2).

Shruti, J.R. and Malige, S.V. (2023). Survey of Big Data Analytics in IoT-Driven Healthcare Applications: A Comparative Approach. In RICE (pp. 79-84).

Shruti and Trivedi, N.K. (2023). Predictive Analytics in Healthcare using Machine Learning. *2023 14th International Conference on Computing Communication and Networking Technologies (ICCCNT)*, 1–5.

Youn, S., Geismar, H.N. and Pinedo, M. (2022). Planning and scheduling in healthcare for better care coordination: Current understanding, trending topics, and future opportunities. *Production and Operations Management, 31*(12), 4407–23.

8 | Redefining Clinical Decision Support Systems through AI
A Futuristic Perspective

This chapter delves into the realm of Clinical Decision Support Systems (CDSS) and explores the integration of Artificial Intelligence (AI) to enhance their capabilities. CDSSs have become vital tools in healthcare, aiding clinicians in making informed decisions regarding diagnosis, treatment, and patient care. The rapid advancements in AI technologies present an opportunity to revolutionize CDSS by providing advanced data analytics, predictive modeling, and decision-making support. The chapter begins by providing an overview of CDSS and their significance in improving healthcare outcomes. It highlights the challenges faced by traditional CDSS, such as limited data processing capabilities and a lack of real-time decision support. The subsequent sections delve into the application of AI techniques in CDSSs. In short, the chapter will look at understanding CDSS and their significance, integration of AI algorithms in clinical decision-making processes, and case studies showcasing the successful implementation of AI-based decision support systems.

Introduction

The healthcare landscape is undergoing a seismic shift with the advent of Artificial Intelligence (AI), redefining the realms of possibility in clinical decision-making. This chapter explores the transformative integration of AI into Clinical Decision Support Systems (CDSS), heralding a new era of precision, efficiency, and patient-centered care in medicine. The integration of Artificial Intelligence (AI) into the healthcare sector promises to catalyze a transformative shift in medical practices and patient care, redefining what is possible within the realms of clinical decision-making (Roopa et al., 2021; Tippur, 2023; Gouripur, 2024). CDSS, traditionally designed to aid healthcare professionals by providing expert insights and evidence-based recommendations, are now on the cusp of a revolutionary evolution. They have undergone significant evolution, with their use becoming more widespread and integrated into electronic medical records and other clinical workflows (Sutton, 2020). These systems have the potential to improve patient care and safety, particularly in the context of public health and genomics (Gupta, 2020; Coiera, 2009). However, their effectiveness is contingent on proper design, implementation, and user training (Berner, 2016; Moon, 2016). The maturation of (EHR) systems and infrastructure standards has facilitated the development of integrated CDSS (Peleg, 2006). Looking ahead, the future of CDSS is likely to be characterized by further advancements in data structuring, knowledge encoding, and information technologies (Middleton, 2016).

This chapter aims to delve into how AI is not just enhancing but fundamentally changing CDSS, offering a futuristic perspective on the potential impacts on precision, efficiency, and patient-centered care. AI technologies, leveraging vast amounts of data and advanced analytical techniques, are poised to enhance the accuracy and timeliness of clinical decisions. For example, machine learning models can predict patient outcomes more accurately by analyzing patterns from past medical records, lab results, and treatment responses. Consider a scenario where AI predicts the risk of sepsis in patients in real time, enabling early intervention and significantly improving survival rates. Another instance is the use of AI in oncology, where it assists in formulating personalized treatment plans based on genetic information, lifestyle, and previous responses to treatment, thereby optimizing therapeutic effectiveness.

However, the integration of AI into CDSS is not without its challenges. Issues such as data privacy, algorithmic bias, and the need for transparency in AI decision-making processes pose significant hurdles. Additionally, there is the problem of integration where existing healthcare infrastructures may need substantial updates to fully leverage AI capabilities. These challenges form a crucial part of the discussion on redefining CDSS through AI. This chapter will explore these aspects through detailed examination and real-world examples, setting the stage for a deep dive into the promises and challenges of AI-enhanced clinical decision support. It will discuss how these systems can be designed to be not only more effective but also equitable and accessible, thus truly advancing the field of medicine into a new era.

Clinical Decision Support Systems (CDSS)

CDSS are software tools that aid healthcare providers in making informed clinical decisions (Alaa, 2016). They are designed to analyze patient data and provide recommendations for diagnosis, prevention, and treatment (Mendonça, 2004). CDSS use patient data to generate case-specific advice, often employing rule-based, probabilistic, and machine-learning techniques (Rigas, 2010). The use of CDSS has been shown to decrease medical errors and improve healthcare processes and patient outcomes (Obeidat, 2015). They can be integrated with EHRs to improve patient safety (García-Jímenez, 2015). However, the workings of CDSSs are not well understood by clinicians, highlighting the need for further discussion and engagement in their development and deployment (Fraccaro, 2015). These systems harness patient data along with extensive medical knowledge bases and sophisticated algorithms to provide recommendations that enhance the accuracy, efficiency, and consistency of patient care. A key feature of CDSS is the integration of data from various sources, such as EHRs, patient monitoring systems, and other medical databases. This allows the systems to offer context-specific advice based on comprehensive patient information. The knowledge bases used by CDSS include guidelines, protocols, and evidence-based best practices, which are continually updated to reflect the latest medical research and clinical guidelines.

The primary function of CDSS is to deliver actionable recommendations or alerts to clinicians. This can range from calculating drug dosages and reminding healthcare providers about clinical guidelines to providing warnings about potential drug interactions or contraindications, as well as offering diagnostic support. CDSS are typically integrated into a healthcare provider's workflow through user-friendly interfaces within EHR systems, ensuring that the decision support is both timely and relevant to the patient being treated. There are two main types of CDSS: knowledge-based systems, which operate on predefined rules, and non-knowledge-based systems, which utilize machine learning to identify patterns and suggestions from large datasets. The benefits of employing CDSS are significant, including improved patient safety, enhanced quality of care, increased healthcare efficiency, and support for healthcare providers in decision-making processes. However, the implementation of such systems also faces challenges. These include issues related to data quality, integration with existing healthcare IT systems, resistance from clinicians to follow computer-generated advice, and the need to keep the medical knowledge base up-to-date. CDSS represent a vital component of modern healthcare, aiming to use data and technology to support clinical processes and improve overall health outcomes.

The Evolution of Clinical Decision Support Systems

The evolution of CDSS from rule-based to AI-driven tools is a complex and ongoing process (Xu et al., 2023; Elhaddad and Hamam, 2024). Early systems in the 1970s focused on cost control and compliance, while the 1980s saw the development of medical knowledge databases. The 2000s brought about the integration of real-time monitoring and physician order entry, and the 2010s saw the use of data mining and knowledge discovery algorithms. Today, CDSS are being developed in two main directions: traditional rule-based and machine learning-based approaches, with the latter showing promise in improving accuracy and trustworthiness. However, there are still challenges to be addressed, such as the need for more accurate and secure CDSS, and the improvement of their clinical role and eligibility in healthcare service. Tracing the history of CDSS provides essential insight into their development from simple, rule-based systems to the sophisticated, AI-driven tools we see today. This evolution reflects broader shifts in technology and healthcare priorities, demonstrating how advances in data processing and analytics have transformed clinical decision-making. Initially, CDSS were straightforward and rule-based, primarily designed to automate manual tasks and mimic basic clinical reasoning. For example, early systems would generate alerts for potential drug interactions by cross-referencing a patient's medication list against a database. These systems relied heavily on a static set of rules and were limited to specific, well-defined tasks such as ensuring prescriptions did not conflict with known allergies or contraindications.

As computing power increased and the availability of digital medical records expanded, CDSS began to incorporate more sophisticated data analytics. This new generation of CDSS could analyze larger datasets, recognizing complex patterns that were not apparent to human observers. Systems started to include algorithms for risk assessment, such as calculating the likelihood of a patient developing a specific condition based on their medical history and demographic data. For instance, tools like the Framingham Heart Study risk calculator, which estimates the 10-year risk of developing cardiovascular disease, are examples of how statistical models have been applied in clinical decision support to guide preventative care strategies. The latest advancement in the evolution of CDSS is the integration of AI, particularly machine learning and natural language processing. This shift represents a quantum leap in the capabilities of these systems, allowing them to process vast amounts of unstructured data, such as clinical notes and radiographic images, and to learn from this data in real time. AI-enabled CDSS can identify subtle patterns in data that human clinicians might miss, offering predictions and recommendations with remarkable accuracy. For example, AI-driven models are now used to predict septic shock in ICU patients, hours before the onset of symptoms, allowing for interventions that can significantly improve patient outcomes.

Moreover, AI has enabled the development of predictive models that can forecast individual patient trajectories, such as predicting the likelihood of readmission or identifying patients at high risk for adverse events. These predictive insights help clinicians tailor interventions more effectively, thereby enhancing personalized care. A notable example is Google's AI model for diabetic retinopathy, which uses deep learning to analyze eye scans and identify early signs of the condition, outperforming traditional screening approaches. Despite these advancements, the integration of AI into CDSS also brings challenges, including issues related to data privacy, the need for robust data to train AI models, and concerns about the "black box" nature of some AI algorithms, where decision-making processes are not transparent. Addressing these challenges is crucial for the next stage of CDSS evolution, which will likely focus on improving interpretability, ensuring equity in healthcare outcomes, and integrating patient preferences more deeply into the decision-making process.

Artificial Intelligence (AI) in Clinical Decision Support Systems (CDSS)

The integration of AI in CDSS is redefining the landscape of healthcare, offering a futuristic perspective that promises to enhance the quality, efficiency, and personalization of patient care. As we look towards the future, it becomes evident that AI will play a pivotal role in transforming CDSS into more dynamic, predictive, and intuitive tools (Figure 1).

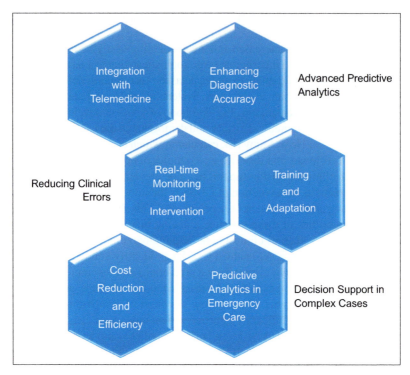

Fig. 1 Artificial Intelligence (AI) in Clinical Decision Support Systems (CDSS).

Advanced Predictive Analytics

CDSS play a crucial role in modern healthcare, enhancing clinical practice by improving safety, reducing costs, and increasing efficiency (Casimir, 2015). These systems are particularly valuable in medical imaging, where they can help clinicians make timely and accurate decisions (Karami, 2015; Mhlanga, 2021, 2023a). CDSS leverage patient data, medical knowledge bases, and advanced algorithms to provide case-specific advice, improving diagnostic efforts and patient safety (Fotiadis, 2006; Musen, 2021; Mhlanga 2023b). They are also increasingly integrated into telemedicine, further enhancing the quality of care (Dinevski, 2017). Despite their potential to benefit healthcare, the widespread adoption and effective use of CDSS are hindered by technological considerations and barriers (Zheng, 2017). However, the use of these systems has been shown to decrease medical errors and improve healthcare processes and patient outcomes (Obeidat, 2015). CDSS are integral tools in modern healthcare, designed to enhance the decision-making processes of healthcare providers through the use of advanced technology and vast data analytics. These systems leverage a combination of patient data, medical knowledge bases, and cutting-edge algorithms to provide recommendations that improve the accuracy, efficiency, and consistency of patient care. One of the core technologies at the heart of CDSS is advanced predictive analytics, particularly those utilizing AI and machine learning. AI algorithms are exceptionally good at analyzing large datasets, such as those comprised of EHRs, to predict patient outcomes. By identifying patterns and correlations that may not be immediately apparent to human observers, these algorithms can facilitate earlier and more accurate diagnoses. For example, in the field of oncology, CDSS can analyze historical data from thousands of patients to predict the likelihood of cancer recurrence. These systems can take into account a multitude of variables including patient age, genetic markers, tumor characteristics, treatment history, and more. By doing so, they provide oncologists with a data-driven assessment of cancer prognosis, which can be crucial for planning follow-up care and deciding on preventive measures.

In cardiology, predictive analytics in CDSS can help in anticipating cardiac events. By analyzing EHR data, such as patient blood pressure readings, cholesterol levels, and genetic information, AI algorithms can predict a patient's risk of heart attack or stroke. This allows cardiologists to intervene earlier with lifestyle advice or medication to mitigate these risks. Furthermore, in managing chronic diseases such as diabetes, CDSS equipped with AI algorithms can forecast potential complications like diabetic retinopathy or kidney damage. These predictions are based on continuous monitoring of the patient's health data over time, allowing for timely preventive measures, which can significantly alter the patient's treatment trajectory and improve quality of life. AI-driven CDSS also excel in emergency settings where quick decision-making is critical. For instance, in emergency departments, CDSS can analyze symptoms, vital signs, and medical histories to quickly identify patients at risk of sepsis, a potentially life-threatening condition. This prompt diagnosis and the subsequent rapid initiation of treatment protocols can be lifesaving.

The integration of CDSS with user-friendly interfaces within healthcare providers' EHR systems ensures that these sophisticated analytics are a seamless part of the clinical workflow, making the decision support timely and highly relevant to the specific patient being treated. Despite these advantages, the deployment of CDSS is not without challenges. The quality of data feeding into these systems is paramount; inaccurate or incomplete data can lead to incorrect predictions. Resistance from healthcare providers, who may be sceptical of relying on algorithmic advice, and the challenge of integrating new systems with existing IT infrastructure are additional hurdles. Moreover, the ethical implications of using AI in healthcare, such as privacy concerns and the potential for bias in algorithmic decisions, require careful consideration. Ensuring that these systems are transparent and that they supplement rather than replace clinician judgment is essential for their successful integration into healthcare practice. CDSS, empowered by AI and advanced predictive analytics, offer tremendous potential to revolutionize healthcare by enhancing the predictive capabilities of medical professionals. These systems not only aid in early diagnosis and preventive healthcare but also ensure that care is timely, efficient, and tailored to the individual needs of patients. As technology evolves, so too will the capabilities of CDSS, further cementing their role as indispensable tools in the field of medicine.

Personalized Medicine

CDSS, augmented by AI, are transforming healthcare through the development and implementation of personalized medicine. By integrating AI algorithms, these systems analyze a wide array of data—ranging from genetic profiles to lifestyle and environmental factors—to tailor treatments specifically to individual patients. This personalized approach not only improves the efficacy of treatments but also minimizes side effects, making it a significant advancement in medical care. Personalized medicine, facilitated by AI in CDSS, is particularly impactful in areas such as oncology, where genetic variations play a crucial role in how different patients respond to treatments. For instance, breast cancer treatment has been revolutionized by the use of CDSS to analyze genetic tests that identify mutations in genes like BRCA1 or BRCA2. Based on this analysis, a treatment plan is personalized, which may include targeted therapies that are more effective for patients with these mutations and less likely to cause adverse reactions compared to standard chemotherapy.

In the field of pharmacogenomics, CDSS with AI capabilities are instrumental. These systems can predict how patients will respond to drugs based on their genetic makeup, preventing adverse drug reactions and ineffective treatments. For example, patients with a specific genetic variant might metabolize certain medications faster or slower than usual, influencing the drug's efficacy and safety. CDSS can guide clinicians in adjusting drug dosages or choosing alternative medications, thus optimizing therapeutic outcomes. The management of chronic diseases such as diabetes also benefits from personalized medicine via CDSS. By considering not only genetic information but also data collected on an individual's lifestyle and environmental factors, CDSS can help predict the progression of the disease and customize management plans. This might include personalized diet and exercise plans, as well as medication regimes tailored to the individual's specific physiological responses, dramatically improving quality of life and disease prognosis. In cardiovascular health, AI-powered CDSS use patient data to personalize treatment plans, which may include recommendations for lifestyle changes, medications, or surgical interventions, based on individual risk factors such as genetic predisposition to heart disease, blood pressure levels, and cholesterol profiles. This approach helps in preventing cardiovascular events with a higher degree of accuracy and personalization.

Despite the promising advances in personalized medicine through CDSS, there are challenges that need to be addressed. These include ensuring the privacy and security of personal health information, the need for extensive and diverse datasets to train AI models effectively, and the integration of these advanced systems into existing healthcare frameworks without disrupting workflows. Additionally, there is the issue of equity in healthcare; personalized medicine requires access to sophisticated tests and treatments that may not be available in all healthcare settings, particularly in low-resource environments. Ensuring that these revolutionary healthcare advancements benefit a broad spectrum of the population is a critical challenge that needs ongoing attention. The integration of AI into CDSS marks a significant leap forward in the move towards personalized medicine. It promises more precise, effective, and safer medical treatments by accounting for the unique genetic, lifestyle, and environmental factors of each patient. As technology continues to advance, the scope and accuracy of personalized medicine will expand, offering unprecedented benefits in the treatment and management of a wide range of diseases. The future of healthcare lies in leveraging these technologies to deliver care that is not only reactive but also predictive and personalized.

Enhancing Diagnostic Accuracy

The integration of AI into CDSS is dramatically enhancing diagnostic accuracy, especially in the fields of radiology and pathology. AI's ability to process and interpret medical imaging with greater accuracy and speed than human practitioners is transforming medical diagnostics, enabling earlier and more accurate detection of diseases (Mhlanga and Dunga, 2020; Mhlanga and Hassan, 2022). In radiology, AI algorithms excel at analyzing complex imaging data quickly and with high precision. These algorithms can detect subtle anomalies in images such as X-rays, CT scans, and MRIs that may be overlooked by human eyes. For example, in the detection of lung cancer, AI can identify minute nodules in lung scans that could be early signs of cancer. Early detection facilitated by AI not only improves the prognosis for patients but also significantly enhances the effectiveness of treatments by catching diseases at their most treatable stages. Similarly, in pathology, AI plays a critical role in analyzing tissue samples under the microscope. Pathologists traditionally examine slides manually, a process that is time-consuming and susceptible to human error, particularly in cases of rare cancers where diagnostic experience may be limited. AI systems, trained on vast datasets of annotated images, can help identify patterns of disease that are consistent with early stages of cancer or other conditions that may be difficult to pinpoint manually. This capability not only speeds up the diagnostic process but also increases its accuracy, offering pathologists a powerful tool to aid their analysis and decision-making.

AI's impact extends beyond just image interpretation. In dermatology, AI-powered tools analyze skin lesion images to detect signs of skin cancer. These tools use deep learning algorithms to distinguish between benign and malignant lesions with a level of precision that matches or sometimes exceeds that of experienced dermatologists. This application of AI can lead to earlier and more accurate diagnoses of skin cancer, improving outcomes through timely treatment. The benefits of AI in enhancing diagnostic accuracy also include reducing the workload on medical professionals and decreasing the likelihood of diagnostic errors. By automating routine and repetitive tasks, AI allows healthcare providers to focus more on patient care and complex cases where human expertise is crucial.

Additionally, AI systems can provide a second opinion in ambiguous cases, adding an extra layer of security and reassurance in the diagnostic process. However, the integration of AI into diagnostic practices also presents challenges. Ensuring the accuracy and reliability of AI algorithms requires continuous training with diverse and expansive datasets to prevent biases in diagnoses. Moreover, the ethical considerations surrounding AI in healthcare—such as patient consent for using personal data and the transparency of AI decision-making processes—must be carefully managed. Despite these challenges, the potential of AI to enhance diagnostic accuracy in medical imaging and pathology is undeniable. As AI technology continues to evolve and integrate more deeply into clinical settings, its role in improving diagnostic precision and patient outcomes is set to expand further. This technological advancement represents a significant stride towards a future where diagnostics are quicker, more accurate, and seamlessly integrated into the overall patient care pathway, thereby revolutionizing the field of medicine.

Real-time Monitoring and Intervention

The integration of AI into CDSS is transforming healthcare by enabling real-time monitoring and intervention (Yang et al., 2024). This is particularly evident in the use of wearable sensors and AI-driven CDSS, which allow for continuous monitoring of patient vitals and early anomaly detection (Haick, 2021; Siddique, 2021). The use of smart materials and AI in healthcare wearables further enhances the potential for early detection and accurate diagnosis of disorders (Zheng et al., 2021). AI and wearable sensors are also revolutionizing healthcare delivery, providing an intelligent framework for assessing patients' general health (Junaid, 2022). In the field of medical imaging, AI-based CDSS using advanced medical imaging and radiomics is enhancing the clinician's capability to make optimal clinical decisions (Shaikh, 2020). The emergence of medical cyber-physical systems (MCPS) is providing a platform for AI algorithms to provide decision support for medical experts and patients (Shishvan, 2023). Despite these advancements, the successful implementation of CDSS relies on technology, training, and ongoing support (Moon, 2020). This paradigm modification in healthcare management practices, particularly in chronic disease management, is significantly enhancing patient outcomes and quality of life. Wearable devices equipped with sensors collect a wealth of data about an individual's health in real time, including heart rate, blood pressure, blood glucose levels, activity levels, and more. AI-driven CDSS analyze this data in real time, continuously monitoring for deviations from normal patterns. When anomalies are detected—such as irregular heart rhythms, sudden spikes or drops in blood glucose levels, or signs of physical distress—these systems can alert healthcare providers or even initiate automated interventions. For example, in the management of diabetes, continuous glucose monitors (CGMs) worn by patients can transmit real-time blood glucose data to AI-driven CDSS. These systems analyze the data and can alert patients and their healthcare providers to potential hypoglycemic or hyperglycemic events before they become severe. In response, the CDSS may suggest adjustments to medication dosages, dietary changes, or other interventions to stabilize blood glucose levels and prevent complications.

Similarly, in the management of heart conditions, wearable electrocardiogram (ECG) monitors can detect abnormal heart rhythms or signs of cardiac distress in real time. AI-driven CDSS can analyze these data streams, identify patterns indicative of a cardiac event, and alert healthcare providers or emergency services for immediate intervention. This timely response can be lifesaving, especially in cases of acute cardiac events like heart attacks or arrhythmias. In addition to acute conditions, real-time monitoring and intervention are invaluable in the management of chronic diseases such as hypertension and chronic obstructive pulmonary disease (COPD). By continuously monitoring blood pressure, oxygen saturation levels, and other relevant parameters, AI-driven CDSS can detect early signs of exacerbations or complications and intervene proactively to prevent their escalation. This proactive approach not only improves patient outcomes but also reduces the need for hospitalizations and emergency room visits, resulting in significant cost savings for healthcare systems.

Furthermore, real-time monitoring and intervention extend beyond physiological parameters to include mental health monitoring and support. AI-driven CDSS can analyze data from wearable devices and smartphone apps to detect changes in mood, behavior, or sleep patterns that may indicate deteriorating mental health. This early detection enables timely interventions such as therapy referrals, medication adjustments, or crisis intervention, improving the overall management of mental health conditions. Despite the numerous benefits, the widespread adoption of real-time monitoring and intervention faces challenges related to data privacy and security, interoperability of healthcare systems, and reimbursement models for remote monitoring services. Overcoming these challenges will require collaboration among stakeholders, including healthcare providers, technology companies, regulators, and insurers, to ensure the safe and effective implementation of AI-driven CDSS in clinical practice. In conclusion, real-time monitoring and intervention facilitated by AI-driven CDSS represent a transformative shift in healthcare delivery, offering personalized and proactive care that improves patient outcomes and reduces healthcare costs. As technology continues to advance and AI algorithms become more sophisticated, the potential for real-time monitoring and intervention to revolutionize healthcare management across a wide range of conditions will only continue to grow.

Predictive Analytics in Emergency Care

The application of AI in CDSS has become increasingly pivotal in transforming emergency care through predictive analytics. The application of AI in CDSS has revolutionized emergency care, particularly in predicting acute medical events like heart attacks and strokes (Janke, 2016). AI has been used to improve stroke diagnosis in emergency departments, reducing treatment delays (Abedi, 2020). It has also been applied to enhance operational efficiencies and patient care in emergency medicine (Tang, 2021). However, the use of AI in emergency medicine raises ethical and risk considerations (Chénais, 2022). AI has been found to be effective in clinical decision support and outcome prediction in stroke care (Yeo, 2021). The integration of AI in emergency care can improve information management and patient care (Coiera, 2013). The collaboration between medical professionals and AI-enabled CDSS is influenced by technological characteristics and human factors (Knop, 2021). By harnessing AI's ability to analyze real-time data streams, healthcare professionals can predict acute medical events like heart attacks or strokes with greater precision and speed. This predictive capability not only enhances the timeliness of interventions but also optimizes the allocation of emergency resources, ultimately improving patient outcomes and the efficiency of emergency services. AI-driven predictive analytics in emergency care operates by continuously analyzing data from a variety of sources, including wearable devices, emergency call systems, and hospital monitoring equipment. These data streams may contain vital signs such as heart rate, blood pressure, oxygen saturation, and (ECGs), which AI systems evaluate in real time to detect signs that precede serious conditions like cardiac events or cerebrovascular accidents (strokes). For instance, sophisticated AI algorithms can analyze subtle changes in an ECG that might indicate the onset of a myocardial infarction (heart attack) before the patient experiences the full magnitude of symptoms. By alerting emergency care providers early, these systems enable pre-emptive interventions such as the administration of clot-dissolving medications or the preparation for immediate surgical procedures, thereby saving crucial time and potentially the patient's life.

Similarly, in the context of stroke prevention, AI models can assess risk factors and warning signs like sudden changes in speech, motor skills, or other neurological functions from data collected through patient monitoring devices or reported symptoms. Early recognition and diagnosis facilitated by AI can expedite lifesaving treatments, such as thrombolysis, which is most effective when administered within a narrow time window from symptom onset. Beyond predicting specific medical events, AI in emergency care predictive analytics significantly enhances resource allocation. By predicting the volume and severity of incoming emergencies, hospitals can better prepare by allocating appropriate staff and resources, thus avoiding both underuse and overstrain of emergency services. For example, AI can forecast peaks in emergency department visits during flu seasons or after major public events, allowing hospitals to adjust staffing levels and resource allocation in anticipation. Moreover, AI-driven predictive analytics can also improve the routing of ambulances in real-time by analyzing traffic data, emergency call locations, and the availability of hospital resources, ensuring that patients are taken to the facility best equipped to handle their specific emergencies in the quickest possible time.

Despite its vast potential, the integration of AI into emergency care predictive analytics presents challenges, including ensuring the accuracy and reliability of AI predictions, protecting patient data privacy, and managing the change in workflow for emergency care providers. Additionally, there is the need for ongoing training and support for emergency personnel to adapt to AI tools and to trust their decision-making capabilities. Predictive analytics powered by AI in emergency care is a ground-breaking advancement that promises to revolutionize the field by predicting acute events before they occur, enabling timely interventions, and optimizing the use of critical emergency resources. As AI technology continues to evolve and integrate more deeply into healthcare systems, its impact on emergency care is expected to grow, offering unprecedented improvements in emergency response times, patient care, and resource management. This evolution marks a significant leap towards a future where emergency care is more proactive, efficient, and aligned with the needs of patients in critical times.

Decision Support in Complex Cases

The integration of AI into CDSS is profoundly impacting the management of complex clinical cases, where patients may present multiple interacting illnesses or conditions. AI systems are instrumental in assisting healthcare providers by analyzing vast amounts of medical literature and patient data, thereby suggesting possible treatment paths that might not be immediately obvious to human clinicians. Complex clinical scenarios often involve multifaceted interactions between various diseases, medications, and patient-specific factors such as age, genetic background, and lifestyle. These scenarios can challenge even the most experienced healthcare providers due to the sheer volume of variables and the potential for unusual disease interactions. AI, with its capacity to process and analyze large datasets rapidly, provides a critical decision-support tool that can offer insights derived from patterns that may not be discernible through traditional methods.

For example, consider a patient with diabetes, heart disease, and renal impairment—a common combination that complicates medical management due to the conflicting requirements of these conditions. AI-driven CDSS can analyze data from similar patient cases, current medical guidelines, and ongoing drug trials to recommend a balanced treatment plan that minimizes the risk of adverse drug interactions while optimizing the management of all conditions. This approach not only supports healthcare providers in their decision-making processes but also enhances patient safety and treatment effectiveness. AI systems can also leverage natural language processing (NLP) to digest and summarize relevant findings from medical research and clinical trials. This capability allows healthcare providers to stay informed about the latest therapeutic options and evidence-based practices without having to spend extensive time reviewing literature. For patients with rare diseases or those exhibiting atypical symptoms, AI can quickly sift through global health data to identify similar cases and suggest diagnostic and treatment strategies that have been effective in comparable scenarios.

In oncology, AI plays a critical role in devising personalized treatment regimens. By analyzing genetic data from tumors alongside historical treatment outcomes, AI models can recommend specific chemotherapy drugs or targeted therapies that are likely to be most effective for a particular patient's cancer type and genetic profile. This precision medicine approach is particularly valuable in complex cancer cases where standard protocols may be less effective. Furthermore, AI systems enhance the capacity for real-time decision-making in critical care settings. In intensive care units, where patients often have multiple acute and chronic conditions, AI-driven CDSS can continuously monitor patient vitals, lab results, and treatment responses to adjust therapeutic strategies dynamically. This real-time adjustment ensures that treatments are adapted to the patient's evolving condition, potentially reducing recovery times and improving outcomes. Despite these advantages, the use of AI in decision support for complex cases must be approached with caution. The dependency on data quality and the need for systems to be free from bias are critical considerations. Additionally, the integration of AI into clinical workflows must be handled sensitively to ensure that it complements, rather than replaces, human judgment. AI in CDSS offers significant potential for improving the management of complex clinical cases by providing comprehensive, data-driven insights that enhance diagnostic accuracy and treatment efficacy. As AI technology continues to advance, its role in supporting healthcare providers in navigating complex patient scenarios is expected to expand, further transforming the landscape of modern medicine. This technological evolution holds the promise of delivering more personalized, efficient, and effective healthcare.

Reducing Clinical Errors

The implementation of AI in CDSS is a pivotal strategy in reducing clinical errors, a critical and persistent concern in healthcare. AI-driven CDSS enhance the accuracy and safety of medical practices by providing evidence-based recommendations and by double-checking prescriptions, diagnoses, and other critical medical decisions. Clinical errors can occur at various points in the patient care process, including diagnostics, medication dispensing, and treatment protocol implementation. These errors not only compromise patient safety but also lead to increased healthcare costs and loss of trust in healthcare systems. By integrating AI into CDSS, healthcare providers are equipped with tools that minimize human error and support decision-making with advanced data analysis and automated oversight.

For instance, in the realm of prescribing medications, AI-driven CDSS can automatically review medication orders to check for potential drug interactions, incorrect dosages, or allergies that a clinician might overlook. By cross-referencing a patient's current medications and historical health records with a comprehensive database of drug information, the system ensures that all prescriptions are safe and appropriate for the patient's specific health profile. This capability is especially vital in settings where patients may be receiving multiple medications, and the risk of drug interactions is significant. Moreover, in diagnostics, AI-driven CDSS can help detect anomalies in lab results or imaging studies that might indicate a rare condition or an early stage of a disease that could easily be missed by a human observer. For example, AI systems can analyze radiographic images with a level of precision that surpasses human capabilities, identifying subtle patterns that could be early signs of conditions like cancer or vascular diseases. These systems can also alert radiologists to review specific areas of an image, thus acting as a second set of eyes that enhances diagnostic accuracy.

AI-driven CDSS also contribute to improving the quality of clinical documentation. By analyzing the notes and data entered into electronic health records, AI can identify inconsistencies or omissions that might lead to errors in patient care. It can prompt healthcare providers to complete necessary fields or correct information that does not align with other patient data, thereby maintaining the integrity and accuracy of medical records. Furthermore, the implementation of AI in emergency care settings shows significant potential for reducing errors. In these high-pressure environments, AI-driven CDSS can provide quick access to patient histories and suggest immediate treatment options that align with the best practices and latest medical guidelines. This is crucial during critical moments where time and accuracy are of the essence, and the risk of oversight is high. Despite the significant advantages, the deployment of AI-driven CDSS must be approached with careful consideration of potential challenges, such as the dependency on the quality of input data and the need to ensure that the AI systems themselves are free from biases that could introduce new types of errors. Additionally, there must be a balance between reliance on technology and the irreplaceable judgment of experienced medical professionals. AI-driven CDSS are instrumental in reducing clinical errors by offering evidence-based recommendations, automating checks for common error points like prescriptions and diagnoses, and supporting healthcare providers with real-time data analysis. As these technologies continue to evolve and integrate into healthcare practices, their role in enhancing patient safety and improving healthcare outcomes will likely grow, marking a significant step forward in the ongoing effort to mitigate clinical errors in the medical field.

Cost Reduction and Efficiency

AI in CDSS can streamline clinical workflows, reduce unnecessary testing, and optimize resource allocation, thereby cutting costs and improving healthcare efficiency. The integration of AI in CDSS is significantly reshaping the healthcare landscape by streamlining clinical workflows, reducing unnecessary testing, and optimizing resource allocation. These improvements are not only enhancing healthcare efficiency but are also contributing to substantial cost reductions across the sector. AI-driven CDSS support the optimization of clinical workflows by automating routine tasks, such as data entry, patient scheduling, and record keeping. This automation frees up healthcare professionals to focus more on patient care rather than administrative duties, thereby increasing the time they can spend with patients. Moreover, AI can prioritize tasks based on urgency and complexity, ensuring that critical cases are attended to promptly, which optimizes the overall workflow and enhances patient outcomes.

One of the key areas where AI significantly impacts cost reduction is through the minimization of unnecessary testing. By analyzing patient data and previous case histories, AI-driven CDSS can provide targeted diagnostic suggestions, reducing the tendency towards ordering broad-spectrum tests that may not be necessary. For example, if AI algorithms determine that the symptoms and medical history of a patient strongly suggest a particular diagnosis, they can recommend specific tests that confirm this diagnosis rather than a battery of general tests. This not only speeds up the diagnosis process but also reduces the costs associated with unnecessary testing. AI also plays a critical role in optimizing resource allocation in hospitals and clinics. By predicting patient inflows and the severity of incoming cases—using historical data and real-time information—AI systems can assist in staff scheduling and the allocation of medical equipment. This ensures that resources are used efficiently, preventing overuse or underutilization, which can be costly.

Additionally, in the realm of inventory management, AI-driven CDSS can forecast the demand for medical supplies and medications, enabling hospitals to maintain optimal inventory levels. This predictive capability helps avoid both excess stocks, which can lead to wastage due to expiry, and stockouts, which can delay treatments. Efficient inventory management not only reduces costs but also improves service delivery in healthcare settings. AI's impact on cost reduction extends into the management of chronic diseases, where continuous monitoring and early intervention can prevent complications that typically lead to expensive emergency care or hospital admissions. For example, AI-driven monitoring systems can track the condition of patients with chronic heart disease, alerting healthcare providers to changes that may indicate an impending heart failure. Early intervention in such cases can prevent costly hospitalizations and intensive treatments. Despite these advancements, the implementation of AI-driven CDSS must be carefully managed to address challenges such as ensuring the privacy of patient data, integrating AI systems with existing healthcare infrastructures, and training staff to effectively use these technologies. There are also ethical considerations regarding the extent to which healthcare decisions should be automated. AI in CDSS offers significant potential for reducing healthcare costs and improving efficiency through the automation of tasks, reduction of unnecessary tests, and optimized resource allocation. As healthcare systems continue to evolve with technological advancements, the role of AI in streamlining operations and enhancing cost-efficiency is likely to expand, fundamentally transforming the way healthcare is delivered and managed.

Training and Adaptation

The effective implementation and utilization of AI in CDSS crucially depend on the training and adaptation of healthcare professionals to these emerging technologies. Ensuring that medical staff are well-educated and comfortable with AI systems is fundamental to maximizing the benefits these tools can offer in improving patient care and enhancing healthcare efficiency. AI-enhanced CDSS represent a significant shift in the traditional healthcare workflow, incorporating complex algorithms to aid in decision-making, diagnosis, treatment planning, and management of healthcare resources. However, the full potential of these systems can only be realized if the healthcare professionals who use them are adequately trained. This training involves not only understanding how to operate the systems but also knowing how to interpret their outputs and integrate this information into clinical practice.

Continuous education and training programs are essential to equip healthcare professionals with the necessary skills and knowledge to effectively interact with AI-driven technologies. These programs should cover the technical aspects of AI systems, including data input, system operation, and troubleshooting, as well as the interpretation of AI-generated recommendations and results. Understanding the underlying principles of AI and how decisions are made helps clinicians to critically assess and effectively incorporate AI suggestions into their clinical decision-making. Moreover, training must address the limitations and ethical considerations of using AI in healthcare. Healthcare providers need to be aware of the potential biases in AI systems, the importance of maintaining patient privacy, and the implications of AI recommendations on patient care. They must be prepared to make informed decisions about when to rely on AI guidance and when to override it based on human judgment and clinical experience. Healthcare institutions can facilitate this adaptation through simulation-based training, workshops, and seminars that provide hands-on experience with AI tools. Regular updates and refresher courses are also vital, as AI technologies and medical guidelines evolve rapidly. Continuous learning opportunities will help healthcare professionals stay current with advancements and ensure that their skills remain relevant. Additionally, the integration of AI training into medical education curriculums can prepare future healthcare professionals from the outset. By incorporating AI literacy as a standard part of medical training, new clinicians will enter the workforce with a strong foundation in using advanced technologies, making them more adept at integrating AI tools into their clinical practice.

The adaptation process also involves organizational change management strategies to help staff adjust to new workflows that incorporate AI. This may include changes in job roles, the introduction of new protocols, and the restructuring of teams to optimize the use of AI-enhanced CDSS. Effective communication, leadership support, and the involvement of healthcare professionals in the design and implementation of AI systems are crucial to ensuring that these changes are successfully adopted. The training and adaptation of healthcare professionals are critical to the success of AI in CDSS. Through continuous education, practical training, and organizational support, healthcare providers can fully leverage the benefits of AI-enhanced systems. This not only improves patient outcomes and operational efficiency but also ensures that the healthcare workforce is confident and competent in using cutting-edge technologies. As AI continues to evolve and become more integrated into healthcare, ongoing education and adaptation will remain essential components of harnessing its full potential.

Integration with Telemedicine

The integration of AI in CDSS is revolutionizing telemedicine by providing robust remote diagnostic and treatment support. This technological synergy is particularly beneficial for extending healthcare services to rural or underserved areas where access to medical specialists and advanced healthcare facilities is limited. AI-enhanced CDSS analyze data from virtual consultations and offers recommendations, thereby significantly improving the reach and quality of telemedicine services. Telemedicine, the practice of delivering healthcare remotely via telecommunications technology, has seen a dramatic increase in adoption due to its convenience and the broader access it provides to healthcare services. When combined with AI-powered CDSS, telemedicine becomes even more powerful. AI algorithms can process and interpret medical data received during virtual consultations, such as symptoms, medical history, and diagnostic tests, to provide accurate assessments and treatment recommendations. For example, in rural communities where patients may have limited access to specialized care, AI-powered telemedicine platforms can perform initial diagnostic evaluations based on symptoms presented during a virtual visit. AI can compare these symptoms with a vast database of medical cases to identify potential conditions. This allows general practitioners or nurses facilitating the telemedicine session to provide informed preliminary care advice, and make better-informed decisions about referring patients to specialists if necessary.

Furthermore, AI-driven CDSS in telemedicine can enhance the management of chronic diseases by providing continuous monitoring and personalized care plans. Patients with chronic conditions such as diabetes or hypertension can use connected devices to regularly submit their health data, which AI systems analyze in real time. These systems can detect deviations from the patient's normal health parameters and alert healthcare providers to potential issues before they become severe, facilitating timely interventions. The integration of AI with telemedicine also extends to mental health services, where AI can analyze verbal and non-verbal cues during virtual therapy sessions to assess a patient's mental state and progress. This analysis helps therapists adjust treatment plans more effectively and provides insights that may be less apparent in traditional in-person sessions. Additionally, AI-powered CDSS can guide patients through self-administered care protocols during telemedicine interactions. For patients recovering from surgery or managing acute conditions at home, AI can provide step-by-step guidance on care procedures, monitor compliance, and evaluate the effectiveness of treatments based on patient-reported outcomes and sensor data.

Despite these advancements, the integration of AI into telemedicine does pose challenges, including ensuring data security and privacy, managing the variability of data quality from remote devices, and addressing the digital divide that may limit access to telemedicine services in some populations. Overcoming these challenges requires robust security protocols, standardization of remote health monitoring devices, and initiatives to increase digital literacy and access.

The integration of AI-powered CDSS with telemedicine represents a significant advancement in healthcare delivery, expanding access to quality medical advice and care, particularly for patients in remote or underserved areas. This combination not only enhances the effectiveness of telemedicine services but also supports a more proactive and personalized approach to healthcare. As these technologies continue to evolve and mature, their potential to transform the healthcare landscape globally is immense, making healthcare more accessible, efficient, and effective.

Ethical and Regulatory Challenges

As AI becomes increasingly integrated into CDSS, a host of ethical and regulatory challenges emerge that require meticulous attention. These challenges revolve around issues such as data privacy, informed consent, and the prevention of biases in AI algorithms, all of which are critical to maintaining trust in healthcare systems and ensuring the safe and fair use of AI in medical settings.

Data Privacy: One of the foremost concerns is the protection of patient data. AI systems require access to vast amounts of personal and medical data to function effectively. Ensuring that this data is handled securely and in compliance with stringent data protection laws, such as the General Data Protection Regulation (GDPR) in Europe or the Health Insurance Portability and Accountability Act (HIPAA) in the United States, is essential. Healthcare providers must implement robust cybersecurity measures to safeguard data against breaches and ensure that patient information is anonymized when used for training AI models.

Informed Consent: Patients must be adequately informed about how their data will be used, particularly when it involves AI systems. They should understand what data will be collected, how it will be used, who will have access to it, and what the potential risks are. Obtaining explicit consent from patients before their data is used for training or operational purposes in AI-driven systems is not just a regulatory requirement but also a fundamental ethical obligation.

Bias in AI Algorithms: AI systems are only as unbiased as the data they are trained on. Historical health data can contain inherent biases related to race, gender, socioeconomic status, and more, which can lead to skewed AI models that perpetuate these biases in clinical recommendations. To counteract this, AI systems must be trained on diverse datasets that accurately represent the entire population. Furthermore, continuous monitoring and updating of AI models are necessary to ensure they do not develop or reinforce undesirable biases over time.

Regulatory Compliance: Regulatory frameworks governing the use of AI in healthcare are still in development and vary significantly across different jurisdictions. Ensuring compliance with these evolving regulations is a significant challenge for healthcare providers. Regulators need to balance the rapid pace of technological innovation with the need to ensure patient safety and ethical standards, necessitating a flexible yet rigorous approach to AI regulation.

Transparency and Accountability: There must be transparency in how AI-driven decisions are made. Healthcare providers and patients should be able to trace and understand the decision-making process of AI systems. This transparency is crucial for accountability, particularly in cases where AI-driven decisions need to be reviewed or contested.

Training Healthcare Providers: Alongside ethical and regulatory concerns, there is a need for ongoing education for healthcare providers regarding AI technologies. Providers must be trained not only on how to use these systems effectively but also on the ethical considerations involved in their deployment. This training will help clinicians make better-informed decisions about when and how to use AI in their practice. While the integration of AI into CDSS offers immense potential to enhance healthcare delivery, it also brings significant ethical and regulatory challenges that must be carefully managed. Addressing these challenges involves a concerted effort from all stakeholders, including healthcare providers, AI developers, regulators, and patients themselves, to ensure that the deployment of AI technologies advances the public good and protects individual rights. As AI continues to evolve, so too must our approaches to these ethical and regulatory issues, ensuring that AI serves as a beneficial tool in the realm of healthcare.

Future Directions

Looking ahead, the integration of AI in CDSS is poised for even greater sophistication, driven by advancements in AI technologies. The potential for expanded applications in genomics, mental health, and the enhancement of user interfaces indicates a transformative trajectory for AI in healthcare. These developments not only aim to enhance the efficiency and effectiveness of healthcare delivery but also promise to revolutionize patient care by offering more personalized and proactive treatments.

Integration with Genomics: One of the most promising future directions for AI in CDSS is its integration with genomics. As genomic data becomes increasingly accessible and affordable, AI can leverage this vast array of information to personalize medical treatments further. For instance, AI systems could analyze genetic variations to predict individual responses to various drugs or to tailor specific therapies for cancer treatment based on a patient's genetic makeup. This could lead to highly effective precision medicine, reducing trial-and-error prescribing and minimizing adverse drug reactions.

Expanded Use in Mental Health: AI is also set to expand significantly in the field of mental health. By analyzing patterns in speech, behavior, and social media usage, AI can help diagnose mental health issues early and suggest personalized treatment plans. For instance, AI-driven CDSS could monitor changes in a patient's language or activity levels that might indicate depression or anxiety, providing alerts for timely intervention. Furthermore, AI could be used to personalize therapeutic techniques, adapting interventions based on real-time feedback from patients about their mental state.

Development of More Intuitive User Interfaces: The effectiveness of AI-driven CDSS also depends on the usability of their interfaces. Future developments are likely to focus on creating more intuitive, user-friendly interfaces that make it easier for healthcare providers to interact with AI systems. This could include the use of NLP to allow clinicians to query AI systems as if they were consulting a human expert, making the integration of AI into daily medical practice smoother and more effective.

Increased Predictive Capabilities: As AI algorithms become more refined, their ability to predict disease progression and outcomes will improve. This will be particularly impactful in chronic disease management, where AI can analyze continuous data streams from wearable devices to predict flare-ups or complications before they occur, allowing for preventative measures to be taken in advance.

Ethical and Regulatory Development: As AI becomes more embedded in healthcare, ethical and regulatory frameworks will need to evolve to address new challenges. This includes ensuring data privacy, managing AI biases, and defining the limits of AI decision-making in clinical settings. The development of international standards and guidelines will be crucial in shaping the global approach to AI in healthcare.

Enhanced Collaboration Tools: Future AI in CDSS will likely incorporate enhanced tools for collaboration among healthcare teams, including telemedicine capabilities. This will be important for complex cases that require multi-disciplinary input, allowing for seamless sharing of patient data and AI-generated insights across different specialists, regardless of geographical barriers. In conclusion, the future of AI in CDSS holds immense promise for transforming healthcare by making it more personalized, predictive, and efficient. As AI technology continues to advance, the integration of these systems into clinical practice will expand, reshaping how care is delivered and offering significant benefits to both patients and healthcare providers. The focus will not only be on technology development but also on ensuring these tools are accessible, equitable, and ethically managed to truly enhance global healthcare outcomes.

Conclusion

This chapter has provided a comprehensive exploration into the realm of CDSS and the transformative integration of AI to augment their capabilities. As vital tools in modern healthcare, CDSS assist clinicians in making informed decisions across various aspects of diagnosis, treatment, and overall patient care. The rapid advancements in AI technologies offer a significant opportunity to revolutionize CDSS by enhancing data analytics, predictive modeling, and decision-making support. Initially, the chapter presented an overview of CDSS, highlighting their critical role in improving healthcare outcomes and addressing the limitations faced by traditional systems, such as restricted data processing capabilities and inadequate real-time decision support. This backdrop set the stage for a deeper investigation into how AI can address these challenges by introducing more dynamic and powerful tools into the healthcare decision-making process. Subsequent sections delved into the specific applications of AI within CDSS, detailing how AI algorithms can improve the efficiency and accuracy of clinical workflows. Through a series of case studies, the chapter demonstrated successful implementations of AI-based decision support systems, showcasing tangible benefits in various medical specialities, including predictive analytics in emergency care, enhanced diagnostic accuracy, and personalized medicine. In conclusion, the integration of AI into CDSS represents a significant advancement in healthcare technology, offering the potential to dramatically enhance clinical decision-making. As AI continues to evolve, it promises to further refine the capabilities of CDSS, making them more responsive and effective. This evolution necessitates ongoing research and adaptation in clinical practices to fully harness the benefits of AI-enhanced CDSS, ensuring that healthcare providers can deliver the highest standard of patient care. As we move forward, it is clear that AI will play an increasingly central role in shaping the future of healthcare, making it essential for medical professionals to remain abreast of these technological developments.

References

Abedi, G., Shojaee, J., Kabir, M.J., Charati, J.Y., Bastani, P., Hazini, A., ... and Asadi, P. (2020). Association between quality of life and palliative care at the cancer patients. Journal of Nursing and Midwifery Sciences, 7(4), 274–80.

Alaa, A.M., Moon, K.H., Hsu, W. and Van Der Schaar, M. (2016). ConfidentCare: a clinical decision support system for personalized breast cancer screening. IEEE Transactions on Multimedia, 18(10), 1942–55.

Berner, C. and Flage, R. (2016). Strengthening quantitative risk assessments by systematic treatment of uncertain assumptions. Reliability Engineering & System Safety, 151, 46–59.

Casimir, P. (2015). Role of Clinical Decision Support Systems in Improving Clinical Practice'. MOJ Clinical & Medical Case Reports, 2(6), 1–6.

Chénais, B. (2022). Transposable elements and human diseases: mechanisms and implication in the response to environmental pollutants. International journal of molecular sciences, 23(5), 2551.

Coiera, E. (2009). Communication in emergency medical teams. Patient Safety in Emergency Medicine. Philadelphia, USA: Lippincot Williams & Wilkins.

Coiera, E. (2013). Social networks, social media, and social diseases. Bmj, 346.

Dinevski, N., Sarnthein, J., Vasella, F., Fierstra, J., Pangalu, A., Holzmann, D., ... and Bozinov, O. (2017). Postoperative neurosurgical infection rates after shared-resource intraoperative magnetic resonance imaging: a single-center experience with 195 cases. World neurosurgery, 103, 275–82.

Elhaddad, M. and Hamam, S. (2024). AI-Driven Clinical Decision Support Systems: An Ongoing Pursuit of Potential. Cureus, 16(4).

Fraccaro, P., Casteleiro, M.A., Ainsworth, J. and Buchan, I. (2015). Adoption of clinical decision support in multimorbidity: a systematic review. JMIR medical informatics, 3(1), e3503.

Garcia-Jimenez, A., Moreno-Conde, A., Martínez-García, A., Marín-León, I., Medrano-Ortega, F.J., and Parra-Calderón, C. L. (2015). Clinical decision support using a terminology server to improve patient safety. In Digital Healthcare Empowering Europeans (pp. 150-154). IOS Press.

Gouripur, K. (2024). The Impact of Artificial Intelligence on Healthcare: A Revolution in Progress. *The North and West London Journal of General Practice, 10*(1).

Gupta, R., Binder, L. and Moriates, C. (2020). Rebuilding trust and relationships in medical centers: a focus on health care affordability. JAMA, *324*(23), 2361–62.

Haick, H. and Tang, N. (2021). Artificial intelligence in medical sensors for clinical decisions. ACS nano, *15*(3), 3557–3567.

Janke, A.T., McNaughton, C.D., Brody, A.M., Welch, R.D. and Levy, P.D. (2016). Trends in the incidence of hypertensive emergencies in US emergency departments from 2006 to 2013. Journal of the American Heart Association, *5*(12), e004511.

Junaid, M., Zhang, Q. and Syed, M.W. (2022). Effects of sustainable supply chain integration on green innovation and firm performance. Sustainable Production and Consumption, 30, 145–157.

Karami, M. (2015). Clinical decision support systems and medical imaging. Radiol Manage, *37*(2), 25–32.

Knop, I., Bansmer, S.E., Hahn, V. and Voigt, C. (2021). Comparison of different droplet measurement techniques in the Braunschweig Icing Wind Tunnel. Atmospheric Measurement Techniques, *14*(2), 1761–81.

Mendonça, E. A. (2004). Clinical decision support systems: perspectives in dentistry. Journal of dental education, *68*(6), 589–97.

Mhlanga, D. (2021). A dynamic analysis of the demand for healthcare in post-apartheid South Africa. *Nursing Reports, 11*(02), 484–94.

Mhlanga, D. (2023a). Artificial Intelligence in Elderly Care: Navigating Ethical and Responsible AI Adoption for Seniors. *SSRN*, 4675564.

Mhlanga, D. (2023b). Digital Transformation in the Healthcare Sector: The Role of Artificial Intelligence for Inclusive Long-term Care around the World, Lessons for Africa. *In*: Mhlanga, D., Ndhlovu, E. (Eds.), *Economic Inclusion in Post-Independence Africa. Advances in African Economic, Social, and Political Development*. Cham: Springer. https://doi.org/10.1007/978-3-031-31431-5_19.

Mhlanga, D. and Dunga, S.H. (2020). Determinants of demand for health insurance in South Africa. *The International Journal of Social Sciences and Humanity Studies, 12*(2), 238–54.

Mhlanga, D. and Hassan, A. (2022). An investigation of the factors influencing the choice of healthcare facility in South Africa. *International Journal of Research in Business and Social Science (2147-4478), 11*(4), 50–58.

Middleton, B., Sittig, D.F. and Wright, A. (2016). Clinical decision support: a 25 year retrospective and a 25 year vision. Yearbook of medical informatics, *25*(S 01), S103–S116.

Moon, C.H. (2016). Relational aesthetics and art therapy. In Approaches to art therapy (pp. 50-68). Routledge.

Moon, J.Y., Yun, E.J., Yoon, D.Y., Seo, Y.L., Cho, Y.K., Lim, K.J. and Hong, J.H. (2020). Analysis of the altmetric top 100 articles with the highest altmetric attention scores in medical imaging journals. Japanese Journal of Radiology, *38*, 630–635.

Musen, M.A., Middleton, B. and Greenes, R.A. (2021). Clinical decision-support systems. In Biomedical informatics: computer applications in health care and biomedicine (pp. 795-840). Cham: Springer International Publishing.

Ndhlovu, E. and Mhlanga, D. (2024). African Agency in Medical Innovation and Practices: From Antiquity to the Present. *African Renaissance, 21*(1), 323–40.

Obeidat, R. (2015). Decision-making preferences of Jordanian women diagnosed with breast cancer. Supportive care in cancer, 23, 2281–85.

Rigas, G., Bougia, P., Baga, D., Tsipouras, M., Tzallas, A., Tripoliti, E., ... and Fotiadis, D.I. (2010, November). A decision support tool for optimal Levodopa administration in Parkinson's disease. In Proceedings of the 10th IEEE International Conference on Information Technology and Applications in Biomedicine (pp. 1-6). IEEE.

Roopa, G.M., Shryavani, K., Pradeep, N. and Diaz, V.G. (2021). Accelerating Translational Medical Research by Leveraging Artificial Intelligence: Digital Healthcare. *In*: *Advanced AI Techniques and Applications in Bioinformatics* (pp. 243–64). CRC Press.

Shaikh, F., Dupont-Roettger, D., Dehmeshki, J., Awan, O., Kubassova, O. and Bisdas, S. (2020). The role of imaging biomarkers derived from advanced imaging and radiomics in the management of brain tumors. Frontiers in oncology, 10, 559946.

Shishvan, O.R., Abdelwahab, A., da Rosa, N.B., Saulnier, G.J., Mueller, J.L., Newell, J.C. and Isaacson, D. (2023). ACT5 electrical impedance tomography system. IEEE Transactions on Biomedical Engineering.

Siddique, A., Shahzad, A., Lawler, J., Mahmoud, K.A., Lee, D.S., Ali, N., ... and Rasool, K. (2021). Unprecedented environmental and energy impacts and challenges of COVID-19 pandemic. Environmental Research, 193, 110443.

Sutton, J.D., Carico, R., Burk, M., Jones, M.M., Wei, X., Neuhauser, M.M., ... and Cunningham, F.E. (2020, January). Inpatient management of uncomplicated skin and soft tissue infections in 34 veterans affairs medical centers: A medication use evaluation. In Open Forum Infectious Diseases (Vol. 7, No. 1, p. ofz554). US: Oxford University Press.

Tang, S., Yu, Y., Chen, Q., Fan, M. and Eisma, M.C. (2021). Correlates of mental health after COVID-19 bereavement in Mainland China. Journal of pain and symptom management, *61*(6), e1-e4.

Tippur, A. (2023). AI-Powered Precision Oncology: Computational Insights Redefining Therapeutic Landscapes. *DHR Proceedings, 3*(S1), 1–10.

Xu, Q., Xie, W., Liao, B., Hu, C., Qin, L., Yang, Z., ... and Luo, A. (2023). Interpretability of clinical decision support systems based on artificial intelligence from technological and medical perspective: A systematic review. *Journal of Healthcare Engineering, 2023*, 1–13.

Yang, K., Al Haddad, C., Alam, R., Brijs, T. and Antoniou, C. (2024). Adaptive intervention algorithms for advanced driver assistance systems. *Safety, 10*(1), 10.

Yeo, G.S., Chao, D.H.M., Siegert, A.M., Koerperich, Z.M., Ericson, M.D., Simonds, S.E., ... and Adan, R.A. (2021). The melanocortin pathway and energy homeostasis: From discovery to obesity therapy. Molecular metabolism, 48, 101206.

Zheng, Y., Tang, N., Omar, R., Hu, Z., Duong, T., Wang, J., ... and Haick, H. (2021). Smart materials enabled with artificial intelligence for healthcare wearables. *Advanced Functional Materials, 31*(51), 2105482.

9 | Disease Diagnosis and AI Applications in Hospital Administration

The field of healthcare is undergoing a transformative shift with the integration of artificial intelligence (AI) into various aspects of hospital administration. One area that has seen remarkable advancements in disease diagnosis is where AI-based applications have proven to be valuable tools for healthcare professionals. This chapter explores the role of AI in disease diagnosis and its broader applications in hospital administration. By leveraging AI technology, hospitals can enhance their efficiency, accuracy, and patient care, ultimately leading to improved healthcare outcomes. In short, this chapter will look at the challenges in disease diagnosis and the potential of AI to address them, machine learning techniques for disease detection and classification and case studies demonstrating the efficacy of AI in disease diagnosis.

Introduction

In the rapidly changing field of healthcare, the pursuit of better patient results and increased operational effectiveness remains the same. Artificial intelligence (AI) is leading the way in this shift and has the potential to completely disrupt the business. This chapter explores the crucial role of AI in disease diagnosis and hospital management, two sectors where precision, effectiveness, and swiftness are of utmost importance. The incorporation of AI into the healthcare sector is occurring at a crucial moment. In light of rising expenses, the prevalence of long-term illnesses, and a growing elderly demographic, healthcare systems globally are in urgent need of inventive remedies (Mlambo and Mhlanga, 2023; Mhlanga, 2023a, 2024). AI technologies, with their capacity to acquire knowledge and adjust accordingly, provide great opportunities to tackle these difficulties using more precise diagnostics, tailored treatment strategies, and efficient hospital operations.

Although AI has the potential to revolutionize healthcare, its implementation poses a multitude of intricate problems and ethical considerations as highlighted in some previous chapters. The precision of AI-powered diagnoses, the confidentiality of patient data, the clarity of AI algorithms, and the fair availability of these emerging technologies are urgent matters that require attention. Moreover, as AI becomes increasingly influential in clinical decision-making, it is crucial to prioritize the integration of these systems with current healthcare practices and the training of healthcare personnel to successfully utilize them. This chapter seeks to offer a thorough examination of how AI is utilized to enhance disease diagnosis accuracy and streamline healthcare delivery. It also addresses the technological, ethical, and operational obstacles associated with its implementation. Through this investigation, our objective is to clarify how AI can not only supplement but also substantially improve the capacities of healthcare systems, revolutionizing them to meet the requirements of the 21st century.

Several scholars support these assertions. According to several scholars (Anwer, 2024; Naveed, 2023; Khanna et al., 2022; Devi et al., 2023; Patil and Shankar, 2023; Jean, 2020; Mishra, 2023), AI technologies have the potential to revolutionize healthcare by improving diagnostics, treatment strategies, and hospital operations. These technologies, including machine learning (ML) and deep learning, can enhance diagnostic accuracy, optimize treatment plans, and predict patient outcomes (Anwer, 2024; Naveed, 2023; Khanna et al., 2022; Devi et al., 2023; Patil and Shankar, 2023; Jean, 2020; Mishra, 2023; Kumar, 2023). They can also automate tasks, streamline hospital operations, and improve patient engagement (Anwer, 2024; Naveed, 2023). However, challenges such as data privacy, algorithmic biases, and ethical considerations need to be addressed to ensure the safe and effective integration of AI in healthcare (Anwer, 2024; Naveed, 2023). Therefore, this chapter explores the diverse and complex function of AI in transforming disease diagnosis and hospital administration, emphasizing its ability to reinvent healthcare models.

AI in Disease Diagnosis: A New Frontier

AI stands as a transformative force in healthcare, particularly in the realm of disease diagnosis. Its ability to augment and sometimes surpass human expertise marks a significant turning point in medical practice. AI is revolutionizing healthcare, particularly in disease diagnosis, by surpassing human expertise and transforming medical practice (Soferman, 2019; Poalelungi, 2023; Bajwa, 2021; Devi, 2023; Francis, 2023; Bhattacharya, 2020; Donel, 2019; Mishra, 2023). It offers predictive analytics, personalized care plans, and rapid image analysis, leading to more accurate and efficient healthcare delivery (Soferman, 2019; Poalelungi, 2023; Bajwa, 2021; Devi, 2023; Francis,2023; Bhattacharya, 2020; Donel, 2019; Mishra, 2023). AI's ability to decipher medical images and combine patient data for tailored diagnostic suggestions is particularly noteworthy (Devi, 2023; Francis, 2023; Mishra, 2023). Despite the need for ethical and fair incorporation, AI's potential to transform healthcare is significant (Devi, 2023; Francis, 2023; Bhattacharya, 2020; Donel, 2019; Mishra, 2023). AI algorithms are adept at analyzing complex data quickly and with a high degree of accuracy, making them invaluable in fields where precision and rapid response are crucial. This part of the chapter explores the current and potential future roles of AI in disease diagnosis, underscoring its revolutionary impact. In radiology, AI's impact is profound. AI algorithms are trained to interpret medical images, such as X-rays, CT scans, and MRIs, with remarkable precision. These tools assist radiologists by identifying subtle patterns that may elude the human eye. For instance, in detecting early-stage cancers, AI can analyze imaging data to pinpoint minute anomalies that signify the presence of tumors. The use of AI in these cases not only enhances diagnostic accuracy but also significantly speeds up the process, allowing for earlier intervention and better patient outcomes.

Pathology has similarly benefited from the advent of AI. Traditional methods of diagnosing diseases from tissue samples can be time-consuming and depend heavily on individual expertise. AI systems, equipped with deep learning capabilities, analyze microscopic images of tissue samples, identifying patterns that indicate disease. Such AI-driven tools help pathologists in diagnosing complex cases, such as differentiating between types of cancer cells, with a level of precision that was previously unattainable. This not only boosts diagnostic accuracy but also standardizes the quality of pathology services across different healthcare settings. The field of genetic testing and personalized medicine has also seen revolutionary changes with AI integration. AI excels in handling and interpreting vast amounts of genetic data, a task that is particularly challenging for humans due to the sheer scale and complexity of genomic information. AI algorithms can quickly identify genetic mutations and link them to specific diseases, facilitating more precise diagnoses and tailored treatment plans. In personalized medicine, AI's ability to analyze patient data and genetic information simultaneously allows for the development of customized medical treatments that are optimized for an individual's unique genetic makeup, enhancing the efficacy of treatments.

Looking ahead, the future applications of AI in disease diagnosis are promising and manifold. Advances in machine learning algorithms and computational power are expected to lead to even more sophisticated AI tools. These advancements may enable AI to not only detect diseases at the earliest stages but also predict susceptibility to certain conditions before they manifest clinically. Such predictive capabilities could shift the focus of healthcare from treatment to prevention, fundamentally altering how diseases are managed. Moreover, as AI technology continues to evolve, there is potential for its application in remote diagnostics, particularly beneficial in underserved or rural areas where specialist medical expertise is scarce. AI-powered mobile apps and devices could enable preliminary diagnoses, guiding patients to seek appropriate medical intervention sooner.

Despite these exciting advancements, the deployment of AI in disease diagnosis does not come without challenges. Issues related to data privacy, the need for robust regulatory frameworks to manage AI applications, and the ethical implications of AI decision-making are all areas that require careful consideration. Additionally, the integration of AI into the healthcare workforce involves significant training and adjustment for healthcare professionals. AI's role in disease diagnosis is already significant and is poised for substantial expansion as technology advances. Its ability to enhance diagnostic accuracy, streamline processes, and personalize patient care is transforming the landscape of healthcare. As we continue to harness AI's potential, it is imperative to navigate its challenges thoughtfully, ensuring that AI serves as a beneficial tool in the quest for better healthcare outcomes.

AI in Disease Diagnosis-Breast Cancer Diagnosis

AI is revolutionizing breast cancer diagnosis through its application in medical imaging analysis, particularly in mammography. Traditional ML and deep learning techniques have been increasingly utilized to improve lesion localization, reduce misdiagnosis rates, and enhance accuracy in mammogram interpretation (Gao, 2023). AI-based models have also been developed to predict breast cancer risk, tumor malignancy, and response to treatment, although challenges remain in their clinical application (Jones, 2022). Despite the lack of a proven algorithm that outperforms human radiologists, AI has the potential to reduce their workload and enhance diagnostic expertise (Bennani-Baiti, 2019). In breast cancer imaging, AI has shown promise in tasks such as tumor volume demarcation, feature extraction, and risk prediction (Sheth, 2020). AI has also been applied to breast pathology, demonstrating success in tasks such as biomarker quantification and treatment response prediction (Yousif, 2021; Mhlanga, 2023b). In the realm of breast cancer detection, AI has shown potential in digital mammography and tomosynthesis, with some algorithms performing on par with human radiologists (Sechopoulos, 2020). The future of AI in breast imaging lies in its potential to improve diagnosis accuracy, reduce reading time, and customize screening programs (Mendes, 2022). As AI continues to evolve, it is expected to play an increasingly important role in clinical breast imaging (Hu, 2021).

AI's role in breast cancer diagnosis stands out as a prime example of how technology is transforming the medical diagnostics field. AI, particularly through ML models and deep learning networks, is increasingly utilized for analyzing medical images like mammograms. These AI systems are adept at detecting subtle variations in images that may not be immediately apparent to human eyes, and they do so with impressive speed and accuracy. Deep learning models are proficient at scanning thousands of mammograms, learning to identify minute abnormalities that could indicate the early stages of breast cancer. AI extends its utility beyond mere diagnosis by also predicting the likelihood of a tumor being benign or malignant based on imaging data and patient history. This capability helps reduce unnecessary biopsies and treatments. Additionally, AI tools serve as a second reader for radiologists, providing a comparative analysis that enhances diagnostic decisions. This collaboration increases confidence in the diagnostic outcomes and minimizes the chances of human error. AI systems significantly improve the detection rates of early-stage breast cancers, which are crucial for effective treatment outcomes. These systems process and evaluate imaging data much faster than traditional methods, thereby reducing wait times and potentially alleviating the anxiety associated with waiting for a diagnosis. In regions where there is a shortage of skilled radiologists, AI can provide expert-level analysis, making high-quality diagnostics more accessible. The effectiveness of AI systems depends heavily on the quality of the data they are trained on. There is a risk that biases in the training data could lead to skewed results, which could disproportionately affect certain groups. Integrating AI tools into existing healthcare infrastructures involves technological and regulatory challenges, as well as necessitating training for medical personnel. Furthermore, managing ethical concerns such as patient privacy, consent, and the potential for over-reliance on technology are critical issues that require careful consideration. AI is expected to become more integrated into routine diagnostics, with improvements in technology making these tools even more reliable and insightful. Research is ongoing to enhance the interpretability of AI decisions and to expand their capabilities to handle a broader range of imaging types and medical conditions.

Skin Cancer Detection

AI applications in dermatology, particularly in the detection of skin cancer, have shown promising results, with some studies reporting accuracy matching or exceeding that of dermatologists (Du-Harpur, 2021; Young, 2020; Jutzi, 2022; Lim, 2021; Brinker, 2020; Eapen, 2020; Ingram, 2020; Gomolin, 2020). These applications have the potential to assist in the diagnosis of skin lesions, particularly at the interface between primary and secondary care (Du-Harpur, 2020; Ingram, 2020). However, real-world clinical validation is currently lacking (Young, 2020). The combination of AI and human assessment has been shown to yield the best results (Brinker, 2020). Despite the potential of AI in dermatology, there are challenges such as systematic biases, standardization, interpretability, and acceptance by physicians and patients (Gomolin, 2020). AI applications have revolutionized various fields of medicine, including dermatology, where they are particularly transformative in detecting skin cancer. AI-powered tools are now routinely used to analyze images of skin lesions and moles, identifying potential melanomas with a precision that matches or even surpasses that of experienced dermatologists. These systems employ deep learning algorithms trained on vast datasets of dermatological images, enabling them to discern subtle patterns and variations in skin lesions that might elude the human eye. This capability significantly enhances the early detection of skin cancers, which is crucial for effective treatment and improved patient outcomes. The field has seen several notable advancements, including the development of AI systems that can differentiate between benign and malignant lesions with high accuracy. For example, a study published in a leading dermatology journal demonstrated that an AI model outperformed a panel of dermatologists in detecting melanoma from dermoscopic images. The model was trained using thousands of images labeled by expert dermatologists, learning to identify malignant features such as irregular growth patterns, asymmetric shapes, and uneven coloring.

Another breakthrough involves the integration of AI with smartphone technology, allowing users to take photographs of their skin lesions and receive instant analyses. This application of AI makes skin cancer screening more accessible, and could potentially increase the rate of early detection among the general population. An app, for example, uses a deep learning algorithm to assess the risk of melanoma based on a photo provided by the user, offering a preliminary evaluation that helps decide whether a professional consultation is necessary. The implementation of AI in skin cancer detection has several impactful benefits which include AI algorithms that can detect nuances in skin lesions that might be missed by the human eye, leading to earlier detection of skin cancer, including melanoma, which is known for its aggressive nature and potential to spread rapidly. Dermatologists can review and diagnose potential skin cancers more quickly with AI assistance, allowing for a higher volume of cases to be managed effectively, which is especially beneficial in areas with limited access to specialized healthcare. AI tools can be used remotely, making diagnostic services accessible to people in rural or underserved regions. This democratization of healthcare helps to reduce disparities in the availability of cancer screening and treatment services. Despite these advances, the integration of AI into clinical practice faces several challenges. One major concern is the potential for algorithm bias, where AI systems might perform differently on diverse populations depending on the data they were trained on. Ensuring that the training datasets are representative of various skin types and conditions is crucial to avoid misdiagnoses. Additionally, the reliance on AI tools raises ethical questions regarding patient privacy and data security. The data used to train these systems often include sensitive personal health information, which must be handled with stringent security measures to prevent breaches that could expose patient data. Furthermore, there is the challenge of gaining trust from both patients and healthcare providers. Building confidence in AI systems involves transparent communication about how these tools work, their benefits, and their limitations. It also requires rigorous testing and validation to prove that AI can be a reliable component of medical diagnostics.

Looking forward, ongoing research and development are focused on enhancing the accuracy and usability of AI in dermatology. Innovations include refining AI algorithms to better understand the context of skin lesions, such as their evolution over time, which can provide more detailed insights into their nature. Researchers are also exploring ways to integrate AI more seamlessly into healthcare workflows, ensuring that these tools support rather than replace the critical role of human clinicians. AI's role in skin cancer detection is a vivid illustration of how technology can extend and enhance the capabilities of traditional medicine. As AI technologies evolve, they promise not only to advance dermatological diagnostics but also to transform the broader landscape of healthcare, driving forward the possibilities of early detection, personalized treatment, and improved patient care.

Diabetic Retinopathy Screening

The application of AI in diabetic retinopathy (DR) screening is a significant advancement, with studies showing that AI systems can perform on par with clinical experts (Bellemo, 2019; Wang, 2020). These systems have the potential to reduce the incidence of preventable blindness (Bellemo, 2019), and improve the identification of DR lesions (Wang, 2020). However, there is a need for more clinical trials to validate these systems (Farahat, 2021). The use of AI in this field is expected to continue to grow, with the potential for further improvements in computing hardware and software (Williamson, 2020). In the realm of ophthalmology, the application of AI systems for the screening of diabetic retinopathy represents a significant advancement. DR is a serious condition that, if left untreated, can lead to blindness. AI models are specifically designed to analyze retinal images to detect signs of this disease. The automation of such screenings not only helps in identifying patients who require further examination by a specialist but also streamlines the workflow in healthcare settings and facilitates early intervention, which is crucial in preventing severe outcomes. AI technologies employed in DR screening utilize sophisticated deep-learning algorithms to analyze detailed images of the retina. These algorithms are trained on thousands of retinal scans, learning to recognize patterns indicative of early or advanced stages of DR. One of the key benefits of using AI in this context is its ability to detect microaneurysms, hemorrhages, and other anomalies that are typically subtle and difficult for the human eye to detect during early stages. A notable example of AI application in this field is an FDA-approved system that automatically detects more than mild DR in adults diagnosed with diabetes. This system uses a deep learning algorithm to analyze images of the patient's retina taken with a specific type of camera, and it provides a diagnostic output indicating whether DR is present. This innovation significantly reduces the burden on healthcare providers by screening patients without the immediate need for a specialist's review, unless the AI system detects potential retinopathy.

The integration of AI into DR screening has shown significant benefits, particularly in enhancing diagnostic accuracy. Studies have demonstrated that AI systems can achieve a level of accuracy comparable to or exceeding that of experienced ophthalmologists, especially in detecting early signs of DR (Deepa, 2023; Li, 2021; Zafar, 2022; Ahmed, 2021; Cuadros, 2020; Padhy, 2019; Huang, 2022; Wang, 2020). This has the potential to revolutionize patient care, leading to improved outcomes and more efficient resource utilization (Deepa, 2023). However, there are still challenges to be addressed, such as the lack of standards for development and evaluation, and the need for real-world evaluation of safety, efficacy, and equity (Li, 2021; Zafar, 2022). Despite these challenges, the use of AI in DR screening holds great promise for the future.

Increased Efficiency: AI-driven screenings can process large volumes of retinal images quickly, reducing the time from screening to diagnosis and allowing for faster intervention. Scalability and accessibility, these AI systems can be deployed in primary care settings, community clinics, or even remote areas, significantly increasing the accessibility of DR screening. This is particularly beneficial in underserved regions where ophthalmologists may not be readily available. Despite its benefits, the use of AI in DR screening is not without challenges. One major concern is the reliability of AI systems across different populations and varying image quality. AI models are dependent on the data they are trained on, and if this data is not diverse or comprehensive enough, the system may not perform well universally. Additionally, there are ethical and privacy concerns related to the use of AI in healthcare, particularly regarding the handling and protection of patient data. Ensuring that patient data used in training and operating these AI systems is securely protected is paramount to maintaining trust and integrity in the process. There are also technical and regulatory hurdles to overcome. AI systems must be continually updated and maintained to keep up with advancements in medical knowledge and imaging technology. Moreover, obtaining regulatory approval for medical AI systems can be complex and time-consuming, requiring extensive validation studies to ensure safety and efficacy. As research continues, future developments in AI for DR screening may focus on integrating more comprehensive data sources, including patient medical histories and genetic information, to enhance diagnostic precision. Additionally, there is ongoing work to improve the interpretability of AI decisions, which could help clinicians better understand and trust AI-generated diagnoses. The use of AI in DR screening exemplifies how technological innovations are increasingly crucial in diagnosing and managing chronic diseases. With ongoing advancements, AI is set to play an even more integral role in ophthalmology, enhancing both the effectiveness of medical interventions and the efficiency of healthcare delivery systems. This progress promises not only to improve patient outcomes but also to transform the landscape of diabetic healthcare management.

Cardiovascular Disease Prediction

AI technology, particularly ML and deep learning, is revolutionizing the prediction and diagnosis of cardiovascular diseases by leveraging vast amounts of data from electronic health records, patient data, and imaging studies. These AI models offer significant insights into the early detection and management of heart-related conditions (Al-Mannai, 2022; Nazir, 2018; Shelke, 2023; Gandham, 2023; Zeron, 2020; Shu, 2021; Ansari, 2021; Doolub, 2023). Despite the potential of AI in this field, challenges such as data quality, model interpretability, generalizability, and ethical issues need to be addressed for widespread adoption (Shelke, 2023; Zeron, 2019; Shu, 2021). AI technology is playing an increasingly pivotal role in the prediction and diagnosis of cardiovascular diseases. By leveraging vast amounts of data from electronic health records, patient data, and imaging studies like ECGs, AI models offer significant insights into the early detection and management of heart-related conditions. These models excel at identifying subtle patterns and indicators of cardiovascular diseases that may not be immediately apparent to human observers, thereby enhancing the accuracy and timeliness of diagnoses. The use of AI in this field involves sophisticated algorithms capable of analyzing complex datasets to predict potential heart conditions. For instance, machine learning models can assess ECG videos to detect early signs of heart failure, changes in heart muscle activity, or abnormalities in heart rhythms that might indicate a higher risk of future cardiovascular events. These predictive insights are invaluable as they allow healthcare providers to implement preventative measures early and tailor treatment plans to the specific needs of individual patients, potentially averting severe health outcomes. A notable development in AI-driven cardiovascular care is its ability to integrate and analyze multiple data types simultaneously. For example, AI systems can combine information from a patient's genetic data, lifestyle choices, and historical health records to provide a comprehensive risk assessment. This holistic approach to health data analysis leads to more personalized and effective patient care.

The implications of AI in cardiovascular care are profound which include:

Improved Diagnostic Accuracy: AI models, through continuous learning and updating, increasingly refine their diagnostic capabilities, leading to higher accuracy in predicting and diagnosing heart diseases.

Proactive Healthcare Management: With the ability to predict potential health issues before they manifest severely, AI enables a more proactive approach to healthcare. This shift from reactive to preventive care can significantly reduce the incidence and severity of cardiovascular diseases.

Customized Treatment Plans: AI's analytical power allows for the customization of treatment plans that cater to the individual nuances of each patient's condition, improving the effectiveness of treatments and patient outcomes. However, deploying AI in cardiovascular disease prediction also involves several challenges. One major concern is the quality and variety of data fed into AI models. If the data is biased or not representative of the broader population, the predictions may not be accurate across different demographics, leading to disparities in healthcare outcomes. Furthermore, there are ethical considerations regarding patient privacy and consent, as AI systems often require access to personal and sensitive health information. Ensuring robust data protection measures and maintaining transparency with patients about how their data is used is crucial to fostering trust and acceptance of AI technologies.

Moreover, there is a need for continuous oversight and regulation to ensure that AI systems in healthcare are safe, and effective, and do not replace the nuanced judgment of human doctors but rather complement it. Looking ahead, ongoing advancements in AI technology promise even greater integration into the healthcare system. Future developments may focus on enhancing the interoperability of AI with existing medical technologies and electronic health systems, improving ease of use and accessibility for healthcare providers. Additionally, as AI algorithms become more sophisticated, they could offer even more detailed and accurate predictions, further transforming the landscape of cardiovascular care. AI's role in cardiovascular disease prediction exemplifies the transformative potential of technology in healthcare, offering new opportunities for early diagnosis and personalized treatment that could significantly improve patient care and outcomes. As technology continues to evolve, AI is poised to become an integral component of modern medical practice, particularly in managing and preventing cardiovascular diseases.

Neurological Disorders

AI technology is revolutionizing the diagnosis and management of neurological disorders, including Alzheimer's and Parkinson's disease. Vashistha (2019) and Patel (2019), both highlight the role of AI in providing fast and effective diagnoses, with Vashistha specifically noting the use of AI in monitoring neurodegenerative functions. Haddad (2020) and Divyashree (2023) emphasize the potential of AI to improve the accuracy and timing of Parkinson's disease diagnosis, with Divyashree's 2-D CNN model achieving a 98% accuracy rate. Raghavendra (2019) and Sylviaa (2023) further underscore the effectiveness of AI in automated diagnosis and prediction of neurological disorders, with Sylviaa's study using an Artificial Neural Network to distinguish different stages of Parkinson's disease. Wang (2020) and Qiu (2020) both demonstrate the potential of AI in diagnosing Alzheimer's disease, with Wang's AI algorithm achieving over 95% accuracy and Qiu's algorithm accurately predicting the risk of Alzheimer's disease. By analyzing brain imaging scans, AI can detect subtle changes in the brain that are often not apparent in the early stages of these diseases. This early detection capability is crucial as it allows for earlier therapeutic interventions, which can significantly improve patient outcomes by slowing the progression of the disease or managing symptoms more effectively. AI models, particularly those using ML and deep learning, are trained on vast arrays of brain imaging data. These models learn to recognize patterns and anomalies associated with neurological conditions that even skilled radiologists might miss. For example, in Alzheimer's disease, AI can detect minute changes in brain volume and specific protein accumulations that are indicators of the disease's progression long before clinical symptoms become apparent. Similarly, for Parkinson's disease, AI tools can analyze movement patterns and brain scans to identify early signs of the disorder, such as slight tremors or rigidity.

The integration of AI into the diagnosis of neurological disorders brings several significant benefits which include early and accurate diagnoses, the ability of AI to analyze complex imaging data quickly and accurately allows for the diagnosis of neurological disorders at much earlier stages than currently possible, which is often key to managing these diseases effectively.

Personalized Treatment Plans: With earlier diagnosis, personalized treatment plans can be developed that are tailored to the specific needs and progression of each patient's condition, potentially altering the disease's impact and improving quality of life.

Enhanced Research Capabilities: AI not only aids in the clinical diagnosis but also enhances research into neurological disorders by identifying new patterns and correlations that may go unnoticed in traditional studies

Looking Forward: AI in the diagnosis of neurological disorders is set to expand. Innovations may include more sophisticated AI models that integrate genetic information, lifestyle data, and longitudinal health records to provide even more accurate diagnoses and predictions. There is also a trend toward developing AI-driven tools that can be used not just in specialized medical centers but also in primary care settings, expanding access to early diagnostics. Moreover, as AI technology evolves, there is potential for these tools to not only diagnose but also predict the onset of neurological conditions before any symptoms appear, profoundly changing how these diseases are managed and treated. The application of AI in diagnosing neurological disorders exemplifies the transformative potential of technology in medical science. It opens up new avenues for managing complex diseases and, most importantly, offers hope for patients and families affected by these challenging conditions, potentially improving outcomes and enhancing quality of life.

Predicting Cardiovascular Disease Risk Factors

AI has significantly transformed the approach to healthcare, particularly in predicting risk factors for cardiovascular diseases (CVDs), which remain a leading cause of death globally. AI, including deep neural networks and ML algorithms, has been shown to improve risk assessment by analyzing large datasets and providing personalized risk forecasts (Shelke, 2023). It has also revolutionized cardiology by offering novel tools for interpreting data and making clinical decisions (Romiti, 2020). In the assessment of coronary artery disease, AI has the potential to overcome the limitations of current risk models by applying computer algorithms to large databases with multidimensional variables (Doolub, 2023). However, the widespread adoption of AI in cardiology is hindered by issues such as data quality, model interpretability, and ethical concerns (Langlais, 2022). Despite these challenges, AI has demonstrated high prediction accuracy in diagnosing and predicting CVDs, particularly when applied to wearable sensor data (Huang, 2022). The use of AI in cardiology is expected to continue to evolve, with the potential to change the way medicine is practiced (Seckanovic, 2020). By harnessing the power of AI, medical professionals can now predict with greater accuracy which patients are at risk of developing CVDs, enabling earlier and more targeted interventions. The application of AI in this field involves sophisticated ML algorithms that analyze vast datasets including not only medical records but also patient demographics, lifestyle choices, genetic information, and even environmental factors. The comprehensive nature of this data allows AI systems to identify patterns and correlations that may not be evident to human analysts. Consider a hypothetical AI model developed to predict the risk of heart attacks. This model, trained on a dataset consisting of thousands of patients over several years, looks at variables such as age, gender, blood pressure, cholesterol levels, smoking status, physical activity, and genetic markers. For instance, a patient named John, a 45-year-old male with a family history of heart disease, high blood pressure, and a sedentary lifestyle, would be identified by the AI as high risk. The model can analyze John's data along with similar profiles to predict his likelihood of having a heart attack within the next decade.

The AI system uses this information to score John's risk, which then informs the healthcare provider's recommendations. Based on AI predictions, John might be advised to start a medically supervised exercise program, adopt a heart-healthy diet, and begin regular monitoring of his blood pressure and cholesterol levels. AI models in this field typically use a variety of ML techniques, including regression analysis, support vector machines, and neural networks, particularly deep learning. These models are trained using historical health data where the outcomes are known, which then allows the models to learn and make predictions about new patients. One real-world example is the use of such technologies in wearable health devices. These devices can continuously collect health data such as heart rate, activity levels, and sleep patterns. AI algorithms analyze this data in real time to provide users with insights into their cardiovascular health, potentially alerting them to seek medical advice if concerning patterns are detected. While AI systems offer significant benefits, they also come with challenges. Data privacy is a major concern as sensitive health data must be protected from unauthorized access. Additionally, there is the issue of bias, if AI models are trained on data that is not representative of the general population, their predictions might not apply to underrepresented groups, potentially leading to disparities in healthcare. Moreover, the reliance on AI should not diminish the role of healthcare providers. Decisions based on AI predictions must be still made in consultation with trained medical professionals who can consider the full context of a patient's health. AI's role in predicting cardiovascular disease risk factors exemplifies the potential of technology to transform healthcare. By enabling early detection and personalized treatment plans, AI not only enhances the quality of care but also improves health outcomes, reduces healthcare costs, and ensures a proactive approach to managing and preventing serious health conditions. Through continuous improvement and ethical management of AI technologies, their full potential can be realized to the benefit of patients worldwide.

Conclusion

In conclusion, the chapter has demonstrated that AI holds substantial promise in transforming hospital administration and improving disease diagnosis. As explored throughout the chapter, AI applications offer considerable advantages by enhancing diagnostic accuracy, efficiency, and overall patient care. With the use of ML techniques for disease detection and classification, along with compelling case studies, AI's efficacy in the healthcare sector is increasingly evident. However, the integration of AI also presents challenges that require careful consideration, including ethical concerns and the need for robust data security measures. Despite these challenges, the potential of AI to revolutionize healthcare practices and outcomes is immense, positioning it as a pivotal tool in modern medicine. This chapter underscores the importance of continued research, investment, and collaboration to harness AI's full potential in disease diagnosis and hospital administration.

References

Ahmed, I. and Liu, T.A. (2021). The impact of COVID-19 on diabetic retinopathy monitoring and treatment. Current diabetes reports, 21, 1–5.

Ansari, M.F., Alankar, B. and Kaur, H. (2021). A prediction of heart disease using machine learning algorithms. In Image Processing and Capsule Networks: ICIPCN 2020 (pp. 497-504). Springer International Publishing.

Anwer, M.S. (2024). Opportunities and Challenges of Artificial Intelligent-powered Technology in Healthcare. *Medical Research Archives, 12*(3).

Bajwa, N.M. (2021). Exploration of Validity Evidence for the P-MEX in a Residency Admissions Process (Doctoral dissertation, University of Illinois at Chicago).

Bellemo, V., Lim, Z.W., Lim, G., Nguyen, Q.D., Xie, Y., Yip, M.Y., ... and Ting, D.S. (2019). Artificial intelligence using deep learning to screen for referable and vision-threatening diabetic retinopathy in Africa: a clinical validation study. The Lancet Digital Health, 1(1), e35–e44.

Bennani-Baiti, B., Krug, B., Giese, D., Hellmich, M., Bartsch, S., Helbich, T.H. and Baltzer, P.A. (2019). Evaluation of 3.0-T MRI brain signal after exposure to gadoterate meglumine in women with high breast cancer risk and screening breast MRI. Radiology, *293*(3), 523–30.

Bhattacharya, M., Sharma, A.R., Mallick, B., Sharma, G., Lee, S.S. and Chakraborty, C. (2020). Immunoinformatics approach to understand molecular interaction between multi-epitopic regions of SARS-CoV-2 spike-protein with TLR4/MD-2 complex. Infection, Genetics and Evolution, 85, 104587.

Brinker, T.J., Faria, B.L., de Faria, O.M., Klode, J., Schadendorf, D., Utikal, J.S., ... and Bernardes-Souza, B. (2020). Effect of a face-aging mobile app–based intervention on skin cancer protection behavior in secondary schools in Brazil: a cluster-randomized clinical trial. JAMA dermatology, *156*(7), 737–45.

Cuadros, J., Bresnick, G., Fleischmann, S., Wolff, G., Khan, M., Cuadros, P. and Pedersen, E.R. (2020). Adherence to Ophthalmology Referral, Treatment and Follow-up: What Happens After Diabetic Retinopathy Screening in the Primary Care Setting? A Retrospective Record Review Study. Investigative Ophthalmology & Visual Science, *61*(7), 3314–14.

Deepa, R. and Sivasamy, A. (2023). Advancements in early detection of diabetes and diabetic retinopathy screening using artificial intelligence. AIP Advances, *13*(11).

Deepa, S., Janet, J., Sumathi, S. and Ananth, J.P. (2023). Hybrid optimization algorithm enabled deep learning approach brain tumor segmentation and classification using MRI. Journal of Digital Imaging, *36*(3), 847–68.

Devi, K.J., Alghamdi, W., Divya, N., Alkhayyat, A., Sayyora, A. and Sathish, T. (2023). Artificial Intelligence in Healthcare: Diagnosis, Treatment, and Prediction. *In: E3S Web of Conferences, 399*, 04043. EDP Sciences.

Divyashree, P. and Dwivedi, P. (2023). Smart Digital Healthcare Solutions Using Medical Imaging and Advanced AI Techniques. In Machine Learning and Deep Learning Techniques for Medical Image Recognition (pp. 76-89). CRC Press.

Donel, J. (2019). Tocophobia: overwhelming fear of pregnancy and childbirth. International Journal of Reproduction, Contraception, Obstetrics and Gynecology, *8*(11), 4641–4646.

Du-Harpur, X., Arthurs, C., Ganier, C., Woolf, R., Laftah, Z., Lakhan, M., ... and Lynch, M.D. (2021). Clinically relevant vulnerabilities of deep machine learning systems for skin cancer diagnosis. The Journal of investigative dermatology, *141*(4), 916.

Eapen, B.R., Sartipi, K. and Archer, N. (2020). Serverless on FHIR: Deploying machine learning models for healthcare on the cloud. arXiv preprint arXiv:2006.04748.

Farahat, Z., Souissi, N., Belmekki, M., Megdiche, K., Benamar, S., Bennani, Y., ... and Ngote, N. (2021, October). Diabetic retinopathy: New perspectives with artificial intelligence. In 2021 Fifth International Conference On Intelligent Computing in Data Sciences (ICDS) (pp. 1-7). IEEE.

Francis, A. (2023). The concept of competitiveness. In The competitiveness of european industry (pp. 5-20). Routledge.

Gandham, R., Manambakam, K.R., Madala, S.V.N., Nannapaneni, N.S., Tokala, S. and Enduri, M.K. (2023, December). Predictive Modeling for Heart Disease Detection with Machine Learning. In 2023 IEEE 15th International Conference on Computational Intelligence and Communication Networks (CICN) (pp. 325-329). IEEE.

Gao, S., Gao, X., Zhu, R., Wu, D., Feng, Z., Jiao, N., ... and Zhu, L. (2023). Microbial genes outperform species and SNVs as diagnostic markers for Crohn's disease on multicohort fecal metagenomes empowered by artificial intelligence. Gut Microbes, 15(1), 2221428.

Gomolin, A., Netchiporouk, E., Gniadecki, R. and Litvinov, I.V. (2020). Artificial intelligence applications in dermatology: where do we stand?. Frontiers in medicine, 7, 100.

Haddad, R., Denys, P., Arlandis, S., Giannantoni, A., Del Popolo, G., Panicker, J.N., ... and Everaert, K. (2020). Nocturia and nocturnal polyuria in neurological patients: from epidemiology to treatment. A systematic review of the literature. European urology focus, 6(5), 922–34.

Haider, M.Z., Al-Mannai, A., Al-Sirhan, S., Elsabagh, A., Nasser, N., Al-Quraishi, N., ... and Al Moustafa, A. E. (2022). Impact of smoking on COVID-19 symptoms in non-vaccinated patients: a matched observational study from Qatar. Journal of multidisciplinary healthcare, 531–40.

Haq, A.U., Li, J.P., Memon, M.H., Nazir, S. and Sun, R. (2018). A hybrid intelligent system framework for the prediction of heart disease using machine learning algorithms. Mobile information systems, 2018(1), 3860146.

Huang, X., Wang, H., She, C., Feng, J., Liu, X., Hu, X. ... and Tao, Y. (2022). Artificial intelligence promotes the diagnosis and screening of diabetic retinopathy. Frontiers in Endocrinology, 13, 946915.

Jean, A. (2020). A brief history of artificial intelligence. *Medicine Sciences (M/S)*, *36*(11), 1059–67.

Jones, S.E. (2022). Mental health, suicidality, and connectedness among high school students during the COVID-19 pandemic—Adolescent Behaviors and Experiences Survey, United States, January–June 2021. MMWR supplements, 71.

Jutzi, M., Raducan, S.D., Zhang, Y., Michel, P. and Arakawa, M. (2022). Constraining surface properties of asteroid (162173) Ryugu from numerical simulations of Hayabusa2 mission impact experiment. Nature communications, 13(1), 7134.

Khanna, N.N., Maindarkar, M.A., Viswanathan, V., Fernandes, J.F.E., Paul, S., Bhagawati, M., ... and Suri, J.S. (2022, December). Economics of artificial intelligence in healthcare: Diagnosis vs. treatment. *In: Healthcare 10*(12), 2493.. MDPI.

Langlais, C. (2022). Impact of Modifiable Diet and Lifestyle Factors on Prostate Cancer Progression and Mortality. University of California, San Francisco.

Li, W.Y., Yang, M., Song, Y.N., Luo, L., Nie, C. and Zhang, M.N. (2021). An online diabetic retinopathy screening tool for patients with type 2 diabetes. International Journal of Ophthalmology, 14(11), 1748.

Lim, S., Bae, J.H., Kwon, H.S. and Nauck, M.A. (2021). COVID-19 and diabetes mellitus: from pathophysiology to clinical management. Nature Reviews Endocrinology, 17(1), 11–30.

Mendes, R., Graça, G., Silva, F., Guerreiro, A.C., Gomes-Alves, P., Serpa, J. ... and Isidro, I.A. (2022). Exploring metabolic signatures of ex vivo tumor tissue cultures for prediction of chemosensitivity in ovarian cancer. Cancers, 14(18), 4460.

Mhlanga, D. (2023a). Financial Technology, Artificial Intelligence, and the Health Sector, Lessons We are Learning on Good Health and Well-Being. *In: FinTech and Artificial Intelligence for Sustainable Development: The Role of Smart Technologies in Achieving Development Goals* (pp. 145–70). Cham: Springer Nature Switzerland.

Mhlanga, D. (2023b). Digital Transformation in the Healthcare Sector: The Role of Artificial Intelligence for Inclusive Long-term Care around the World, Lessons for Africa. *In: Economic Inclusion in Post-Independence Africa: An Inclusive Approach to Economic Development* (pp. 347–62). Cham: Springer Nature Switzerland.

Mhlanga, D. (2024). Generative AI for Emerging Researchers: The Promises, Ethics, and Risks. *Ethics, and Risks* (February 24). *SSRN*. 4737492. https://ssrn.com/abstract=4737492 or http://dx.doi.org/10.2139/ssrn.4737492.

Mishra, V., Ugemuge, S. and Tiwade, Y. (2023). Artificial intelligence changing the future of healthcare diagnostics. *Journal of Cellular Biotechnology* (Preprint), 1–8.

Mlambo, F. and Mhlanga, D. (2023). A Machine Learning Approach for Predicting Emissions Based on GDP: A Case of South Africa in Comparison with the United Kingdom. In: *The Fourth Industrial Revolution in Africa: Exploring the Development Implications of Smart Technologies in Africa* (pp. 91–116). Cham: Springer Nature Switzerland.

Naveed, M.A. (2023). Transforming Healthcare through Artificial Intelligence and Machine Learning. *Pakistan Journal of Health Sciences*, 4(05), 01. https://doi.org/10.54393/pjhs.v4i05.844

Ndhlovu, E. and Mhlanga, D. (2024). African Agency in Medical Innovation and Practices: From Antiquity to the Present. *African Renaissance* (1744–2532), *21*(1).

Padhy, S.K., Takkar, B., Chawla, R. and Kumar, A. (2019). Artificial intelligence in diabetic retinopathy: A natural step to the future. Indian journal of ophthalmology, *67*(7), 1004–1009.

Patil, S. and Shankar, H. (2023). Transforming healthcare: Harnessing the power of AI in the modern era. *International Journal of Multidisciplinary Sciences and Arts*, *2*(1), 60–70.

Patel, A., Surti, N. and Mahajan, A. (2019). Intranasal drug delivery: Novel delivery route for effective management of neurological disorders. Journal of Drug Delivery Science and Technology, 52, 130–37.

Poalelungi, D.G., Musat, C.L., Fulga, A., Neagu, M., Neagu, A.I., Piraianu, A.I. and Fulga, I. (2023). Advancing patient care: how artificial intelligence is transforming healthcare. Journal of personalized medicine, *13*(8), 1214.

Qiu C., Cui C., Hautefort C., et al. Olfactory and Gustatory Dysfunction as an Early Identifier of COVID-19 in Adults and Children: An International Multicenter Study. Otolaryngology–Head and Neck Surgery. 2020; *163*(4): 714–721. doi:10.1177/0194599820934376

Romiti, S., Vinciguerra, M., Saade, W., Anso Cortajarena, I. and Greco, E. (2020). Artificial intelligence (AI) and cardiovascular diseases: an unexpected alliance. Cardiology Research and Practice, 2020(1), 4972346.

Sechopoulos, I. and Mann, R.M. (2020). Stand-alone artificial intelligence-The future of breast cancer screening? The Breast, 49, 254–60.

Shelke, A., Shelke, S., Acharya, S. and Shukla, S. (2023). Synergistic Epidemic or Syndemic: An Emerging Pattern of Human Diseases. Cureus, *15*(11).

Sheth, R.A., Murthy, R., Hong, D.S., Patel, S., Overman, M.J., Diab, A., ... and Tam, A. (2020). Assessment of image-guided intratumoral delivery of immunotherapeutics in patients with cancer. JAMA Network Open, *3*(7), e207911–e207911.

Shu, S., Ren, J. and Song, J. (2021). Clinical application of machine learning-based artificial intelligence in the diagnosis, prediction, and classification of cardiovascular diseases. Circulation Journal, *85*(9), 1416–25.

Soferman, R. (2019). The transformative impact of artificial intelligence on healthcare outcomes. Journal of Clinical Engineering, *44*(3), E1–E3.

Sylvia, M.T., Soundharia, R., Bhat, R.V. and Marak, F. (2023). Myocardial bridging in cases of sudden death and its association with clinicopathologic characteristics. Heart Views, *24*(1), 6–10.

Vashistha, R., Yadav, D., Chhabra, D. and Shukla, P. (2019). Artificial intelligence integration for neurodegenerative disorders. In Leveraging Biomedical and Healthcare Data (pp. 77–89). Academic Press.

Wang, S., Wang, X., Hu, Y., Shen, Y., Yang, Z., Gan, M. and Lei, B. (2020). Diabetic retinopathy diagnosis using multichannel generative adversarial network with semisupervision. IEEE Transactions on Automation Science and Engineering, *18*(2), 574–85.

Wang, S., Zhang, Y., Lei, S., Zhu, H., Li, J., Wang, Q., ... and Pan, H. (2020). Performance of deep neural network-based artificial intelligence method in diabetic retinopathy screening: a systematic review and meta-analysis of diagnostic test accuracy. European Journal of Endocrinology, *183*(1), 41–49.

Williamson, E.J., Walker, A.J., Bhaskaran, K., Bacon, S., Bates, C., Morton, C.E., ... and Goldacre, B. (2020). Factors associated with COVID-19-related death using OpenSAFELY. Nature, *584*(7821), 430–36.

Young, T., Soorapanth, S., Wilkerson, J., Millburg, L., Roberts, T. and Morgareidge, D. (2020). The costs and value of modelling-based design in healthcare delivery: Five case studies from the US. Health Systems, 9(3), 253–62.

Yousif, N., Niederseer, D., Davies, A., El Issa, M., Sidia, B., Noor, H.A., ... and Obeid, S. (2021). Impact of malignancy on clinical outcomes in patients with acute coronary syndromes. International journal of cardiology, 328, 8–13.

Zafar, S., Mahjoub, H., Mehta, N., Domalpally, A. and Channa, R. (2022). Artificial intelligence algorithms in diabetic retinopathy screening. Current Diabetes Reports, 22(6), 267–74.

Zeron, R.M.C. and Serrano, C.V. (2020). Artificial intelligence in the diagnosis of cardiovascular disease. Revista da Associação Médica Brasileira, 65, 1438–41.

10 | AI in Healthcare Finance and Billing
Enhancing Efficiency and Accuracy

The integration of artificial intelligence (AI) technologies into healthcare finance and billing processes has brought about significant advancements in terms of efficiency, accuracy, and cost-effectiveness. This chapter explores the transformative role of AI in healthcare finance and billing, highlighting its potential to streamline administrative tasks, minimize errors, and optimize revenue cycles. The chapter begins by providing an overview of the current challenges and complexities faced by healthcare organizations in managing financial operations and billing procedures. It highlights the labor-intensive nature of manual processes, the risk of human errors, and the impact of regulatory compliance on revenue management. Subsequently, the chapter delves into the application of AI in healthcare finance and billing. The chapter will look in detail at the following, AI for revenue cycle management, fraud detection and prevention in billing, AI-driven cost analysis and financial forecasting, and insurance claims processing and reimbursement

Introduction

In the rapidly evolving landscape of healthcare, financial operations play a critical role in sustaining service delivery and organizational viability. Yet, managing these financial operations, especially in billing and revenue cycles, presents significant challenges. Traditional methods are often labor-intensive, error-prone, and subject to complex regulatory requirements that can stymie efficiency and threaten financial stability. As healthcare providers seek more resilient and adaptive systems, the emergence of artificial intelligence (AI) offers unprecedented opportunities to transform healthcare finance and billing processes. The healthcare industry is facing significant challenges in managing financial operations, particularly in billing and revenue cycles, due to their labor-intensive and error-prone nature (Macapagal, 2022; Buker 2023). The emergence of AI offers potential solutions to these challenges, with the ability to alleviate revenue cycle management issues (Konda et al., 2018). However, the transformation of healthcare finance and billing processes requires a structured model that considers factors such as value-based financing and accountable care models (Tan and Le, 2019). Information technology, including AI, is crucial in addressing the rising costs and complexity of the healthcare industry (Bigus et al., 2011). To improve financial management, healthcare organizations need to become more efficient and reduce costs while maintaining quality care (Pelt et al., 2014). The use of financial information systems can provide a competitive advantage (Ryckman, 1990), and disruptive innovation can help healthcare providers adapt to changes in the marketplace (Kenagy, 2002).

This chapter explores the integration of AI into healthcare finance and billing, aiming to enhance the efficiency and accuracy of these essential functions. By examining the intersection of AI technologies with the intricate dynamics of healthcare billing systems, this discourse underscores the transformative potential of AI across various facets of financial operations. The healthcare finance and billing systems are rife with operational inefficiencies, leading to significant financial and service quality impacts (Conway et al., 2008; Westgate, 2020; Yannamani, 2019; Patel, 2023). These inefficiencies are largely due to manual processes, which are time-consuming and error-prone (Conway, 2008; Westgate, 2011; Nieto-Salazar, 2023; Patel, 2022). These systems are characterized by their dependency on manual processes that not only consume substantial time and resources but also leave ample room for human error. Such errors can lead to incorrect billing, delayed reimbursements, and ultimately, financial losses. Additionally, healthcare billing is heavily regulated, requiring adherence to stringent compliance measures that complicate the financial landscape further.

In particular, administrative complexity and misaligned incentives in the US healthcare system contribute to these inefficiencies (Patel, 2023). Organizational factors such as insufficient workspace, poor process design, and lack of integration in internal supply chains also play a role (Tucker, 2014). The cost of these inefficiencies is estimated to be substantial, with healthcare claims processes, payment, and reconciliation alone eating up to 10–14% of physician practice revenue (Bonvissuto, 2011). These inefficiencies can also impact patients, leading to a poor experience with the billing department (Abrahams, 2014). To address these issues, there is a need for standardization and simplification of health administrative activities, as well as the promotion of high-productivity innovation (Patel, 2023). As the volume of data generated by healthcare services continues to grow exponentially, traditional systems struggle to keep pace, often resulting in bottlenecks that delay processing and impede cash flow. Moreover, the lack of predictive analytics in traditional systems hampers effective financial forecasting and strategic planning. These challenges highlight the pressing need for innovative solutions that can revolutionize healthcare finance management. In response to these complexities, AI presents a suite of capabilities, from automating routine tasks to employing sophisticated algorithms for fraud detection and financial forecasting. This chapter will delve into how AI technologies are being harnessed to streamline administrative tasks, minimize errors, and optimize revenue cycles, thereby fostering a more efficient and accurate system for healthcare finance and billing.

Background and Context

The landscape of healthcare finance and billing has long been fraught with challenges. Traditionally, the management of these systems has relied heavily on manual processes which are not only time-consuming but also prone to human error, resulting in significant inefficiencies and financial losses. For example, manual entry of billing information is susceptible to typos or misinterpretation of handwritten notes, which can lead to claim rejections or delays that frustrate patients and strain the resources of healthcare providers. The complexity of healthcare billing is further exacerbated by constantly evolving regulations that demand meticulous compliance and rigorous documentation. Healthcare providers must navigate a labyrinth of coding standards like ICD-10 (International Classification of Diseases) and CPT (Current Procedural Terminology), where a single miscode can lead to denied claims or audits, impacting financial stability and operational efficiency. Additionally, the diverse and changing insurance policies complicate the claims process, requiring billing departments to stay continually updated and adaptable.

As healthcare costs continue to escalate globally, the financial strain on healthcare systems intensifies, highlighting the urgent need for streamlined operations that do not compromise the quality of patient care. In this challenging environment, the evolution of technology, particularly through digital record-keeping and advanced data analytics, has been pivotal. Electronic Health Records (EHRs) have replaced paper files, reducing the risk of lost information and facilitating quicker access to patient histories, which is crucial for accurate billing and coding. The advent of AI has further revolutionized this domain by integrating with these technological advancements. AI technologies are now being employed to automate routine tasks such as data entry and claims processing, drastically reducing the scope for human error and freeing up staff to focus on more complex and patient-centric tasks. For instance, AI-powered tools are capable of extracting relevant information from EHRs to ensure accurate billing codes are applied, which helps in minimizing claim denials. Moreover, AI algorithms can analyze historical data to identify patterns that lead to denials, allowing healthcare providers to pre-emptively address potential issues.

Beyond routine automation, AI is also making strides in more sophisticated areas like fraud detection and financial forecasting. Advanced AI systems can scrutinize billing patterns to detect anomalies that may indicate fraudulent activities, safeguarding against financial loss. Furthermore, AI-driven predictive analytics are being used to forecast future revenue streams and patient influx, enabling healthcare facilities to better manage resources and plan strategically. These technological advancements not only promise to alleviate the traditional burdens of healthcare billing but also pave the way for more efficient, accurate, and cost-effective financial operations. By leveraging AI, healthcare providers can not only improve their financial health but also enhance patient satisfaction through faster and more accurate billing processes.

The Need for AI in Healthcare Finance

Healthcare finance and billing are fraught with challenges that stem from the need for regulatory compliance, accuracy in coding and billing, effective management of patient data, and ensuring timely reimbursements. The challenges in healthcare finance and billing, including regulatory compliance, coding accuracy, patient data management, and timely reimbursements, have been well-documented (Holmes, 1921; Baselski, 2024; Holmes, 2021; Baselski, 2024; James, 2022; Szarfman, 2022; Palmer, 2023; Classen, 2024). These challenges are further complicated by the need for effective records retention (Tilley, 1994; Bg, 1994), the complexity of E/M coding guidelines (Sosa, 2000), and the multi-disciplinary nature of CPT coding (Shrake, 1999; Kl, 1999). State legislators and regulators have also grappled with the issue of timely payment of healthcare claims (Morgan, 2002; MacEachern, 2003). A lack of formal education in residency curriculum, inadequate clinical documentation, and a lack of feedback systems have been identified as common reasons for inaccurate billing (Burks, 2022). These challenges are magnified by the exponential increase in patient data and the growing complexity of healthcare services offered. The traditional methods, characterized by manual inputs and linear processing, are increasingly inadequate. They are not only error-prone and time-consuming but also lead to delayed payments and a higher rate of denied claims. These inefficiencies can significantly undermine the financial health of healthcare institutions, while simultaneously affecting patient satisfaction and trust.

For instance, a typical scenario in a busy hospital setting involves the manual entry of vast amounts of data from patient interactions into billing systems. Each entry point represents a potential for error—whether it's a miskeyed procedure code or incorrect patient information—that can lead to claim denials. Such denials not only delay the reimbursement process but also require additional resources to address and rectify the errors, further straining the hospital's administrative capacity. AI offers a robust solution to these persistent issues. By automating processes, AI can significantly reduce the human error associated with data entry and processing. AI systems are designed to handle large volumes of data with precision, ensuring that coding and billing are conducted accurately and in compliance with the latest regulatory standards. Furthermore, AI can manage the increasing scale and complexity of data more effectively than traditional systems. A practical example of AI's application can be found in its ability to analyze large datasets to identify patterns and anomalies that might indicate potential claim denials before they occur. For example, AI-driven systems can pre-emptively flag claims that are likely to be rejected based on historical data and trends, allowing healthcare providers to correct any issues before submission.

Additionally, AI technologies have been instrumental in streamlining the billing process itself. By employing machine learning algorithms, AI can automate the extraction and processing of billing information from EHRs, ensuring that all billable procedures are accurately captured and submitted. This level of automation not only speeds up the billing process but also reduces the administrative burden on staff, allowing them to focus on more critical patient-care tasks. Moreover, AI's capability in predictive analytics can be harnessed to forecast future billing challenges and adapt to regulatory changes, ensuring continuous compliance. For example, AI models can be trained to anticipate changes in healthcare regulations and adapt billing practices accordingly, thus maintaining a seamless workflow and avoiding potential compliance issues. The integration of AI into healthcare finance is not merely an option but a necessity in today's complex healthcare environment. By enhancing the accuracy, efficiency, and reliability of financial operations, AI not only improves the financial footing of healthcare providers but also significantly boosts patient satisfaction by reducing errors and expediting service delivery.

Overview of AI Applications in Healthcare Finance

The applications of AI in healthcare finance are as diverse as they are transformative. At the core of these innovations is the automation of billing and claims processing systems. The transformative potential of AI in healthcare finance is evident in its ability to automate billing and claims processing systems, reducing administrative burden and improving accuracy (Kilanko, 2023). AI-driven solutions are reshaping the industry, leading to improved patient outcomes and greater efficiency (Sarkar, 2023). These solutions are being applied in diagnosis, treatment recommendations, patient engagement, and adherence, as well as administrative activities (Davenport, 2020). The use of AI in healthcare finance extends to various areas, including patient care, clinical and non-clinical research, medical imaging, and medicine (Roy, 2021). AI is also being used to improve clinical workflows, manage claims, detect fraud, and predict hospital-acquired infections (Hussain, 2020). The technology's ability to predict, understand, learn, and act on novel relationships between genetic codes is transforming healthcare (Shaheen, 2021). However, the implementation of AI in healthcare finance also presents challenges, such as data privacy and algorithm bias (Kilanko, 2023). AI-powered systems are designed to handle these routine yet critical tasks with unprecedented accuracy and speed. By automating the entry, processing, and verification of billing data, AI reduces the administrative burden on healthcare facilities and minimizes errors that can lead to claim denials and financial losses. For instance, a hospital using AI to automate its billing systems could see a significant reduction in the time it takes to process claims, from several days to just a few hours, drastically cutting down on the payment cycle.

Fraud detection represents another critical application of AI in this sector. Traditional methods of detecting fraud often involve manual reviews and random audits, which are not only labor-intensive but also less effective in catching sophisticated schemes. AI algorithms excel in analyzing vast amounts of billing and claims data to identify patterns, outliers, and inconsistencies that might suggest fraudulent activities. For example, an AI system could flag a provider who submits unusually high claims for a particular procedure compared to peers or historical data, prompting further investigation. This capability not only protects revenue but also ensures the integrity of healthcare operations. Predictive analytics is revolutionizing revenue management in healthcare. By leveraging historical financial data, AI systems can forecast future trends and potential disruptions in the revenue cycle, allowing healthcare providers to proactively adjust their financial strategies. This might include predicting periods of high claim denials or changes in patient inflow, enabling hospitals to allocate resources more effectively and maintain financial stability.

Personalized patient billing is another innovative use of AI in healthcare finance. This approach uses AI to consider each patient's insurance coverage details, past payment history, and even socio-economic factors to customize billing statements and payment plans. Such personalization not only enhances patient satisfaction by providing clear, understandable, and tailored billing information but also improves payment collection rates. For example, an AI system might adjust a billing plan based on a patient's financial behavior, offering early payment discounts or extended payment plans as needed. These diverse applications of AI in healthcare finance underscore the technology's critical role in enhancing operational efficiency, protecting financial assets, and improving patient relations. By harnessing the power of AI, healthcare providers can navigate the complexities of modern financial operations more effectively, ensuring that they not only survive but thrive in today's challenging economic landscape.

Benefits of AI in Healthcare Finance

The introduction of AI into healthcare finance brings numerous benefits. The most significant is the enhancement of efficiency. By automating routine tasks, AI allows healthcare staff to focus on more complex and patient-centric activities. The introduction of AI into healthcare finance has numerous benefits, with the most significant being the enhancement of efficiency. AI can streamline billing operations, reduce administrative burden, and optimize reimbursement strategies (Kilanko, 2023). It also plays a crucial role in transforming operations in the healthcare industry, particularly in early disease detection, drug development, personalized treatment, and remote monitoring (Mohan, 2024). AI's potential in healthcare is further underscored by its ability to support decision-making, optimize business processes, and deliver personalized treatment plans (Kara, 2023). The technology's impact on clinical practice, error reduction, and efficiency improvement is also highlighted (Madhvi, 2024). AI's transformative potential in reshaping the industry is evident in its applications, which range from administrative task optimization to personalized medicine and improved diagnostics (Sarkar, 2023). However, the successful application of AI in healthcare requires effective planning and strategies (Lee, 2021). Despite the challenges and ethical dilemmas, AI has a concrete impact on patient care and healthcare systems, improving patient care delivery and enhancing medical logistics (Jeyaraj, 2023). In terms of accuracy, AI reduces the risk of human error in billing and claims processing, leading to fewer denied claims and smoother revenue cycles. Cost reduction is another critical benefit. AI's ability to optimize billing processes and predict financial trends helps healthcare providers manage resources more effectively, leading to cost savings. From a patient perspective, AI-driven processes can lead to a better understanding of billing and more personalized payment options, enhancing the overall patient experience. The integration of AI in healthcare finance and billing is revolutionizing the industry by enhancing efficiency and accuracy.

Automated Billing and Claims Processing

In the complex ecosystem of healthcare finance, billing and claims processing are critical yet cumbersome activities that are prone to inefficiency and errors when handled manually. The introduction of AI algorithms has revolutionized these processes by automating tasks that traditionally required extensive human intervention, thus significantly enhancing both speed and accuracy. One of the primary benefits of AI in billing and claims processing is its ability to streamline operations. AI systems can quickly extract and process data from various sources, including EHRs, patient management systems, and insurance databases. For example, an AI algorithm can automatically pull diagnostic codes and treatment information from EHRs, apply the appropriate billing codes, and process the claim with the patient's insurance provider without manual input. This automation significantly reduces the processing time from several days or weeks to just a few hours, dramatically accelerating the reimbursement cycle.

Manual data entry is susceptible to numerous errors, from typographical mistakes to misinterpretation of handwritten notes or codes. These errors can lead to incorrect billing, claim denials, and substantial financial losses for healthcare providers. Manual data entry in healthcare is prone to errors, including transcription mistakes and misinterpretation of handwritten notes (Vecellio, 2021). These errors can lead to incorrect billing, claim denials, and substantial financial losses for healthcare providers (Sunder, 2020). The integration of EHR systems has the potential to reduce these errors (Arsoniadis, 2017). However, the quality of data entered in EHR-integrated handoff notes can still be compromised, with an average of 1.7 errors per note (Arsoniadis, 2017). The use of health information technologies, such as computer-based medical records and decision support software, can help reduce these errors (Sutton, 2020). Despite the potential for errors, the use of automated medical billing systems can help control and reduce these errors (Schwartz, 1921). AI algorithms help minimize these errors by ensuring that data is accurately extracted and interpreted. AI systems are equipped with natural language processing (NLP) capabilities that can understand and process medical terminology from unstructured data sources, thereby reducing inaccuracies in coding and billing. A notable implementation of AI in automated billing is seen at a large hospital network in the United States, which integrated AI to handle its outpatient billing. The AI system was programmed to identify billing codes based on clinical documentation automatically. As a result, the network saw a 30% reduction in claim denials within the first six months of implementation, alongside a significant decrease in the time required to close billing cycles.

Another example is a cloud-based AI solution used by a multispecialty clinic to automate the end-to-end claims process. The AI system not only identified and corrected potential errors before submission but also tracked the claim through every stage of the insurance cycle. This proactive approach prevented delays and denials, improving cash flow and operational efficiency. Beyond basic automation, AI in billing and claims processing can adapt and learn from historical data, which enables continuous improvement in billing accuracy and compliance. AI systems can analyze past claims that were denied and identify patterns or common issues that led to these denials. Using this information, AI can flag similar future claims before submission, allowing for pre-emptive correction. The implementation of AI-driven automated billing and claims processing transforms the financial landscape of healthcare providers. By reducing manual labor, minimizing errors, and speeding up reimbursement, healthcare organizations can allocate more resources to patient care and other critical areas. Moreover, the reduction in processing time and error rates significantly boosts the financial health of these organizations by improving cash flow and reducing revenue lost to denials and corrections. AI-driven automation in healthcare billing and claims processing not only enhances operational efficiency but also supports a more robust financial strategy for healthcare providers, ultimately contributing to better patient care and satisfaction.

Fraud Detection

In the realm of healthcare finance, fraud detection stands as a critical function where AI systems excel significantly. By leveraging the ability to analyze vast amounts of data, AI is adept at uncovering anomalies and patterns that are indicative of fraudulent activities—tasks that might be too subtle or complex for human auditors to detect reliably. The sophistication of AI in recognizing deviations from normal patterns allows it to identify suspicious claims or billing practices that could potentially go unnoticed. AI-powered fraud detection systems work by continuously scanning billing and claims data across multiple platforms and systems. They employ complex algorithms to analyze historical and real-time data, which includes comparing current claims with historical billing data, looking for outliers, or irregular patterns that deviate from the norm. For instance, an AI system might flag a claim if it notices charges for unusually high frequencies of a particular procedure that do not correlate with the patient's medical history or diagnoses.

Moreover, AI can integrate and cross-reference data from different sources, such as patient records, payment histories, and even external databases, to create a comprehensive view of a patient's or provider's interactions. This capability significantly enhances the ability to detect fraud. For example, it can identify instances where providers bill for services that were never rendered or claim for a higher level of service than what was actually provided. These AI systems are particularly adept at recognizing complex schemes, such as when different services are billed under separate claims to avoid detection, a practice that might be challenging for a human to spot without extensive cross-referencing. Another significant advantage of AI in fraud detection is its capacity for learning and adaptation. AI systems utilize machine learning algorithms that learn over time from identified instances of fraud, enhancing their ability to detect new and evolving fraudulent tactics. This feature is vital in the dynamic field of healthcare, where fraudulent strategies frequently change as perpetrators find new loopholes or ways to circumvent traditional detection measures.

The deployment of AI for fraud detection not only protects healthcare organizations financially by preventing losses due to fraud but also plays an essential role in maintaining the integrity of healthcare systems and the trust of patients. As healthcare fraud can lead to higher insurance premiums and out-of-pocket expenses for patients, effective fraud detection ensures that resources are used for legitimate, necessary medical services. Thus, AI's role in fraud detection in healthcare finance represents a substantial advancement in combating fraud effectively and efficiently. It provides a powerful tool for healthcare providers and insurers, ensuring that the focus remains on delivering quality care rather than resolving discrepancies and fraudulent activities. This application of AI not only enhances operational efficiency but also reinforces a system of integrity and trust, which are fundamental to the healthcare industry.

Predictive Analytics for Revenue Management

Predictive analytics powered by AI is transforming revenue management in healthcare by allowing organizations to analyze historical data and predict future trends in healthcare spending and revenue. This capability enables healthcare providers to better plan their budgets and financial strategies, optimizing their financial performance and ensuring sustainability in an increasingly complex healthcare environment. AI-driven predictive analytics works by harnessing vast amounts of historical financial data, such as past billing records, payment cycles, patient demographics, and service utilization rates. By applying machine learning algorithms to this data, AI systems can identify patterns and trends that may not be apparent through manual analysis. For example, an AI model might analyze years of billing data to predict seasonal fluctuations in service demand or identify the likelihood of revenue dips and spikes. This information is crucial for healthcare organizations to anticipate changes and adapt their strategies accordingly.

The predictive capabilities of AI extend beyond simple trend analysis. These systems can also help healthcare organizations forecast the impact of external factors such as regulatory changes, new treatment modalities, or shifts in insurance policies. For instance, if a new healthcare regulation is set to take effect, AI can simulate its potential financial impact based on historical data, allowing the organization to adjust its operational and financial planning proactively. Additionally, AI-driven analytics can predict patient payment behaviors, which is invaluable for managing cash flow and reducing the incidence of bad debt. By analyzing individual patient payment histories and broader economic conditions, AI systems can identify patients who might be at risk of defaulting on payments. This allows healthcare facilities to engage with these patients early, possibly offering tailored payment plans or financial counseling, thus improving collection rates and patient satisfaction. Predictive analytics also aids in resource allocation. By predicting busy periods or potential increases in certain types of healthcare services, hospitals can ensure that they have adequate staff and resources to meet patient needs without unnecessary expenditures on unused capacity. This strategic resource management is vital for maintaining operational efficiency and high-quality patient care. Moreover, AI-enhanced predictive analytics helps healthcare organizations to innovate their financial strategies. By providing a deep understanding of financial dynamics and patient care trends, these tools empower healthcare providers to explore new services or business models that could lead to improved healthcare outcomes and revenue streams. The application of predictive analytics in healthcare finance using AI is a powerful tool for navigating the future. It not only provides healthcare organizations with the insights needed to make informed financial decisions but also supports a proactive approach to financial management. This leads to improved operational efficiency, better patient care, and the financial health of the organization, ensuring it can thrive even in the face of healthcare's dynamic challenges.

Personalized Patient Billing

Personalized patient billing, facilitated by AI, represents a significant shift in how healthcare finance operations manage patient interactions and financial transactions. By tailoring billing processes to individual patients, taking into account factors like their insurance coverage, financial situation, and payment history, AI enables a more personalized, efficient, and patient-centered approach to billing. This personalized approach not only improves patient satisfaction but also increases the likelihood of timely payments, enhancing the financial stability of healthcare providers. AI achieves this by integrating and analyzing data from various sources including patient registration information, insurance details, past payment behaviors, and even socio-economic data. For example, AI systems can automatically adjust billing statements based on a patient's insurance plan details, ensuring that the billing is accurate and compliant with the insurance policies. This reduces the chances of billing errors that could lead to disputes or delays in payment.

Moreover, AI can identify patients who may need more flexible payment options based on their historical payment patterns and current financial assessments. For patients identified as having financial difficulties, AI can trigger options for tailored payment plans such as extended terms or adjusted payment schedules. This not only helps patients manage their healthcare expenses better but also improves collection rates for healthcare providers by reducing the incidence of unpaid bills. In addition to improving billing accuracy and payment flexibility, personalized patient billing can also enhance overall patient experience and satisfaction. By using AI to streamline the billing process, patients receive clearer, more understandable bills. AI can help in breaking down the charges in simpler terms, explaining the costs associated with treatment, and pre-emptively answering common questions through automated patient communication tools. This transparency helps build trust and reduces confusion, which are common with traditional billing practices.

An example of AI-driven personalized billing can be seen in a healthcare system that implemented an AI tool to segment patients based on their risk of non-payment and their preferred communication methods. The system sends out billing communications tailored to each segment, using the preferred channels—be it email, text message, or postal mail—and language that best suits the patient's profile. This approach has led to a measurable increase in patient satisfaction scores and a decrease in days' sales outstanding (DSO), showcasing the direct benefits of personalized communication. AI's role in personalized patient billing also extends to compliance and ethical considerations, ensuring that all patients are treated fairly and that their data is used responsibly to better their treatment and payment experience. By addressing each patient's unique financial needs and providing tailored billing solutions, AI is setting a new standard in healthcare finance that prioritizes patient welfare and financial efficiency. This shift towards personalized patient billing, driven by AI, is not just a technological upgrade but a fundamental rethinking of how healthcare financial interactions should be managed to benefit both the provider and the patient. This approach not only secures the financial health of healthcare institutions but also contributes to a more positive healthcare experience for patients.

Error Reduction

Error reduction is a critical application of AI in healthcare finance, especially in the realm of billing and claims processing. AI algorithms are adept at cross-checking patient data, treatments, and billing codes to ensure that claims are processed accurately the first time around. AI has the potential to revolutionize medical billing by reducing errors and improving financial outcomes (Kilanko, 2023; Mlambo et al., 2023). Machine learning techniques can predict and prevent errors in health insurance claims processing, resulting in significant cost savings (Kumar, 2021). Big data analytics can be leveraged to detect fraud, abuse, waste, and errors in health insurance claims, leading to reduced losses and enhanced patient care (Srinivasan, 2022; Mhlanga 2023a). Lean Six Sigma methodology can be used to automate data input processes, reducing errors and processing time (Duc, 2022; Mhlanga 2023b). The application of AI in healthcare can also help prevent medical errors and improve patient safety (Ahmad, 2023; Mhlanga, 2023c). This capability significantly reduces the chances of errors that can lead to rejected claims or the need for reprocessing, thus streamlining operations and improving financial efficiency for healthcare providers. AI systems enhance error reduction by integrating with EHRs and other healthcare databases to automatically verify and validate every piece of data entered into a claim. For example, AI can ensure that the treatment codes and diagnostic codes entered are not only appropriate for the diagnosis but also allowable under the patient's current insurance policy. This kind of cross-referencing prevents common mistakes such as mismatched codes or outdated procedural codes that often result in claim denials.

Furthermore, AI-powered tools utilize advanced algorithms and machine learning to learn from historical billing data. This enables the system to recognize patterns that might indicate potential errors or common points of failure. For instance, if a particular type of claim is frequently rejected due to a specific data entry error, the AI system can flag similar future entries for additional review before submission. This proactive approach to error management not only reduces the frequency of claims denials but also lessens the administrative burden associated with correcting and resubmitting claims. An illustrative example of how AI contributes to error reduction can be seen in a hospital that implemented an AI solution to automatically review all outgoing claims for errors. The system checks for discrepancies such as incorrect patient identifiers, mismatched treatment and diagnosis codes, and incomplete patient information. Since the implementation of this AI tool, the hospital has reported a 40% decrease in billing errors and a corresponding increase in the speed of claim approvals. AI's role in error reduction also extends to improving the accuracy of billing documents. By ensuring that bills are correct when first issued, AI reduces the need for subsequent corrections and adjustments, which can be costly and time-consuming. This not only facilitates smoother financial operations but also enhances patient trust and satisfaction, as patients are less likely to encounter errors in their billing statements. Additionally, AI's ability to integrate with and pull data from multiple sources ensures a comprehensive review process. It can cross-verify information from the patient's medical history, treatment logs, pharmacy records, and previous claims, ensuring that all aspects of the billing are accurate and consistent. This level of thoroughness is challenging to achieve with manual processes but is seamlessly managed by AI systems. The use of AI for error reduction in healthcare billing and claims processing is transforming the landscape of healthcare finance. By minimizing errors, AI helps healthcare providers avoid costly rework and claims denials, ensures faster reimbursement, and maintains a high level of accuracy in financial records. This ultimately leads to improved operational efficiency, reduced costs, and enhanced patient satisfaction, reinforcing the financial stability of healthcare institutions.

Enhanced Patient Communication

Enhanced patient communication through the use of AI-powered chatbots and virtual assistants represent a significant advancement in healthcare finance, particularly in the context of billing inquiries and patient interactions. These AI tools are designed to provide patients with instant and accurate answers to billing questions, greatly reducing the workload on human staff and notably improving the patient experience. AI chatbots and virtual assistants are becoming increasingly common in healthcare settings due to their efficiency and capability to handle high volumes of inquiries without fatigue. These systems are programmed to understand and respond to a wide range of patient questions, from basic inquiries about billing statements to more complex questions regarding insurance coverage and payment options. For instance, if a patient is confused about a charge on their bill, the AI can instantly provide a detailed explanation of the service charged, how it is covered by their insurance, and even guide them through the payment process if necessary. These virtual assistants are accessible 24/7, providing a significant advantage over traditional call centers that operate within limited hours. Patients can get immediate answers at any time, which not only enhances satisfaction but also empowers them with the information they need to manage their healthcare finances better. This accessibility is particularly beneficial for managing small issues that can be resolved quickly without needing to escalate to human staff, thereby freeing up human resources to focus on more complex cases and improving overall operational efficiency.

Moreover, AI-powered communication tools can personalize interactions based on the patient's history and preferences, which improves the quality of service. For example, if a patient frequently inquires about certain types of charges, the AI can recognize these patterns and proactively provide information related to these inquiries in future interactions. This level of personalized communication helps build trust and loyalty, as patients feel that their specific needs are understood and addressed effectively. An example of successful implementation of such AI tools can be seen in a regional hospital that introduced an AI chatbot to handle all initial patient billing inquiries. The chatbot is integrated with the hospital's billing system and is capable of pulling up specific patient bills, outlining payment methods, and even setting up payment plans automatically. Since its implementation, the hospital has noted a 50% reduction in calls requiring human intervention, a significant increase in patient satisfaction ratings, and a noticeable decrease in administrative costs. In addition to handling inquiries, these AI systems also have the capability to send out automated reminders for upcoming bills, explain payment options, and provide updates on changes to billing policies or insurance requirements. This proactive communication ensures that patients are well-informed and can manage their payments more effectively, reducing the incidence of late payments and financial complications. In summary, the deployment of AI-powered chatbots and virtual assistants in healthcare finance enhances patient communication by providing quick, accurate, and personalized responses to billing inquiries. This not only improves patient satisfaction but also optimizes the efficiency of healthcare providers by reducing the workload on human staff and allowing them to concentrate on more critical tasks.

Streamlining Administrative Processes

Streamlining administrative processes in healthcare finance through AI involves automating a wide range of routine tasks, such as data entry, appointment scheduling, and insurance verification. This technological integration significantly frees up staff to focus on more complex and critical tasks, enhancing overall operational efficiency and reducing the potential for human error. AI-driven automation takes over the repetitive and time-consuming tasks that traditionally consume substantial staff hours. For example, AI systems can automatically enter patient information into databases, pull relevant data for billing purposes, and update patient records without manual intervention. This automation reduces the likelihood of data entry errors, which are common in manual processes and can lead to billing issues or inaccuracies in patient records. In appointment scheduling, AI tools can analyze patterns in appointment durations and frequencies to optimize the booking process. They can automatically adjust the scheduling based on the type of visit required, provider availability, and patient preferences, all while accounting for cancellations and rescheduling. This level of automation not only improves the efficiency of the scheduling process but also enhances patient satisfaction by reducing wait times and ensuring that they can see their preferred providers at convenient times.

Insurance verification is another critical area where AI can make a significant impact. Traditionally, verifying patient insurance involves checking details against multiple databases and often requires communication with insurance companies, which can be both time-consuming and prone to errors. AI simplifies this process by automating the verification steps, ensuring that the patient's insurance coverage is checked and confirmed in real-time. This automation speeds up the check-in process, reduces the administrative burden on staff, and minimizes the risk of billing issues due to incorrect insurance information. By automating these routine tasks, AI allows healthcare staff to redirect their focus towards more value-added activities, such as patient care, complex problem-solving, and strategic planning. This not only improves the efficiency of healthcare services but also contributes to a more satisfying work environment for staff, who can engage in more meaningful and rewarding work. Furthermore, the introduction of AI in streamlining administrative tasks also leads to cost savings for healthcare organizations. Reduced need for extensive administrative staff and decreased incidence of errors lead to lower operational costs and improved financial performance. These savings can then be redirected into improving patient care services or investing in further technological advancements. The use of AI to automate routine tasks in healthcare finance is transforming the landscape of administrative operations. By taking over mundane tasks, AI enables healthcare organizations to focus their human resources on areas that require human expertise and judgment, ultimately leading to improved efficiency, reduced costs, and enhanced patient and staff satisfaction.

Cost Reduction

AI's role in reducing costs in healthcare is pivotal, particularly in how it automates routine tasks and enhances the accuracy of administrative processes. This dual capability not only helps in cutting down the overhead administrative expenses but also contributes to broader cost savings that can lead to lower healthcare costs for patients and more efficient resource utilization for providers. AI's role in reducing healthcare costs is pivotal, as it automates routine tasks and enhances the accuracy of administrative processes (Kilanko, 2023). This dual capability not only cuts down on overhead administrative expenses but also contributes to broader cost savings, leading to lower healthcare costs for patients and more efficient resource utilization for providers (Sarkar, 2023). AI's transformative potential in medical billing, including streamlining operations and enhancing accuracy, is particularly noteworthy (Mohan, 2023). The technology's impact in areas such as medical imaging, personalized medicine, and EHRs is also significant, with the potential to further reduce costs and improve patient outcomes (Pendy, 2023). The use of AI in health tech, including machine learning and NLP, is expected to further enhance the performance of clinical and operational workflows (Velagaleti, 2023). The integration of AI into various healthcare domains, from medical imaging to drug discovery, virtual health assistants, and remote patient monitoring, has demonstrated transformative potential in improving patient care and healthcare delivery (Jeyaraj, 2023). However, the potential violations while utilizing personal patient data must be addressed while modifying this technology (Kuganesan, 2021). Automation, a key feature of AI, takes over tasks such as data entry, appointment scheduling, claims processing, and insurance verification—activities traditionally done manually, which are labor-intensive and prone to human error. By streamlining these processes, AI reduces the need for extensive staff hours and the associated labor costs. For instance, AI systems can handle the input and management of patient data seamlessly, freeing up administrative staff to focus on more complex tasks that require human intervention. This not only speeds up the process but also minimizes the likelihood of errors that could lead to costly rectifications or claim denials.

Further, AI enhances the accuracy of billing and coding in healthcare finance. Mistakes in these areas often result in denied claims or the need for reprocessing, both of which impose additional costs and delays in revenue flow for healthcare institutions. AI's ability to analyze vast datasets ensures that billing is done correctly the first time, reducing the incidence of denials and rework. For example, AI systems use pattern recognition to identify discrepancies or common errors in claim submissions based on historical data, enabling proactive corrections before claims are submitted. The impact of AI in reducing administrative costs extends to resource allocation as well. With AI handling routine and repetitive tasks, healthcare facilities can allocate their human resources to areas that add more value, such as patient care and strategic decision-making. This optimized allocation not only improves the quality of care provided but also increases the operational efficiency of the healthcare facility.

Moreover, the cost reductions achieved through AI can be passed on to patients, lowering the overall cost of healthcare. By reducing the administrative burden and the associated costs, healthcare providers can offer services at more competitive prices or invest more in patient care services, which can lead to better health outcomes and higher patient satisfaction. Additionally, AI's capabilities in predictive analytics further aid in cost reduction by forecasting future trends in healthcare utilization. This allows healthcare providers to better plan and allocate resources, avoiding overspending on unnecessary supplies or understaffing that could lead to overtime costs. For example, AI can predict peak periods of demand in certain departments and help manage staffing levels accordingly to maintain efficiency without incurring extra costs. AI significantly contributes to cost reduction in healthcare by automating routine tasks, improving accuracy, and optimizing resource allocation. These advancements not only reduce the financial strain on healthcare systems but also make healthcare more affordable for patients, representing a win-win for all stakeholders involved.

Compliance and Reporting

AI systems play a crucial role in ensuring compliance and accuracy in reporting within the healthcare industry, particularly as it relates to the ever-evolving landscape of healthcare regulations and billing codes. By being programmed to stay current with these changes, AI helps healthcare providers maintain compliance with regulatory requirements, thus avoiding potential legal issues and penalties that can arise from non-compliance. Healthcare regulations and billing codes are complex and frequently updated to reflect new medical discoveries, policy changes, and government directives. Keeping up with these changes manually is not only challenging and resource-intensive but also prone to errors. AI systems, however, can be continuously updated with the latest regulatory and coding information without the lag that might affect human-operated systems. This capability ensures that billing processes are always compliant with the most current standards, reducing the risk of costly billing errors or violations of regulatory mandates. For example, AI can automatically update the database of billing codes used by healthcare providers. When a physician enters a treatment or diagnosis, the AI system can suggest the appropriate billing codes based on the latest updates, ensuring that the billing is accurate and up-to-date. This helps in submitting correct claims the first time, which reduces the need for rework and resubmission, thus enhancing operational efficiency.

Moreover, AI's role in compliance extends to more comprehensive reporting responsibilities. AI systems can generate detailed reports that provide insights into compliance metrics, billing accuracy, and other critical operational aspects. These reports are invaluable not only for internal audits but also for regulatory reviews, ensuring that healthcare providers can demonstrate compliance with all applicable laws and regulations. The accuracy and timeliness of AI-driven reporting also enable healthcare organizations to respond more swiftly to regulatory changes. If a new regulation requires additional documentation or a change in how services are billed, AI systems can adjust their operations accordingly and provide feedback on the impact of these changes in real-time. This agility is crucial for maintaining compliance in a sector where non-compliance can result in significant fines and damage to reputation. Furthermore, AI systems enhance the transparency of the compliance process. By maintaining accurate records and providing easy access to historical data, AI facilitates a clear audit trail that can be reviewed by external regulators or internal compliance officers. This transparency not only helps in identifying and rectifying compliance issues more efficiently but also builds trust among stakeholders, including patients, regulators, and insurance companies. AI significantly enhances compliance and reporting in healthcare by keeping systems up-to-date with the latest regulations and billing codes, ensuring accuracy in billing and reporting, and providing the agility to adapt to regulatory changes. These capabilities not only safeguard healthcare providers against compliance risks but also boost overall operational efficiency, making AI an indispensable tool in modern healthcare administration.

Data Security

The implementation of AI significantly enhances the security of financial data within healthcare settings, a sector where data privacy and protection are paramount due to the sensitivity of the information handled. The use of AI in healthcare settings, particularly in the protection of sensitive financial data, has been a topic of significant research. Gopalan (2021) and Al-Kuwari (2021) highlight the potential of AI in enhancing cybersecurity and preserving data privacy. Seh (2021) and Abdelaziz (2023) further emphasize the role of AI in proactive security mechanisms and the integration of information security and management. Alruwaili (2020) and Selvanambi (2021) propose the use of AI in combination with multi-agent systems and blockchain technology to ensure the privacy and safety of EHRs. Hlávka (2020) and Murdoch (2021) discuss the challenges and potential policy responses in the implementation of AI in healthcare, particularly in relation to security, privacy, and information sharing. AI systems contribute to safeguarding data by monitoring network activities continuously and detecting any unusual access patterns or potential breaches, thus providing an extra layer of security that is both proactive and adaptive. AI-powered security systems are designed to analyze vast quantities of data transactions in real time, identifying deviations from normal behavior that could indicate a security threat. For example, an AI system can detect if an unusually large volume of patient records is being accessed or downloaded, which could suggest a potential data breach. Upon detecting such anomalies, the AI system can automatically initiate protocols to restrict access or alert security personnel to investigate the issue further, preventing data leakage before it becomes a more serious breach.

Moreover, AI enhances data security through advanced encryption methods and intelligent threat detection systems that evolve with emerging security threats. Traditional safety measures often lag behind sophisticated cyber attacks but AI systems learn from each attempt and adapt, improving their detection capabilities over time. This learning ability allows AI to stay ahead of cyber criminals who continuously refine their methods to exploit new vulnerabilities. AI's role in data security is also critical in managing access controls. By analyzing user behavior and access patterns, AI can ensure that only authorized personnel have access to sensitive financial data. It can recognize patterns associated with specific roles within the healthcare organization and flag any actions that deviate from established norms, such as accessing data not relevant to a user's duties. In addition to monitoring and detection, AI can also be utilized for predictive security measures. It can forecast potential security risks based on trends and patterns identified in data access and usage, allowing healthcare organizations to fortify their defences proactively before any actual threat materializes. This predictive capability not only mitigates risks but also optimizes the allocation of security resources, ensuring that protective measures are concentrated where they are most needed. Another example of AI's utility in data security is its integration into compliance frameworks. AI systems can ensure that all data handling within the organization adheres to strict regulatory standards, such as HIPAA in the United States, by automating compliance checks and reporting any discrepancies in real time. This not only helps prevent violations but also builds trust with patients and partners by upholding high standards of data privacy and security. The implementation of AI transforms the landscape of data security in healthcare finance by offering sophisticated, real-time monitoring and detection capabilities, predictive security measures, and enhanced compliance assurance. This proactive and adaptive approach not only protects sensitive financial data from the ever-evolving threats of cyber attacks but also supports the overall integrity and reliability of healthcare financial operations.

Conclusion

Throughout this chapter, we have explored the significant impact that AI has on the field of healthcare finance and billing. As we have seen, AI does not merely enhance existing processes—it transforms them. By integrating AI technologies, healthcare organizations can tackle the inherent challenges of the industry, including the labor-intensive nature of manual processes, the risk of human errors, and the stringent demands of regulatory compliance. AI's applications within healthcare finance—from automating billing and claims processing to enhancing fraud detection, enabling predictive analytics for revenue management, and streamlining insurance claims and reimbursements—illustrate a broad spectrum of benefits. These applications not only boost efficiency and accuracy but also contribute significantly to cost-effectiveness, reducing financial waste, and optimizing resource use across the board. Moreover, the deployment of AI in healthcare finance extends beyond operational enhancements. It plays a crucial role in securing patient data, ensuring compliance with evolving regulations, and improving the overall patient experience through personalized billing and enhanced communication. By doing so, AI not only supports the financial health of healthcare providers but also elevates the standard of care delivered to patients. As healthcare continues to evolve, so too will the capabilities of AI. With every improvement in AI technology, new possibilities emerge for its application in healthcare finance, promising even greater efficiency, accuracy, and patient satisfaction in the future. The ongoing integration of AI into healthcare finance and billing is not just a trend but a profound shift towards more resilient, responsive, and patient-centered healthcare systems. The transformative role of AI in healthcare finance and billing is clear and compelling. It is an essential tool in the modernization of healthcare, driving improvements that benefit providers, payers, and patients alike. The continued advancement and adoption of AI technologies are likely to redefine the standards of healthcare finance, setting a new benchmark for efficiency, accuracy, and patient care in the years to come.

References

Abdelaziz, A. and Mahmoud, A.N. (2023). Data Security in Healthcare Systems: Integration of Information Security and Information Management. Journal of Cybersecurity & Information Management, *11*(2).

Abrahams, J.M. (2023). The future of private practice neurosurgery and the pitfalls of private equity. Journal of Neurosurgery, *140*(4), 1198–1203.

Ahmed, A., Xi, R., Hou, M., Shah, S.A. and Hameed, S. (2023). Harnessing big data analytics for healthcare: A comprehensive review of frameworks, implications, applications, and impacts. IEEE Access.

Al-Kuwari, S. (2021). Privacy-preserving AI in healthcare. In Multiple Perspectives on Artificial Intelligence in Healthcare: Opportunities and Challenges (pp. 65-77). Cham: Springer International Publishing.

Alruwaili, F.F. (2020). e-Learning Chain: A Secure Blockchain Approach to e-Learning & Certification Systems. e. Learning, 11, 16.

Anderson, D.L., Bonvissuto, G.L., Brizuela, M.A., Chiossone, G., Cibils, A.F., Cid, M.S., ... and Villagra, E.S. (2011). Perspectives on rangeland management education and research in Argentina. Rangelands, 33(1), 2–12.

Baselski, V.S., Weissfeld, A.S. and Sorrell, F. (2024). Correct coding of billable services in the clinical laboratory. Clinical laboratory management, 443–59.

Bigus, J.P., Campbell, M., Carmeli, B., Cefkin, M., Chang, H., Chen-Ritzo, C.H., ... and Zhu, X. (2011). Information technology for healthcare transformation. *IBM Journal of Research and Development*, *55*(5), 6–14.

Buker, K.L. (2023). *Financial Impact When a Health System Automates Manual Insurance Verification Processes*. Doctoral dissertation. Northcentral University.

Classen, D.C., Rhee, C., Dantes, R.B. and Benin, A.L. (2024). Healthcare-associated infections and conditions in the era of digital measurement. Infection Control & Hospital Epidemiology, *45*(1), 3–8.

Conway, D.I., Petticrew, M., Marlborough, H., Berthiller, J., Hashibe, M. and Macpherson, L.M. (2008). Socioeconomic inequalities and oral cancer risk: A systematic review and meta-analysis of case-control studies. *International Journal of Cancer*, *122*(12), 2811–19.

Davenport, T., Guha, A., Grewal, D. and Bressgott, T. (2020). How artificial intelligence will change the future of marketing. Journal of the Academy of Marketing Science, 48, 24–42.

Duc, M.L. and Thu, M.N. (2022). Application of lean six sigma for improve productivity at the mechanical plant. A case study. Manufacturing Technology, *22*(2), 124–38.

Gopalan, R.S. (2021). Blockchain and Cybersecurity. In Securing IoT in Industry 4.0 Applications with Blockchain (pp. 221-245). Auerbach Publications.

Hlávka, J.P. (2020). Security, privacy, and information-sharing aspects of healthcare artificial intelligence. In Artificial intelligence in healthcare (pp. 235-270). Academic Press.

Holmes, J.H., Beinlich, J., Boland, M.R., Bowles, K.H., Chen, Y., Cook, T.S., ... and Moore, J.H. (2021). Why is the electronic health record so challenging for research and clinical care?. Methods of information in medicine, *60*(01/02), 32–48.

Hussain, I. (2020). Attitude of university students and teachers towards instructional role of artificial intelligence. International Journal of Distance Education and E-Learning, *5*(2), 158–77.

J.H., Beinlich, J., Boland, M.R., Bowles, K.H., Chen, Y., Cook, T.S., ... and Moore, J.H. (2021). Why is the electronic health record so challenging for research and clinical care?. Methods of information in medicine, 60(01/02), 032-048.

James, C.E. (2022). Improving Medical Record Documentation Behaviors and Subsequent Medical Billing Errors in Community-Based Dialysis Facilities: The Educational Approach. Trident University International.

Jeyaraj, R., Balasubramaniam, A., MA, A.K., Guizani, N. and Paul, A. (2023). Resource management in cloud and cloud-influenced technologies for internet of things applications. ACM Computing Surveys, 55(12), 1–37.

Kara, P.A., Ognjanovic, I., Maindorfer, I., Mantas, J., Wippelhauser, A., Šendelj, R., ... and Bokor, L. (2023). The present and future of a digital Montenegro: analysis of C-ITS, agriculture, and healthcare. Eng, 4(1), 341–66.

Kenagy, G.P. (2002). HIV among transgendered people. *AIDS Care*, 14(1), 127–34.

Kilanko, V. (2023). Government Response and Perspective on Autonomous Vehicles. In Government Response to Disruptive Innovation: Perspectives and Examinations (pp. 137-153). IGI Global.

Konda, P., Das, S., Suganthan GC, P., Martinkus, P., Ardalan, A., Ballard, J. R., ... and Raghavendra, V. (2018). Technical perspective: Toward building entity matching management systems. *ACM SIGMOD Record*, 47(1), 33–40.

Kuganesan, N., Dlamini, S., Tillekeratne, L.V. and Taylor, W.R. (2021). Tumor suppressor p53 promotes ferroptosis in oxidative stress conditions independent of modulation of ferroptosis by p21, CDKs, RB, and E2F. Journal of Biological Chemistry, 297(6).

Kumar, M.D., Bassi, N. and Singh, O.P. (2021). Rethinking on the methodology for assessing global water and food challenges. In Global Water Resources (pp. 325-342). Routledge.

Macapagal, K. (2022). *Assessing the Relationship between Automated Technology Expenditure and Revenue Cycle Performance*. Doctoral dissertation. Walden University.

Madhavi, T. and Bhatt, D. (2024, June). Managing the Challenges and Opportunities of Leadership for Organizational Success in the Age of Artificial Intelligence. In 2024 16th International Conference on Electronics, Computers and Artificial Intelligence (ECAI) (pp. 1-6). IEEE.

Mhlanga, D. (2023a). Artificial Intelligence in Elderly Care: Navigating Ethical and Responsible AI Adoption for Seniors. *SSRN*, 4675564. http://dx.doi.org/10.2139/ssrn.4675564.

Mhlanga, D. (2023b). Digital Transformation in the Healthcare Sector: The Role of Artificial Intelligence for Inclusive Long-term Care around the World, Lessons for Africa. *In: Economic Inclusion in Post-Independence Africa: An Inclusive Approach to Economic Development* (pp. 347–62). Cham: Springer Nature Switzerland.

Mhlanga, D. (2023c). Artificial Intelligence and Machine Learning in Making Transport, Safer, Cleaner, More Reliable, and Efficient in Emerging Markets. *In: FinTech and Artificial Intelligence for Sustainable Development: The Role of Smart Technologies in Achieving Development Goals* (193–211).

Mlambo, F., Chironda, C., George, J. and Mhlanga, D. (2023). The Role of Machine Learning and Artificial Intelligence in Improving Health Outcomes in Africa During and After the Pandemic: What are We Learning on the Attainment of Sustainable Development Goals? *In: The Fourth Industrial Revolution in Africa: Exploring the Development Implications of Smart Technologies in Africa* (pp. 117–49). Cham: Springer Nature Switzerland.

Mohan, S. (2024). Passive Ambitions, Active Limitations: Defence AI in India. In The Very Long Game: 25 Case Studies on the Global State of Defense AI (pp. 445–463). Cham: Springer Nature Switzerland.

Murdoch, S. (2021). Cybersecurity Information Sharing: Voluntary Beginnings and a Mandatory Future.

Nieto-Salazar, M.A., Ordóñez, K.N.A., Carcamo, Z.D.S., Cristina, A., Ordóñez, A., Saldana, E.A., ... and Garza12, D.A.D.L. (2023). Neurological dysfunction associated with vitamin deficiencies: a narrative review. Open Access J Neurol Neurosurg, 18, 1–9.

Palmer, C.F. (2023). Billing, Coding, and Reimbursement in Eye Telehealth Programs. In Ocular Telehealth (pp. 175–184). Elsevier.

Patel, S.Y., Huskamp, H.A., Frakt, A.B., Auerbach, D.I., Neprash, H.T., Barnett, M.L., ... and Mehrotra, A. (2022). Frequency of Indirect Billing to Medicare for Nurse Practitioner and Physician Assistant Office Visits: Study examines the frequency of indirect billing to Medicare for nurse practitioner and physician assistant office visits. Health Affairs, 41(6), 805–13.

Pelt, C.E., Anderson, A.W., Anderson, M.B., Van Dine, C. and Peters, C.L. (2014). Postoperative falls after total knee arthroplasty in patients with a femoral nerve catheter: Can we reduce the incidence? *The Journal of Arthroplasty*, 29(6), 1154–57.

Pendy, B. (2023). Artificial Intelligence in Health Sector of USA. Jurnal Indonesia Sosial Sains, 4(3).

Roy, J. and Saha, S. (2021). Integration of artificial intelligence with meta classifiers for the gully erosion susceptibility assessment in Hinglo river basin, Eastern India. Advances in Space Research, 67(1), 316–33.

Ryckman, T.A. (1990, January). Designation and convention: A chapter of early logical empiricism. *In: PSA: Proceedings of the Biennial Meeting of the Philosophy of Science Association, 1990*(2), 149–157. Cambridge University Press.

Sarkar, S.M., Dhar, B.K., Crowley, S.S., Ayittey, F.K. and Gazi, M.A.I. (2023). Psychological adjustment and guidance for ageing urban women. Ageing International, 48(1), 222–30.

Sarkar, S., Ganapathysubramanian, B., Singh, A., Fotouhi, F., Kar, S., Nagasubramanian, K., ... and Singh, A.K. (2023). Cyber-agricultural systems for crop breeding and sustainable production. Trends in Plant Science.

Schwartz, L.N., Shaffer, J.D. and Bukhman, G. (2021). The origins of the 4 × 4 framework for noncommunicable disease at the World Health Organization. SSM-Population Health, 13, 100731.

Seh, A.H., Al-Amri, J.F., Subahi, A.F., Agrawal, A., Kumar, R. and Khan, R.A. (2021). Machine learning based framework for maintaining privacy of healthcare data. Intelligent Automation & Soft Computing, 29(3), 697–712.

Selvanambi, R., Bhutani, S. and Veauli, K. (2021). Security and privacy for Electronic Healthcare Records using AI in Blockchain. In Applications of Artificial Intelligence for Smart Technology (pp. 90–102). IGI Global.

Shaheen, M.Y. (2021). Applications of Artificial Intelligence (AI) in healthcare: A review. ScienceOpen Preprints.

Srinivasan, A. (2022). The Indian Institutes of Technology: a sociology of knowledge perspective. In Reclaiming Public Universities (pp. 143–163). Routledge India.

Sunder M.V. and Kunnath, N.R. (2020). Six Sigma to reduce claims processing errors in a healthcare payer firm. Production Planning & Control, 31(6), 496–511.

Sutton, R.T., Pincock, D., Baumgart, D.C., Sadowski, D.C., Fedorak, R.N. and Kroeker, K.I. (2020). An overview of clinical decision support systems: benefits, risks, and strategies for success. NPJ digital medicine, 3(1), 17.

Szarfman, A., Levine, J.G., Tonning, J.M., Weichold, F., Bloom, J.C., Soreth, J.M., ... and Altman, R.B. (2022). Recommendations for achieving interoperable and shareable medical data in the USA. Communications Medicine, 2(1), 86.

Tan, M. and Le, Q. (2019, May). Efficientnet: Rethinking model scaling for convolutional neural networks. *In: International Conference on Machine Learning* (pp. 6105–6114). PMLR.

Tucker, A.L., Heisler, W.S. and Janisse, L.D. (2014). Organizational factors that contribute to operational failures in hospitals. Harvard Business School working paper series# 14–23.

Vecellio, D.J., Bardenhagen, E.K., Lerman, B. and Brown, R.D. (2021). The role of outdoor microclimatic features at long-term care facilities in advancing the health of its residents: An integrative review and future strategies. Environmental research, 201, 111583.

Velagaleti, S. (2023, March). A Low Power APB with an Area Efficient Structure. In 2023 2nd International Conference for Innovation in Technology (INOCON) (pp. 1-6). IEEE.

Westgate, C.J. (2020). Popular music fans and the value of concert tickets. *Popular Music and Society*, 43(1), 57–77.

11 | Ethical Considerations in AI-enabled Healthcare

The integration of artificial intelligence (AI) in healthcare is rapidly transforming medical diagnosis, treatment, and management, offering unprecedented opportunities to enhance patient care. However, this technological advancement also brings forth complex ethical challenges that need to be addressed to ensure responsible and equitable implementation. This chapter aims to provide a comprehensive framework for understanding the ethical implications of AI in healthcare. It seeks to guide stakeholders in navigating the ethical dilemmas associated with privacy, data security, patient consent, transparency, fairness, and accountability in AI systems. Through a detailed examination of current practices and emerging trends, this chapter identifies the primary ethical concerns related to AI in healthcare. It highlights the need for robust privacy protections, unbiased algorithms, and transparent AI processes to maintain public trust and ensure equitable access to AI-driven healthcare solutions. The ethical integration of AI in healthcare is essential for realizing its full potential to improve patient outcomes. Addressing ethical challenges through regulatory frameworks and ethical guidelines is crucial. A balanced approach that mitigates risks, while embracing AI's benefits, will be key to achieving responsible and equitable healthcare advancements.

Introduction

The acceleration of Artificial Intelligence (AI) research and its application in healthcare across continents like Europe, North America, and Asia is profound (Čartolovni et al., 2022). The potential of AI in enhancing healthcare delivery has been demonstrated through its success in areas such as dermatological assessments, emergency risk predictions, and notably in breast cancer detection, where it has outperformed traditional radiological assessments. The World Medical Association, during its 70th General Assembly in 2019, proposed the term "augmented intelligence" to emphasize AI's role in supporting and enhancing clinical decision-making processes. However, the rapid advancement of AI technologies in healthcare also brings to light significant ethical and regulatory challenges. These challenges become particularly acute when abstract ethical principles are insufficiently tailored to the specific needs of healthcare, potentially leading to "ethical whitewashing" where important societal concerns may be oversimplified or ignored (Čartolovni et al., 2022). Additionally, the opaque nature of many AI algorithms, often referred to as "black box" models, poses serious issues for transparency and accountability, crucial in high-stakes fields such as healthcare where decisions have life-or-death implications (Li et al., 2022).

Global regulatory bodies have begun to address these challenges, with directives like the European Commission's *Ethics Guidelines for Trustworthy AI*, the US *Report on the Future of Artificial Intelligence*, and the *Beijing AI Principles* by the Chinese government, each contributing to a framework aiming to ensure that AI technologies honor human values and rights (Li et al., 2022; Mhlanga, 2023a). Moreover, recent global health crises such as the COVID-19 pandemic have underscored the importance of AI in managing public health emergencies through enhanced disease surveillance and response mechanisms (Borda et al., 2022; Mhlanga, 2023b; Ndhlovu and Mhlanga, 2024). This situation highlights the need for a responsible AI framework that considers the ethical, social, and technical dimensions of AI applications in healthcare. This chapter will further explore these dimensions, focusing on safeguarding patient privacy, ensuring the accuracy and fairness of AI algorithms, and maintaining transparency and accountability in AI decision-making processes. It aims to provide a comprehensive overview of the ethical landscape in AI-enabled healthcare, encouraging a thoughtful and informed approach to integrating AI technologies in a manner that truly benefits patients and aligns with broader societal values.

Data Privacy and Security in AI-enabled Healthcare

Patient data is inherently sensitive, containing information that is deeply personal and often linked to the individual's identity. As such, the privacy and security of this data are paramount. AI systems in healthcare often require vast amounts of data for training and operation, which amplifies concerns regarding the collection, storage, and utilization of this information. The use of AI in healthcare, while promising, raises significant concerns about patient data privacy and security (Rickert, 2020). The need for vast amounts of data for AI training and operation amplifies these concerns (Hill, 2024). Technical considerations such as data storage, cloud usage, and AI pipeline design are crucial in addressing these challenges (Segijn, 2022; Mhlanga 2024). The combination of sensor-embedded AI and secure server-distributed AI offers a potential solution (Gembaczka, 2019). The role of AI in handling large volumes of sensitive patient data is increasingly important (Kejriwal, 2022). However, the limitations of sharing biomedical data for AI development in healthcare must also be considered (Pereira, 2021). Healthcare data is typically collected through various means, such as electronic health records (EHRs), diagnostic tools, and increasingly, wearable technology that continuously monitors patient vitals. For example, wearable devices like smartwatches can track heart rate and physical activity, providing valuable data for AI models that predict heart conditions. However, this also raises ethical questions about consent—patients must be fully informed about what data is being collected and how it will be used. Implementing dynamic consent models, where patients can adjust their consent preferences in real time based on the use of their data, is one approach to addressing these concerns. Once collected, data must be securely stored and managed. Hospitals might use encrypted databases on secure servers or cloud storage solutions with strict access controls. For instance, a large hospital network might use cloud services provided by vendors who specialize in compliant healthcare solutions, ensuring that data is encrypted both in transit and at rest. Despite these precautions, the risk of breaches remains, necessitating robust security protocols and constant vigilance.

The use of patient data extends beyond the initial collection point, contributing to AI-driven diagnostics, treatment plans, and longitudinal health studies. A notable example is the use of AI in predictive analytics to identify patients at high risk of chronic illnesses like diabetes, based on their health data trends. Data sharing is equally critical, as it enables collaboration between healthcare providers, researchers, and even across borders. However, it is crucial that all parties adhere to agreed-upon ethical standards to protect patient privacy. The sharing of anonymized datasets for research purposes, under frameworks such as the GDPR (general data protection regulation), ensures that patient identities remain confidential while supporting medical advances. Anonymization of data involves stripping away personally identifiable information. Techniques like k-anonymity ensure that data cannot be linked back to an individual without considerable effort. For example, a dataset used for training an AI system in recognizing dermatological diseases could be anonymized to remove all patient identifiers before it is used, reducing the risk of data misuse. Despite the robustness of these techniques, the threat of re-identification persists, especially with the advent of sophisticated re-identification algorithms. Compliance with regulations such as HIPAA in the United States and GDPR in Europe is non-negotiable. These regulations define the framework within which data must be handled, imposing strict penalties for breaches. They ensure that entities handling patient data have adequate safeguards in place and that patients have rights over their data, including the right to access and the right to be forgotten. For instance, a European hospital using AI to monitor patient recovery must comply with GDPR, ensuring that all data handling practices are transparent and subject to patient consent.

The employment of advanced technological safeguards is crucial. Technologies such as blockchain can offer unique solutions for maintaining patient data integrity and traceability. For example, blockchain could be used to create a decentralized and tamper-proof ledger of patient data access and usage, ensuring transparency and security. Similarly, techniques like secure multi-party computation allow for data to be used in AI models without ever exposing the underlying data to AI providers. In the field of radiology, AI systems are used to enhance the accuracy of diagnoses from imaging studies such as X-rays and MRIs. For instance, an AI system developed to detect anomalies in chest X-rays must handle sensitive data with care. Hospitals implementing such systems ensure that all images are de-identified before they are fed into the AI, with access to the AI system tightly controlled and monitored. Regular audits are conducted to ensure that the system adheres to all necessary privacy and security regulations. This thorough exploration of data privacy and security within AI-enabled healthcare illustrates the multifaceted approach required to address these critical issues. By examining real-world applications and the strategies implemented to safeguard sensitive information, this section underscores the importance of maintaining high ethical standards in the utilization of AI in healthcare.

Bias and Discrimination in AI-enabled Healthcare

AI algorithms have the potential to revolutionize healthcare by improving diagnostic accuracy, predicting patient outcomes, and personalizing treatment plans. However, they also carry the risk of perpetuating and even amplifying existing biases present in the training data. AI algorithms have the potential to revolutionize healthcare by improving diagnostic accuracy, predicting patient outcomes, and personalizing treatment plans (Tiwari, 2023). However, they also carry the risk of perpetuating and even amplifying existing biases present in the training data (Norori, 2021). These biases can lead to fatal outcomes, misdiagnoses, and lack of generalization (Nelson, 2022). The sources of bias in AI algorithms in healthcare include social determinants of health, data collection, pre-processing, development, and validation (Nazer, 2023). To mitigate these biases, it is important to address contextual bias, such as differences in care between high-resource and low-resource settings (Price, 2020). The responsible development, implementation, and maintenance of AI in the clinical enterprise is crucial (Matheny, 2023). However, the potential disruption to medical training and the need for physicians to understand AI platforms and limitations are also important considerations (Arora, 2023; Giordano, 2021).

These biases can lead to significant disparities in healthcare outcomes across different demographics, such as race, gender, or socio-economic status. Bias in AI can originate from various sources, including the ways in which data is collected, imbalances in the datasets themselves, and the subjective decisions made by those who design and deploy these systems. For example, if an AI model for diagnosing skin conditions is trained primarily on datasets comprising images from lighter-skinned individuals, it may perform inadequately when assessing conditions on darker-skinned patients. This can result in delayed or incorrect diagnoses for these patients, thereby exacerbating existing health disparities. The impact of such biases is not trivial and can manifest in several ways, including disparities in treatment recommendations, risk assessments, and diagnostic accuracy. A particularly illustrative case involved a healthcare algorithm used by several U.S. hospitals that was found to systematically favor white patients over black patients in referrals to advanced care programs. This was because the algorithm used healthcare spending as a proxy for health needs, inadvertently ignoring the lower healthcare access and spending among black patients due to socio-economic factors.

To mitigate these biases, a comprehensive strategy must be employed. This includes collecting more diverse data to ensure that AI systems are trained on datasets representative of all patient groups. Additionally, conducting regular and independent audits of these AI algorithms is essential to identify and rectify biases. These audits help maintain transparency and allow for the ongoing adjustment of algorithms as they learn and evolve. Furthermore, the development of AI in healthcare must adhere to strict ethical guidelines, involving a wide range of stakeholders, including ethicists and representatives from diverse patient groups, during the development process. Such inclusivity not only helps foresee potential biases but also fosters broader acceptance of the technology. Governments and regulatory bodies also play a crucial role in this landscape by establishing standards and regulations that enforce fairness and non-discrimination in AI applications. For instance, the European Union has set forth guidelines for a trustworthy AI, which include fairness as a fundamental criterion. An illustrative example of how bias can affect healthcare outcomes is seen in the diagnostics of heart disease. Traditionally, many diagnostic tools were based on data predominantly from male patients, leading to underdiagnosis and undertreatment of heart disease in women, who often present different symptoms. Recognizing this, researchers developed an AI model that was trained on gender-specific data, which significantly improved diagnostic accuracy for women. Educational initiatives are also critical. Training healthcare professionals on the potential biases of AI tools and the implications for patient care can empower them to use these technologies more judiciously. Understanding the limitations and potential pitfalls of AI can help clinicians make better-informed decisions and advocate for the development of more equitable AI tools. In conclusion, while AI holds great promise for enhancing healthcare delivery, it is imperative to address the biases that these systems may inherit or develop. By taking a proactive and comprehensive approach that includes diverse data collection, ethical development, regular auditing, and stringent regulatory oversight, the healthcare industry can leverage AI to benefit all patients equitably, regardless of their demographic characteristics.

Transparency and Explainability

Transparency and explainability are foundational to the successful integration of AI systems in healthcare. These principles are crucial not only for building trust among patients and healthcare providers but also for ensuring that the rationale behind AI-based decisions is thoroughly understood and appropriately scrutinized. AI systems often operate as complex "black boxes", where the decision-making process is not easily discernible by users. This opacity can be a significant barrier in healthcare settings, where understanding the basis of diagnostic or treatment decisions is essential for trust and accountability. For instance, if an AI tool is used to recommend a particular course of treatment, both the patient and the physician must be able to understand why this recommendation was made. Without this understanding, there can be a reluctance to accept the AI's advice, regardless of its potential benefits. The need for transparency starts with the way AI systems are designed and the data they are trained on. Healthcare providers and patients must have access to information about the data sources, the types of algorithms used, and the validation measures that have been applied to ensure the system's reliability. For example, if an AI system is developed to predict the onset of diabetic complications, it should be clear what patient data the model was trained on, what factors it considers in its predictions, and how accurate it has been in clinical trials.

Explainability extends to the outputs of AI systems. It's important that these systems not only provide decisions, recommendations, or predictions but also offer explanations that are understandable to a non-technical audience. Techniques such as feature importance scores, which highlight what variables most influenced an AI's decision, can be invaluable. For example, an AI system used for diagnosing lung cancer might reveal that certain imaging features, patient demographics, and genetic markers are the key factors influencing its diagnoses. This type of transparency allows clinicians to make more informed decisions about when to rely on AI guidance and when to question it. Moreover, the push for greater explainability has led to the development of new tools and methodologies designed to open up the "black box" of AI. These include model-agnostic methods that can be applied to any machine learning model to explain its behavior, such as LIME (Local Interpretable Model-agnostic Explanations) and SHAP (SHapley Additive exPlanations). These tools help to demystify AI decisions by showing how different features contribute to the outcome of the model. Furthermore, regulatory bodies are beginning to require more transparency in AI systems as a condition for their deployment in healthcare. For instance, the European Union's GDPR includes provisions that can be interpreted to require explanations of decisions made by AI systems that affect EU citizens. This regulatory push enhances the drive towards more transparent and explainable AI in healthcare. Educational efforts are also essential to ensure that healthcare professionals are equipped to understand and work with AI systems. Training programs that focus on the basics of AI technology, how it can be applied in healthcare, and how to interpret its outputs are crucial. These programs help bridge the gap between the capabilities of AI technologies and the practical needs of clinical practice. Ensuring that AI systems in healthcare are transparent and their decisions explainable is critical for fostering trust, facilitating user acceptance, and ensuring that these technologies are used ethically and effectively. By emphasizing these principles in the development and implementation of AI tools, the healthcare sector can better leverage the profound capabilities of AI to improve patient outcomes and enhance the delivery of care.

Patient Autonomy and Consent

Patient autonomy and informed consent are cornerstones of ethical healthcare practice, and the integration of AI technologies into healthcare environments underscores the importance of these principles. Patients have a fundamental right to understand how AI is being used in their care, including the potential risks and benefits associated with AI-enabled healthcare. In the context of AI, informed consent involves more than just the traditional approach of informing patients about treatment options; it also requires explaining the role of AI systems in their diagnosis, treatment, or prognosis. This is especially crucial given the complexity and novelty of AI applications, which might not be immediately understandable to patients without a technical background. For instance, consider a scenario where an AI system is used to analyze medical images to detect early signs of cancer. Patients must be informed not only about the capabilities and limitations of the AI system but also about how it works, the data it uses, and the implications of its findings. They should be made aware of how the AI's analysis might influence their treatment options and the potential consequences of relying on AI-generated insights.

Moreover, discussing the potential risks is equally important. This includes explaining the possibility of errors or uncertainties in AI predictions and how such issues might be addressed in the clinical workflow. For example, if an AI model predicts a high probability of a patient having a certain genetic disorder, patients need to understand the accuracy of these predictions and the possibility of false positives or negatives, which could lead to unnecessary anxiety or inappropriate treatment. The process of obtaining informed consent for AI in healthcare also needs to address the privacy concerns that come with the use of extensive data sets. Patients should be informed about what data will be used, how it will be protected, who will have access to it, and how long it will be stored. This transparency is vital to building trust and ensuring that patients feel comfortable with the use of AI tools in their medical care. Furthermore, the dynamic nature of AI, where algorithms can learn and adapt over time, presents unique challenges for informed consent. It's not just a one-time process but rather an ongoing conversation between healthcare providers and patients. As AI systems evolve, the information on which consent is based might change, necessitating regular updates to patients about how these changes could impact their care. Effective communication is crucial in this process. Healthcare providers must ensure that explanations are given in clear, understandable language, avoiding technical jargon that could confuse patients. Additionally, visual aids or decision aids can be used to help explain how AI works and its role in patient care. These tools can facilitate better understanding and help patients make more informed decisions about their treatment options. In summary, maintaining patient autonomy in the age of AI-driven healthcare means ensuring that patients are fully informed and actively consenting to the use of AI technologies in their care. By thoroughly addressing the potential risks and benefits and ensuring ongoing communication, healthcare providers can uphold the ethical standards of patient care while harnessing the advantages of AI technologies.

Accountability and Liability

In the rapidly evolving landscape of AI-enabled healthcare, the issues of accountability and liability are paramount. As AI systems increasingly influence decision-making in healthcare, it becomes crucial to establish clear guidelines on who is responsible for the decisions made by these systems, particularly when they lead to adverse outcomes like incorrect diagnoses or inappropriate treatments. Accountability in the context of AI involves several layers, including the developers who create the algorithms, the healthcare providers who use them, and the regulatory bodies that oversee their application. Each has a role in ensuring that AI systems function as intended and do not harm patients. For example, if an AI diagnostic tool incorrectly identifies a benign tumor as malignant, leading to unnecessary surgery, the question arises: Who is responsible? Is it the developers for potentially providing a flawed algorithm, the healthcare provider for relying on the AI's decision, or the hospital administration for implementing the technology? To address such complexities, it is essential to have robust legal and regulatory frameworks that can assign liability appropriately. These frameworks should consider the unique aspects of AI, such as the ability of algorithms to learn and adapt over time, which might shift how responsibility is assigned. For instance, if an AI system learns from new data and develops a bias that leads to a misdiagnosis, determining liability becomes more complicated.

Moreover, the principles of accountability extend beyond legal liability to include ethical responsibility. Healthcare providers need to ensure that they do not blindly trust AI systems but instead use them as tools to augment their professional judgment. This means providers must stay informed about the limitations and capabilities of the AI systems they use and should verify AI-generated recommendations against their clinical expertise and patient context. Furthermore, transparency plays a critical role in accountability. Both healthcare providers and patients should have access to information about how AI systems make decisions. This transparency not only builds trust but also simplifies the process of determining liability when things go wrong. For instance, if an AI system's decision-making process is opaque, it can be challenging to assess whether an error was due to a mistake in the data input by the healthcare provider, a flaw in the algorithm itself, or an error in how the algorithm was applied. To ensure accountability, ongoing monitoring and evaluation of AI systems are necessary. This can be achieved through regular audits and performance assessments to ensure that AI systems continue to operate safely and effectively. These evaluations can help identify potential issues before they lead to harmful outcomes, thereby mitigating the risk of liability. Training and education also play critical roles in managing accountability. Healthcare providers must be adequately trained on how to use AI systems responsibly and how to interpret their outputs. This training should cover the ethical considerations of using AI in healthcare, including understanding when and how to rely on AI recommendations. In summary, establishing clear accountability and liability in AI-enabled healthcare requires a multifaceted approach that includes legal, ethical, and operational considerations. By developing comprehensive policies, fostering transparency, and ensuring continuous education and monitoring, the healthcare sector can responsibly leverage the benefits of AI while minimizing the risks associated with its use.

Accessibility and Equity

The integration of AI technologies in healthcare holds great promise for improving patient outcomes and optimizing healthcare systems. However, there is a significant risk that these technologies could inadvertently widen health disparities if they are not made accessible to diverse groups or if they fail to address the needs of varied populations. One of the central challenges with AI in healthcare is ensuring that these technologies are accessible to everyone, regardless of socioeconomic status, geographic location, race, or age. For instance, advanced AI diagnostic tools may be available in urban hospitals but completely absent in rural or under-resourced areas. This can exacerbate existing disparities in healthcare quality between urban and rural populations. Moreover, the design and development of AI systems often reflect the biases of their creators, typically involving data that might not be representative of diverse patient populations. For example, if an AI system is trained primarily on data from patients of a certain ethnic background, its accuracy and effectiveness may be lower for individuals from different ethnic backgrounds. This could lead to poorer healthcare outcomes for minority groups, further entrenching health inequities.

Addressing these issues requires a concerted effort to ensure that AI healthcare technologies are developed with inclusivity in mind. This includes using diverse datasets that are representative of the global population and involving stakeholders from varied demographics in the design and testing phases. For example, including diverse healthcare professionals and patients in the development process can provide insights that enhance the cultural competence and inclusivity of AI systems. Moreover, there must be policies and initiatives aimed at improving the accessibility of AI technologies. Governments and healthcare organizations can play a crucial role here by investing in infrastructure that supports the widespread deployment of AI in healthcare, especially in underserved areas. Subsidies or financial assistance programs can also help ensure that all healthcare facilities, including those in economically disadvantaged regions, can access advanced AI tools. Education and training are also critical in addressing accessibility and equity issues. Healthcare providers in all settings must be trained on how to effectively use AI technologies and understand their limitations. This training should be made widely available to ensure that providers, regardless of their location or the type of facility they work in, can leverage AI to improve patient care. Public awareness campaigns can also help patients understand how AI might be used in their healthcare and advocate for equitable access to these technologies. Informing patients about how AI is being used to manage their health and the potential benefits can help increase acceptance and demand for these technologies, which in turn can drive more equitable distribution. In conclusion, while AI technologies have the potential to transform healthcare, deliberate actions are needed to prevent these advances from widening existing disparities. By focusing on inclusivity in development, enhancing accessibility, and providing comprehensive training and education, healthcare stakeholders can ensure that AI technologies benefit all segments of the population equally.

Sustainability

Implementing AI in healthcare requires a thoughtful approach that includes considering the long-term sustainability of these technologies. This includes not only the environmental impact of running large AI models but also the ongoing costs associated with updating and maintaining these systems. The implementation of AI in healthcare requires a thoughtful approach, considering both the environmental impact and long-term sustainability (Richie, 2022; Mhlanga and Ndhlovu, 2023). This includes addressing potential risks and ethical considerations (Morley, 2021), and ensuring that healthcare organizations are AI-capable (Novak, 2023). The development and implementation of AI in low- and middle-income countries should be guided by responsible, sustainable, and inclusive principles (Alami, 2020). A sociotechnical systems approach is also crucial for effective AI application in healthcare (Salwei, 2023). From a policy perspective, there is a need to address issues such as accuracy, fairness, transparency, data privacy, and workforce disruption (Aggarwal, 2021). As AI becomes increasingly integrated into healthcare, understanding and mitigating its potential downsides is crucial for ensuring that its deployment is both beneficial and sustainable. AI systems, particularly those involving large datasets and complex algorithms, require significant computational power. This can lead to substantial energy consumption, which in turn has a notable environmental impact. Data centers that power AI operations often consume vast amounts of electricity, much of which comes from non-renewable sources. This environmental cost must be factored into the deployment of AI technologies in healthcare. For instance, developing more energy-efficient AI models and utilizing green data centers powered by renewable energy sources are steps that can help reduce the carbon footprint associated with these technologies. Moreover, the financial sustainability of implementing AI in healthcare is another critical consideration. AI systems require not only initial investment in technology but also ongoing expenses for maintenance, updates, and training of personnel to use them effectively. These costs can be prohibitive, especially for smaller healthcare providers or those in lower-income regions. To address this, healthcare organizations can consider partnerships with AI providers that offer scalable solutions or subscription-based models that spread out costs over time and include regular updates and support.

Additionally, the sustainability of AI in healthcare extends to the human resources required to manage and utilize these systems effectively. Continuous training and professional development are necessary to ensure that healthcare providers are equipped to work with AI technologies. This involves not only understanding how to operate these systems but also staying updated on the latest advancements and best practices in AI healthcare applications. Healthcare organizations must also consider the long-term implications of dependency on AI technologies. As AI systems become more embedded in healthcare processes, ensuring that these systems do not become obsolete or incompatible with other technologies is vital. This requires a commitment to ongoing investment in technology upgrades and integration with other digital health systems. Furthermore, ethical sustainability is an aspect that cannot be overlooked. This encompasses ensuring that AI systems are used in ways that are ethical and that they continue to align with the values and needs of society. For instance, continuous monitoring of AI applications for potential biases or adverse effects on patient care is essential to maintain the ethical integrity of healthcare services. In conclusion, the sustainability of AI in healthcare involves a balanced approach that considers environmental, financial, human resource, and ethical aspects. By adopting strategies that minimize environmental impact, ensure financial viability, provide for continuous training and professional development, and uphold ethical standards, healthcare organizations can effectively integrate AI technologies in a way that is sustainable and beneficial over the long term.

Clinical Validation and Safety

The integration of AI tools in healthcare necessitates rigorous clinical validation to ensure that these technologies are safe and effective for patient care. This critical process involves extensive testing and peer review, which are essential to establish the accuracy and reliability of AI systems across diverse clinical settings. Clinical validation of AI tools starts with extensive testing using diverse datasets that represent the full spectrum of patients who might use healthcare services. This testing is designed to identify any potential biases or errors in the AI system and ensure that it performs well across different demographics, including various ages, races, ethnicities, and medical histories. For example, an AI system developed to diagnose diabetic retinopathy must be tested on images from patients of different ethnic backgrounds who have varying stages of the disease to ensure that it can accurately detect the condition in a wide range of scenarios. Once initial testing is complete, AI tools often undergo peer review before they can be widely implemented in clinical settings. This review process involves experts in the field scrutinizing the development and testing methodologies used by the AI tool to ensure that they meet the high standards necessary for medical applications. The peer review also typically includes an assessment of the clinical relevance of the AI tool's capabilities, such as its ability to improve diagnostic accuracy or enhance treatment planning.

Moreover, AI tools must be validated not only for their technical performance but also for their integration into clinical workflows. This involves piloting the tools in real-world clinical settings to understand how they interact with existing healthcare infrastructure, including EHRs, diagnostic equipment, and healthcare IT systems. For instance, an AI tool that assists in radiological imaging needs to be compatible with the imaging software and hardware used in hospitals, and it must seamlessly integrate into the radiologists' workflow without causing disruptions or delays. In addition to internal testing and peer review, clinical validation of AI tools often involves regulatory review by bodies such as the Food and Drug Administration (FDA) in the United States, or the European Medicines Agency

(EMA) in the European Union. These regulatory agencies assess the safety and efficacy of AI tools based on stringent criteria before they can be approved for clinical use. This regulatory oversight ensures that AI tools meet all necessary safety standards and are consistently reliable in a variety of clinical environments. Finally, the process of clinical validation must be ongoing. As AI tools are used over time, continuous monitoring is essential to ensure they remain effective and safe. This involves regularly updating the AI algorithms as new data becomes available and reassessing the tools to ensure they continue to perform as expected. For example, an AI system used for predicting cardiovascular risks must be periodically updated to incorporate the latest research findings and patient data to maintain its accuracy and relevance. In conclusion, rigorous clinical validation is crucial for ensuring the safety and effectiveness of AI tools in healthcare. Through extensive testing, peer review, integration trials, regulatory approval, and continuous monitoring, healthcare providers can confidently deploy AI technologies that enhance patient outcomes and improve the efficiency of healthcare services.

Conclusion

The transformative potential of AI in healthcare is immense, promising to revolutionize medical practices and improve patient care. However, this potential can only be fully realized if the ethical challenges associated with AI implementation are adequately addressed. This chapter underscores the importance of developing and adhering to ethical guidelines and regulatory frameworks that ensure the responsible use of AI in healthcare. The goal is to foster an environment where AI technologies can be leveraged to their fullest potential while safeguarding patient rights and trust. The analysis reveals that addressing ethical concerns such as patient privacy, data security, algorithmic bias, and transparency is critical for the successful integration of AI in healthcare. Ensuring fairness and accountability in AI systems is also essential to maintain public trust and achieve equitable healthcare outcomes. A thoughtful and informed approach to AI integration in healthcare is necessary to harness its benefits while mitigating ethical risks. Regulatory frameworks and ethical guidelines must evolve alongside technological advancements to protect patient rights and ensure public trust. By balancing the potential benefits of AI with rigorous ethical considerations, the healthcare industry can achieve significant advancements in patient care and overall health outcomes.

References

Aggarwal, N., Aguiar, O.D., Bauswein, A., Cella, G., Clesse, S., Cruise, A.M. ... and White, G. (2021). Challenges and opportunities of gravitational-wave searches at MHz to GHz frequencies. Living reviews in relativity, 24, 1–74.

Alami, A. (2020, June). The sustainability of quality in free and open source software. In Proceedings of the ACM/IEEE 42nd International Conference on Software Engineering: Companion Proceedings (pp. 222-225).

Arora, A., Alderman, J.E., Palmer, J., Ganapathi, S., Laws, E., Mccradden, M. D., ... and Liu, X. (2023). The value of standards for health datasets in artificial intelligence-based applications. *Nature Medicine*, *29*(11), 2929–38.

Benbya, H., Davenport, T. H., and Pachidi, S. (2020). Artificial intelligence in organizations: Current state and future opportunities. MIS Quarterly Executive, *19*(4).

Borda, A., Molnar, A., Neesham, C. and Kostkova, P. (2022). Ethical Issues in AI-enabled Disease Surveillance: Perspectives from Global Health. *Applied Sciences*, *12*(8), 3890.

Čartolovni, A., Tomičić, A. and Mosler, E.L. (2022). Ethical, legal, and social considerations of AI-based medical decision-support tools: A scoping review. *International Journal of Medical Informatics*, *161*, 104738.

Gembaczka, P. and Krupp, L. (2023). The internet is full of things. Physics Today, *76*(7), 54–55.

Giordano, C., Brennan, M., Mohamed, B., Rashidi, P., Modave, F. and Tighe, P. (2021). Accessing artificial intelligence for clinical decision-making. Frontiers in digital health, 3, 645232.

Hill, D.L. (2024). AI in imaging: the regulatory landscape. British Journal of Radiology, *97*(1155), 483–91.

Kejriwal, M. (2022). Knowledge graphs: A practical review of the research landscape. Information, *13*(4), 161.

Li, F., Ruijs, N. and Lu, Y. (2022). Ethics and AI: A systematic review on ethical concerns and related strategies for designing with AI in healthcare. *AI*, *4*(1), 28–53.

Matheny, K.T. (2023). A seat at the table: Lessons from Tennessee's rapid achievement and equity gains. Education Policy Analysis Archives, 31.

Mhlanga, D. (2023a). Digital Transformation in the Healthcare Sector: The Role of Artificial Intelligence for Inclusive Long-term Care around the World, Lessons for Africa. *In*: *Economic Inclusion in Post-Independence Africa: An Inclusive Approach to Economic Development* (pp. 347–62). Cham: Springer Nature Switzerland.

Mhlanga, D. (2023b). *Responsible Industry 4.0: A Framework for Human-centered Artificial Intelligence*. Taylor and Francis.

Mhlanga, D. (2024). Big Data and Financial Technology (Fintech) Towards Financial Inclusion. *SSRN*. 4697365. https://ssrn.com/abstract=4697365 or http://dx.doi.org/10.2139/ssrn.4697365.

Mhlanga, D., Ndhlovu, E. (2023). Economic Inclusion: Transforming the Lives of the Poor and How to Make Economic Inclusion Work in Africa. *In*: Mhlanga, D., Ndhlovu, E. (Eds.), *Economic Inclusion in Post-Independence Africa. Advances in African Economic, Social and Political Development*. Cham: Springer. https://doi.org/10.1007/978-3-031-31431-5_2.

Morley, A. (2021). Procuring for change: An exploration of the innovation potential of sustainable food procurement. Journal of Cleaner Production, 279, 123410.

Nazer, L.H., Zatarah, R., Waldrip, S., Ke, J.X.C., Moukheiber, M., Khanna, A.K., ... and Mathur, P. (2023). Bias in artificial intelligence algorithms and recommendations for mitigation. PLOS Digital Health, 2(6), e0000278.

Ndhlovu, E. and Mhlanga, D. (2024). African Agency in Medical Innovation and Practices: From Antiquity to the Present. *African Renaissance* (1744–2532), *21*(1).

Nelson, A.P., Gray, R.J., Ruffle, J.K., Watkins, H.C., Herron, D., Sorros, N., ... and Nachev, P. (2022). Deep forecasting of translational impact in medical research. Patterns, *3*(5).

Norori, N., Hu, Q., Aellen, F.M., Faraci, F.D. and Tzovara, A. (2021). Addressing bias in big data and AI for health care: A call for open science. Patterns, *2*(10).

Novak, D. and Mohammadian, H.D. (2023). Risks and forecasts of global temperature increase and climate challenges: Insights from the 5th wave theory and Novak triangle. Progress in Energy & Fuels, *12*(2), 3316.

Pereira, V. and Bamel, U. (2021). Extending the resource and knowledge based view: A critical analysis into its theoretical evolution and future research directions. Journal of Business Research, 132, 557–70.

Price-Haywood, E.G., Burton, J., Fort, D. and Seoane, L. (2020). Hospitalization and mortality among black patients and white patients with COVID-19. New England Journal of Medicine, *382*(26), 2534–43.

Richie, C. (2022). Environmental sustainability and the carbon emissions of pharmaceuticals. Journal of Medical Ethics, 48(5), 334–37.

Rickert, D.A., Singh, V., Thirukumaran, M., Grandy, J.J., Belinato, J.R., Lashgari, M. and Pawliszyn, J. (2020). Comprehensive analysis of multiresidue pesticides from process water obtained from wastewater treatment facilities using solid-phase microextraction. Environmental Science & Technology, 54(24), 15789–99.

Salwei, M.E., Hoonakker, P.L., Pulia, M., Wiegmann, D., Patterson, B.W. and Carayon, P. (2023). Post-implementation usability evaluation of a human factors-based clinical decision support for pulmonary embolism (PE) diagnosis (Dx): PE Dx Study Part 1. Human Factors in Healthcare, 4, 100056.

Segijn, C.M. and Van Ooijen, I. (2022). Differences in consumer knowledge and perceptions of personalized advertising: Comparing online behavioural advertising and synced advertising. Journal of Marketing Communications, 28(2), 207–26.

Taivalsaari, A., Mikkonen, T. and Pautasso, C. (2021, May). Towards seamless IoT device-edge-cloud continuum: Software architecture options of IoT devices revisited. In International Conference on Web Engineering (pp. 82–98). Cham: Springer International Publishing.

Tiwari, S., Bahuguna, P.C. and Srivastava, R. (2023). Smart manufacturing and sustainability: a bibliometric analysis. Benchmarking: An International Journal, 30(9), 3281–3301.

12 Overcoming Barriers to AI Adoption in Healthcare

In this chapter, the book explores the several complex obstacles that prevent the widespread use of Artificial Intelligence (AI) in the healthcare industry. Despite the potential for significant technical advancements, this sector faces a variety of hindrances. This chapter provides a comprehensive analysis of the technological, ethical, regulatory, and cultural barriers that hinder the integration of AI into healthcare systems. It also presents strategic options to overcome these issues. The text highlights the need of technological progress in safeguarding data privacy, addressing the issue of biased data, and effectively incorporating AI into current IT systems. In addition, the chapter emphasizes the importance of government and governance in creating a favorable climate for the adoption of AI. It also includes comments on the economic effects, such as cost-benefit evaluations and potential savings. The importance of collaborative frameworks in uniting healthcare professionals, AI developers, regulators, and patients is also explored. These frameworks ensure that AI technologies are customized to fulfill clinical requirements, adhere to ethical norms, and comply with regulations.

Introduction

As we stand on the precipice of a technological revolution in healthcare, the transformative potential of Artificial Intelligence (AI) is palpable. Promising to enhance patient care, optimize treatment outcomes, and streamline operations, AI holds the key to a myriad of advancements in the healthcare sector. Yet, the journey toward its widespread adoption is not without obstacles. Chapter 12, "Overcoming Barriers to AI Adoption in Healthcare", offers a thorough exploration of these impediments, delving into the complex interplay of technical, ethical, regulatory, and cultural challenges that stand in the way. The integration of AI into healthcare systems faces significant technical hurdles, such as concerns over data privacy, the need for vast amounts of high-quality data, and the complexities of merging AI with existing IT infrastructures (Bianco, 2021). Ethical considerations are equally daunting, with issues such as maintaining patient confidentiality, addressing biases in AI algorithms, and ensuring equitable access to AI-driven healthcare solutions at the forefront (Pan, 2016; Mhlanga 2023a, Mhlanga 2023b). Additionally, the regulatory landscape presents its own set of challenges, demanding robust and adaptable frameworks that keep pace with rapid technological advancements while safeguarding patient safety and legal compliance (Haider, 2020).

Moreover, cultural and organizational barriers cannot be overlooked. Establishing a culture of innovation and trust among healthcare professionals and patients is crucial. This chapter discusses effective change management strategies, the importance of upskilling healthcare staff, and ways to foster patient trust in AI-driven care (Mathur and Geerts, 2023). Navigating these multifaceted challenges requires innovative solutions and best practices, which this chapter seeks to highlight through cutting-edge research and pioneering case studies. The collaborative efforts of healthcare leaders, policymakers, and AI technologists are essential in harnessing AI's potential to transform healthcare. This chapter not only maps out the obstacles but also serves as a guide, offering actionable insights and strategies to overcome these barriers, ensuring AI's role as a force for good in advancing global health and well-being.

AI Integration Success Stories in Healthcare

The integration of AI in healthcare, particularly in diagnostic imaging, has shown significant potential to enhance medical outcomes, streamline operations, and personalize patient care (Davenport, 2020; Pesapane, 2018; Pinto-Coelho, 2023; Coppola, 2021; Arora, 2018; Alloghani, 2019; Thrall, 2018; Najjar, 2023). AI's ability to analyze X-rays, MRIs, and CT scans with high accuracy has been a key driver of this potential (Davenport, 2019; Pesapane, 2018; Pinto-Coelho, 2023; Coppola, 2021; Arora, 2020; Alloghani, 2019; Thrall, 2018; Najjar, 2023). Despite concerns about job displacement and ethical considerations, the benefits of AI in medical imaging are clear, with the potential to improve diagnostic accuracy, patient outcomes, and the quality of work life for radiologists (Davenport, 2019; Pesapane, 2018; Pinto-Coelho, 2023; Coppola, 2021; Arora, 2020; Alloghani, 2019; Thrall, 2018; Najjar, 2023). One of the most notable applications is in diagnostic imaging. AI algorithms are now able to analyze X-rays, MRIs, and CT scans with accuracy that rivals, and sometimes surpasses, human radiologists. This technology not only speeds up the diagnostic process but also improves detection rates of diseases such as cancer, leading to earlier and potentially more effective treatments. Another area where AI has made significant strides is in patient data management. By utilizing AI to manage and analyze large datasets, healthcare providers can identify trends, predict patient outcomes, and tailor treatments to individual needs. This use of AI in predictive analytics can significantly enhance preventive medicine and manage chronic diseases by anticipating complications before they become severe. AI is also revolutionizing drug discovery and development. Through machine learning algorithms, AI can predict how different chemicals will interact much quicker than traditional methods. This acceleration reduces the time and cost associated with bringing new drugs to market, thereby benefiting patients sooner than expected.

Telemedicine has also benefitted from AI, particularly during the COVID-19 pandemic. AI-powered chatbots have been used to pre-screen patients and provide basic healthcare advice, reducing the burden on healthcare facilities and ensuring patients receive timely care. However, the successful integration of

AI in healthcare does not come without challenges. Issues such as data privacy, ethical concerns, and the need for substantial initial investment must be carefully addressed. Moreover, for AI to be truly effective, there must be an ongoing collaboration between technologists and healthcare professionals to ensure that the solutions developed are practical and meet actual needs. AI holds tremendous promise for the future of healthcare, offering innovative solutions that improve efficiency, accuracy, and patient outcomes. However, its success depends on strategic planning, overcoming technical and ethical challenges, and fostering strong collaborations across disciplines.

AI-powered Clinical Decision Support at TidalHealth Peninsula Regional

TidalHealth Peninsula Regional's collaboration with IBM to integrate Watson Micromedex into its Clinical Decision Support system is a significant step towards enhancing patient care. This AI-driven tool, which can seamlessly analyze vast amounts of patient data, aligns with the growing emphasis on personalized medicine and evidence-based practice (Yesha, 2014; Castañeda, 2015). The integration of Watson Micromedex with Electronic Medical Records (EMRs) is crucial for achieving semantic interoperability and ensuring data security (Jung, 2016; Mhlanga 2022a). The proposed architecture for a distributed clinical decision support system, which includes data mining techniques and knowledge bases, could further enhance the capabilities of TidalHealth's system (El-Sappagh, 2014; Mhlanga 2022b). The use of Soft Computing techniques, such as Fuzzy Cognitive Maps, could also be explored to improve the system's efficiency (Stylios, 2014). Lastly, the application of a UMLS-based Knowledge Acquisition Tool could facilitate the creation and maintenance of the knowledge base within the system (Achour, 2001; Mhlanga 2022c).

TidalHealth Peninsula Regional has collaborated with IBM to enhance its Clinical Decision Support systems by integrating Watson Micromedex, a sophisticated AI-driven tool. This tool is designed to seamlessly integrate with EMRs, enabling it to analyze vast amounts of patient data efficiently. The primary goal is to furnish healthcare providers with pertinent clinical insights and information, facilitating more informed decision-making processes. Prior to this integration, clinicians at TidalHealth often found themselves spending a significant amount of time navigating through EMRs to locate necessary information. This extensive search process, typically taking between three to four minutes per query, significantly detracted from the time available for direct patient interactions. The introduction of Watson Micromedex has markedly improved this situation by reducing the time required to access clinical information to less than one minute per search. This substantial reduction in search time has allowed clinicians to reallocate a greater portion of their time to providing direct care to patients, thereby enhancing the overall efficiency of healthcare delivery at TidalHealth Peninsula Regional.

AI Streamlining Prior Authorizations with Cohere Health

Cohere Health is leveraging AI to transform the process of prior authorizations in healthcare, making it more efficient and patient-centered. Their innovative platform, Cohere Unify, utilizes AI to meticulously analyze patient data and forecast healthcare requirements. This advanced system generates evidence-based care pathways and expedites the pre-approval of essential medical services. Traditionally, the prior authorization process has been fraught with delays and inefficiencies, often hindering timely access to necessary medical treatments. These delays can be critical, especially for patients requiring urgent care. By integrating AI, Cohere Unify anticipates the specific care needs of patients, thereby streamlining the approval process. As a result, Cohere's AI-enhanced system not only minimizes the waiting time for approvals but also ensures that patients receive the required treatments without unnecessary delays. This approach significantly improves the overall efficacy of healthcare delivery and patient satisfaction.

Blueprint for Successful AI Integration in Healthcare

The highlighted cases provide crucial insights into the successful integration of AI within healthcare systems. To effectively implement AI, it is essential to pinpoint specific problems that AI can address, such as enhancing clinician workflows or streamlining administrative procedures. Effective AI implementation often requires robust partnerships between healthcare providers and AI technology companies. These collaborations foster innovation and facilitate tailored solutions that meet specific healthcare needs. AI technologies depend heavily on access to high-quality, comprehensive data. It's imperative to establish a strong data infrastructure that not only supports AI algorithms but also ensures the privacy and security of patient data. AI is designed to augment, not replace, human decision-making in healthcare. The integration of AI should enhance the capabilities of healthcare professionals, not diminish their role, and ensure that AI-generated recommendations are transparent and can be easily understood by medical professionals. This transparency is vital for trust and effective utilization in clinical settings. It's crucial to address potential biases in AI algorithms and strive for equitable access to AI-powered healthcare solutions. This involves continuous monitoring and adjustment to ensure fairness and effectiveness across diverse patient groups. By adhering to these principles and drawing lessons from successful case studies, healthcare organizations can leverage AI to significantly enhance patient care, increase clinician efficiency, and improve the overall delivery of healthcare services.

Role of Government and Policymaking

The integration of AI in healthcare is profoundly influenced by government regulations and policies, which can either facilitate or impede this technological adoption. A proactive approach from government bodies is essential to foster an environment that nurtures AI innovation and application in the healthcare industry, where AI promises to enhance diagnostic accuracy, improve treatment efficacy, and optimize management systems. Government roles in facilitating AI integration are multifaceted, including providing funding for research and development and adjusting policies to accommodate the burgeoning technology. For example, the U.S. government's American AI Initiative aims to sustain and enhance the country's AI technology capabilities, accompanied by substantial funding that benefits both research institutions and private enterprises focusing on healthcare applications. Moreover, policy adjustments are critical in shaping a regulatory environment that supports the safe and effective use of AI, with privacy and data security at the forefront. The European General Data Protection Regulation (GDPR) has set a standard in protecting and managing extensive personal health data processed by AI systems. Such regulations ensure that AI tools in healthcare are developed with an inherent focus on data privacy, shaping their development from inception. Countries like Singapore and the UK illustrate the successful implementation of AI in healthcare, driven by supportive government policies. Singapore's Smart Nation initiative and the UK's National Health Service partnerships with AI companies demonstrate practical applications of AI that streamline operations and enhance patient care, showcasing how government policies can bridge AI capabilities with healthcare needs.

Public-private partnerships (PPPs) serve as a vital conduit for the integration of AI in healthcare, leveraging the regulatory and policymaking prowess of the public sector with the technical and innovative capabilities of the private sector. An exemplary partnership is that between the U.S. Veterans Affairs and DeepMind technologies, focusing on AI research to predict patient deterioration in hospitals. Such collaborations not only spur innovation but also ensure that these innovations are practical and beneficial, improving patient outcomes and care efficiencies. As AI becomes more pervasive in healthcare, ethical guidelines and fair practices become increasingly critical. Governments must ensure that AI systems are developed and implemented ethically, without reinforcing existing health disparities. Policies need to address AI algorithm biases and promote access to AI-driven healthcare solutions across all population segments. The European Union's Ethics Guidelines for Trustworthy AI exemplifies efforts to make AI systems transparent, fair, and accountable, promoting public trust and broader acceptance. In essence, the government's role in the AI healthcare integration is indispensable. By facilitating research through funding, adjusting policies to support AI adoption, fostering PPPs, and setting ethical standards, governments can profoundly influence the pace and effectiveness of AI adoption in healthcare. This proactive involvement is crucial for leveraging AI's full potential to transform healthcare delivery, making systems more efficient, responsive, and patient-centric, thereby ensuring that the benefits of AI are widespread and equitable.

Technological Advancements to Address Barriers

Technological advancements in the realm of AI are rapidly evolving to address some of the most significant technical barriers that have impeded its broader adoption in healthcare. These advancements are particularly focused on enhancing data privacy, handling biased data, and streamlining the integration of AI technologies with existing healthcare IT infrastructures. One of the key advancements is the development of improved algorithms that bolster data privacy. As healthcare systems handle sensitive patient information, ensuring privacy is paramount. Innovations such as federated learning, where AI models are trained across multiple decentralized devices or servers without exchanging data samples, offer promising solutions. This means that sensitive data does not need to leave the hospital or clinic, thus maintaining patient confidentiality while still benefiting from the insights gained through AI.

Addressing biased data is another critical area where technological advancements are making significant strides. AI systems are only as good as the data they are trained on, and historically, some datasets have included biases that could lead to unequal treatment outcomes. New machine learning algorithms and data processing techniques are being developed to identify, correct, and ultimately prevent biased data from influencing AI-driven decisions. Techniques such as synthetic data generation are also being employed to create balanced datasets where historical data may be lacking or biased, ensuring fairer AI outcomes. Furthermore, the integration of AI technologies into existing healthcare IT infrastructures has been a notable challenge, often due to compatibility issues between new AI tools and old systems. New integration protocols and standards are being developed to simplify this merger. These protocols ensure that AI tools can communicate seamlessly with different healthcare databases and software, facilitating smoother data flows and interoperability. Such protocols are designed to be adaptable, allowing for easier updates and scalability as technology advances. These technological advancements are crucial for the successful integration of AI in healthcare. They not only enhance the functionality and effectiveness of AI applications but also ensure that these innovations can be implemented ethically and equitably (Alowais et al., 2023). By overcoming these barriers, the healthcare industry can harness the full potential of AI to improve patient outcomes, enhance the efficiency of healthcare services, and foster more personalized and predictive medicine. As these technologies continue to evolve, they will play a pivotal role in shaping the future of healthcare, making it more responsive and tailored to individual patient needs.

Economic Impact Analysis

The adoption of AI in healthcare presents a complex landscape of economic impacts that can significantly alter the financial dynamics of the sector. This analysis explores the cost-benefit implications, potential cost savings, and economic incentives that encourage the integration of AI technologies into healthcare systems. Starting with cost-benefit analyses, the initial investment in AI technologies can be substantial, involving not only the costs of the technologies themselves but also the integration, training, and ongoing maintenance. However, the benefits often outweigh these costs significantly. AI can enhance diagnostic accuracy, reduce redundant procedures, and optimize treatment plans, which in turn can lead to a decrease in unnecessary spending. For example, AI-driven diagnostic tools can analyze medical imaging faster and often more accurately than human counterparts, reducing the time and resources spent on diagnosing patients and allowing for earlier interventions that are less costly and more effective.

Potential cost savings from AI adoption in healthcare are substantial. AI can streamline administrative processes, such as scheduling, billing, and compliance monitoring, which traditionally consume a significant portion of healthcare budgets. By automating these tasks, healthcare facilities can reduce labor costs and minimize errors, leading to further savings. Moreover, AI applications in patient monitoring and care can lead to shorter hospital stays and less frequent readmissions, directly reducing healthcare costs associated with prolonged hospital care. Economic incentives for adopting AI technologies in healthcare are also significant. Governments and healthcare policymakers are increasingly recognizing the value of AI in improving the efficiency and quality of care. Incentives such as tax breaks, grants, and subsidies are often offered to healthcare providers to offset the costs of adopting new technologies. Additionally, reimbursement policies are being adjusted to favor treatments that incorporate AI, providing a direct financial benefit to healthcare providers who adopt these technologies. Moreover, the competitive advantage gained through AI can also be considered an economic incentive. Healthcare providers that adopt AI can offer faster, more accurate diagnostics and personalized treatment plans, attracting more patients, and potentially allowing providers to charge a premium for these advanced services. The economic impact of AI in healthcare extends beyond direct financial calculations. The broader societal benefits, such as improved health outcomes, greater accessibility to healthcare services, and advancements in medical research, contribute to long-term economic growth. By reducing the burden of disease and enhancing the quality of life, AI in healthcare can contribute to a more productive workforce and a reduction in healthcare-related social security costs. In conclusion, the economic impacts of AI adoption in healthcare are both direct and indirect, affecting various aspects of healthcare economics from cost savings and efficiency gains to broader societal benefits. The financial implications are significant, providing strong incentives for the continued expansion and integration of AI technologies in healthcare settings. As AI continues to evolve, its potential to transform the healthcare landscape economically will likely expand, making it an increasingly critical component of healthcare strategy.

Overcoming Barriers to the Adoption of AI in Healthcare Involves Addressing Several Key Challenges

Data Privacy and Security

Ensuring the privacy and security of patient data is a critical concern in healthcare, particularly with the integration of AI systems. Compliance with regulatory frameworks like HIPAA in the United States, GDPR in Europe, and various other local data protection laws is essential. Healthcare providers are tasked with ensuring that AI systems adhere to these stringent regulations, and that data is securely managed during storage and transmission. The complexity of safeguarding patient data requires a multifaceted approach that combines both technical and organizational strategies. Technical measures such as access control, authentication, and encryption are vital components of a robust security strategy (Verykios, 2008; Burger, 2011; Garrison, 1970; Gupta, 2021; Patokar, 2018; Dai, 2013). These measures help in securing data against unauthorized access and breaches. In addition to these security measures, privacy-preserving data management techniques play a crucial role. Techniques such as anonymization, which strips identifying information from data, and securing user consent for data usage are critical for maintaining privacy (Verykios, 2008). These practices help in minimizing the risks associated with data handling and ensure compliance with legal standards. The challenges posed by big data in healthcare—characterized by its large volume, wide variety, and high velocity—further underscore the need for stringent security measures (Jha, 2017). The sheer scale and complexity of data collected in healthcare necessitate advanced security protocols to protect sensitive information effectively. This comprehensive approach ensures that as healthcare providers continue to adopt AI technologies, they can maintain the trust of their patients by safeguarding their personal health information against potential threats.

Integration with Existing Systems

Integrating AI solutions into existing healthcare IT systems presents a significant challenge due to the diverse range of software and platforms in use across healthcare settings. For AI technologies to be widely adopted and effectively utilized, they must be compatible with these pre-existing systems.

Developing AI tools that can seamlessly integrate is crucial. These tools need to be designed with flexibility and adaptability in mind, allowing them to function effectively within the various IT infrastructures that are already in place. This compatibility is essential not only for the operational functionality of AI but also for its ability to communicate and share data across different platforms, which is vital for the comprehensive analysis and treatment planning that AI offers. To achieve this seamless integration, AI developers must focus on creating interoperable systems that can easily connect with different healthcare databases and software. This often involves using standard data formats and common programming interfaces, which help bridge the gap between new AI applications and older systems. By ensuring that AI tools can integrate without disrupting existing workflows, healthcare providers can enhance their service delivery without significant overhauls or downtime, thereby facilitating smoother transitions and broader acceptance of AI technology in healthcare.

The challenge of integrating AI solutions into existing healthcare IT systems is addressed by a range of studies. Yates (1998) and McHenry (1994) both propose methods for integrating separately developed software systems, with a focus on maintaining data consistency. Yang (2010) and Манвелидзе (2013) present approaches that improve adaptability and compatibility, with Yang specifically focusing on multi-platform and interdisciplinary systems. Langer (2011) and Meng (2009) offer strategies for interfacing new systems with pre-existing applications, with Meng's Five-Layers Architecture based on SOA and BPM emphasizing the reuse and integration of existing computer software resources. Tyson (2011) and Bodorik (1990) explore the integration of multiple heterogeneous and autonomous systems, with Tyson's model-driven approach and Bodorik's tool for integrating existing databases both aiming to improve the integration process.

Clinical Validation and Trust

AI systems must be clinically validated to ensure that their recommendations are accurate and reliable. This involves extensive testing and peer-reviewed research. Building trust among healthcare professionals is also essential, as they need to be confident in the AI's recommendations. A range of studies have explored the concept of trust in healthcare, particularly in the context of patient-physician relationships and medical technology. Thom (2011) and Anderson (1990) both developed and validated scales to measure trust in physicians, with the former focusing on the physician's trust in the patient. Robie (2012) emphasized the importance of transparency in building trust, particularly in psychiatry research. Montague (2010) and Richmond (2022) developed and validated instruments to measure patients' trust in medical technology and healthcare providers, respectively. O'Mathúna (2009) highlighted the need for responsible, ethical, and professional conduct in clinical research to build trust. Zarin (2013) emphasized the importance of trial registration and adherence to protocols in clinical trials to ensure trustworthiness. These studies collectively underscore the significance of trust and transparency in healthcare, and the need for rigorous validation of instruments and protocols to build and maintain trust.

Cost and ROI Considerations

Implementing AI solutions in healthcare can involve substantial expenses. Healthcare organizations need to carefully evaluate the return on investment (ROI) when considering these technologies. This evaluation includes considering the upfront costs of the technology, as well as the expenses related to training staff and maintaining the systems over time. To justify the investment in AI, it's crucial for healthcare organizations to demonstrate how these technologies can enhance operational efficiency, reduce errors, and improve patient outcomes. For example, AI-driven systems can streamline diagnostic processes, leading to quicker and more accurate diagnoses. This can significantly reduce the costs associated with misdiagnosis or delayed treatment. Moreover, AI can automate routine tasks, such as data entry and patient scheduling, which frees up healthcare professionals to focus more on patient care rather than administrative duties. This increase in efficiency can lead to reduced operational costs and improved patient satisfaction.

Additionally, AI's ability to analyze vast amounts of data can lead to better patient outcomes by identifying effective treatment plans based on patterns that may not be evident to human observers. This capability can decrease the likelihood of costly complications or readmissions, providing a substantial financial benefit. Thus, while the initial costs of implementing AI in healthcare can be high, the potential for significant ROI through improved efficiency, reduced errors, and better patient outcomes can make these investments worthwhile. This highlights the importance of strategic planning and careful consideration of both the immediate and long-term financial impacts of AI technology adoption in healthcare settings.

Ethical and Legal Implications

The use of AI in healthcare brings with it a complex array of ethical and legal implications that need careful consideration. Ethical concerns primarily revolve around decision-making processes and the potential for bias within AI algorithms. These issues raise questions about fairness, transparency, and accountability in AI-driven healthcare solutions. From an ethical standpoint, it is crucial to ensure that AI systems make decisions in a manner that is just and equitable. There is a risk that AI algorithms could perpetuate or even exacerbate existing biases if they are trained on datasets that are not representative of diverse populations. This could lead to unequal treatment outcomes, which not only undermines the effectiveness of healthcare but also compromises ethical standards. Legally, the use of AI in healthcare introduces potential liabilities, particularly in cases of misdiagnoses or errors that could harm patients. Determining liability when an AI system is involved is complex. Traditional legal frameworks are based on human decision-making, and adapting these to include AI-driven decisions is an ongoing challenge. Healthcare providers and AI developers must navigate these legal waters carefully to ensure compliance with existing laws and to prepare for new regulations that might emerge as AI becomes more embedded in healthcare. Moreover, there are questions about who is responsible when AI-driven healthcare tools fail. Is it the developers, the healthcare providers, or the manufacturers of the AI systems? Addressing these questions requires a clear legal framework that delineates responsibility and ensures that patient safety is paramount. In summary, both the ethical and legal implications of AI in healthcare demand rigorous scrutiny and proactive management. Ensuring that AI systems operate within ethical boundaries and have robust legal frameworks in place is crucial for maintaining trust in AI as a tool for enhancing healthcare outcomes. This includes rigorous testing of AI systems for biases, continuous monitoring of their decisions, and the development of legal standards that can adapt to the evolving nature of AI technologies in healthcare.

User Training and Adoption

Training healthcare professionals to effectively use AI systems is crucial for the successful integration of this technology in healthcare settings. This training encompasses not only the technical aspects of operating the AI software but also the interpretative skills necessary to understand and utilize the outputs of AI systems. For AI to truly enhance healthcare services, users must be proficient in both—using the technology and making informed decisions based on the insights it provides. To encourage the adoption of AI, it is essential to demonstrate its benefits clearly to healthcare providers. Showing tangible improvements in efficiency, accuracy, and patient outcomes can help overcome skepticism and resistance to new technologies. For instance, if AI can significantly reduce the time taken to diagnose diseases or predict patient deterioration earlier, these benefits should be highlighted to illustrate the direct impact of AI on enhancing healthcare delivery. Involving healthcare professionals in the development and implementation process of AI systems can also foster greater acceptance and smoother integration. When users are part of the development process, they can provide valuable insights into practical needs and challenges, ensuring that the AI solutions developed are truly user-friendly and effective in a real-world clinical setting. Moreover, user involvement helps tailor the training programs to the specific needs of the professionals who will use these systems daily. This tailored training can address specific concerns and questions, making the learning process more relevant and engaging for healthcare providers. Ultimately, comprehensive training and inclusive development processes are the key to ensuring that healthcare professionals are not only comfortable using AI technologies but also fully equipped to leverage these tools to improve patient care and operational efficiency.

Access and Equity

Ensuring access and equity in the deployment of AI solutions in healthcare is critical. It is important that these technologies are accessible to all healthcare providers, not just those in well-resourced, high-tech environments but also those working in low-resource settings. This broad accessibility can help prevent the widening of existing disparities in healthcare quality. Moreover, addressing potential biases in AI algorithms is essential to ensure that they perform equitably across diverse patient populations. AI systems often depend on large datasets for training, and if these datasets are not representative of the global population, there is a risk that the AI will perform less effectively for underrepresented groups. This can lead to disparities in healthcare outcomes, where certain populations may not receive the same quality of care due to biased AI decision-making. To promote equity, developers must rigorously test AI algorithms across a variety of demographic groups, ensuring that the system's performance is consistent regardless of the patient's background. Additionally, continuous monitoring and updating of AI systems are necessary to address any biases that may emerge over time.

Making AI solutions accessible in low-resource settings involves not only adapting the technology to work with less infrastructure but also ensuring that the cost of AI tools does not put them out of reach for these environments. Strategies to achieve this could include developing low-cost AI solutions or providing financial assistance, such as grants or subsidies, to healthcare providers in these areas. Ultimately, a concerted effort to address both access and equity will help ensure that AI technologies benefit all segments of the population equally, enhancing overall healthcare delivery and preventing the exacerbation of existing healthcare inequalities.

Interdisciplinary Collaboration

Developing effective AI solutions in healthcare hinges on the collaboration between technologists, clinicians, and other stakeholders. This interdisciplinary approach is crucial to ensure that the AI tools developed are both technologically sophisticated and clinically relevant. Technologists contribute their expertise in AI and computational technologies, crafting the backbone of AI solutions. However, for these solutions to be effective in a healthcare setting, they must meet the practical and nuanced needs of clinical practice. Clinicians, who bring their deep understanding of patient care, medical protocols, and healthcare workflows, are essential in guiding the development of AI so that it aligns with real-world medical scenarios and enhances patient outcomes. Moreover, the involvement of other stakeholders such as ethicists, regulatory experts, and even patients themselves enriches the development process. Ethicists ensure that the AI solutions uphold ethical standards and consider patient rights, especially concerning privacy and consent. Regulatory experts help navigate the complex landscape of healthcare regulations, ensuring that AI tools comply with all legal requirements. Patient involvement can offer insights into user experience and expectations, making AI tools more user-friendly and accepted by the broader public. This collaborative process bridges the gap between technical possibilities and clinical needs, leading to the creation of AI applications that are not only innovative but also practical and beneficial within the healthcare context. It encourages a holistic view of technology development, where every aspect of healthcare delivery, including efficacy, usability, ethics, and compliance, is considered. Through such interdisciplinary collaboration, AI in healthcare can truly fulfill its promise of transforming care delivery and improving patient outcomes.

Scalability and Flexibility

AI systems in healthcare need to be designed with scalability and flexibility at their core to effectively handle the diverse and dynamic nature of medical data and healthcare environments. Scalability is essential because these systems must be capable of managing varying volumes of data, ranging from small datasets in individual clinics to vast amounts of information generated by large hospitals. As healthcare providers continue to digitize more aspects of patient care, the ability of AI systems to scale up efficiently is crucial to maintaining performance without compromising speed or accuracy. Flexibility is equally important, as it ensures that AI systems can be adapted to different healthcare settings—such as hospitals, clinics, and remote care environments. This adaptability allows AI tools to be customized to meet specific clinical needs and cater to varying patient demographics. For example, an AI application used in a large urban hospital might need to be configured differently when deployed in a small rural clinic or used for home-based care. This customization could involve adjusting the algorithms to reflect different patient population characteristics or integrating with various types of healthcare IT systems. This scalability and flexibility not only enhance the functionality of AI systems but also broaden their applicability across different healthcare scenarios. By ensuring that AI tools can both scale with growing data requirements and flexibly adapt to diverse clinical environments, healthcare organizations can maximize their investment in AI, making it a powerful tool that supports a wide range of clinical activities and contributes to improved patient care outcomes.

Data Quality and Standardization

In the realm of healthcare, the effectiveness of AI models hinges significantly on the quality and standardization of the data they are trained on. High-quality, standardized data is crucial because AI systems rely on this data to learn, make predictions, and support decision-making processes. However, healthcare data often originates from a multitude of sources, each with varying formats and degrees of accuracy, which can lead to inconsistencies and challenges in data integration. To address these challenges, significant efforts must be made to standardize data collection practices across different healthcare settings. Standardization involves creating common protocols for data entry, storage, and exchange, ensuring that data from various sources is compatible and can be seamlessly integrated. This uniformity is essential for developing AI models that are robust, reliable, and applicable across different healthcare environments. Moreover, ensuring the quality of data is equally important. This means that data must be accurate, complete, and timely, reflecting the true state of patient health and healthcare processes. Quality control measures, such as regular audits, validation processes, and the use of advanced data cleaning techniques, are necessary to maintain the integrity of the data used for training AI. By focusing on improving data quality and standardization, healthcare organizations can enhance the training of AI models, making them more effective and capable of delivering accurate insights and predictions. This, in turn, supports better clinical decision-making and contributes to the overall improvement of patient care and healthcare operations.

Regulatory Approval and Compliance

Gaining regulatory approval for AI-based medical devices and software represents a complex and critical step in bringing these technologies into clinical use.

Developers of AI solutions in healthcare must navigate through rigorous approval processes established by regulatory bodies such as the FDA in the U.S. or the EMA in Europe. These organizations set stringent standards to ensure that medical technologies are safe and effective before they can be deployed in healthcare settings. The process involves a thorough evaluation of the AI system, including its design, development, intended use, and potential impacts on patient care. This evaluation is designed to assess not just the technical efficacy of the AI system but also its reliability, accuracy, and potential risks. For example, the FDA requires that AI-based devices demonstrate substantial equivalence to existing technologies or prove their safety and effectiveness through clinical trials, depending on the type of device and its application. Ensuring compliance with these regulatory standards is crucial for several reasons. Firstly, it safeguards patient safety by preventing the use of untested or unreliable technologies in sensitive clinical environments. Secondly, regulatory approval lends credibility to AI technologies, which can help in their adoption by healthcare providers wary of implementing new and relatively unproven tools. Moreover, compliance with regulatory standards often requires ongoing monitoring and reporting of the performance of AI systems, which can help in identifying any unforeseen issues or areas for improvement after the AI system has been deployed. This ongoing process helps maintain high standards of patient care and ensures that AI technologies continue to meet the evolving needs of healthcare providers and patients. Navigating these regulatory landscapes can be daunting, but it is a necessary step to ensure that AI technologies are both effective in clinical settings and meet the high safety standards required for medical devices and software. For developers, understanding and adhering to these regulatory requirements is essential to successfully bring AI solutions to market and gain acceptance in the healthcare community.

Public Perception and Patient Consent

Addressing public concerns about the use of AI in healthcare is crucial for its successful integration and acceptance. It is essential that patients are fully informed about how their data is used and the role AI plays in their care. This transparency is vital for building trust between healthcare providers and patients, especially given the sensitivity surrounding personal health information and the potential implications of AI decision-making. Obtaining patient consent is a fundamental aspect of this process. Patients must have a clear understanding of what data will be collected, how it will be used, and what aspects of their care are influenced by AI. This means providing easily understandable information and ensuring that consent is obtained in a way that respects patient autonomy and choice. Moreover, healthcare providers must be proactive in communicating the benefits and potential risks associated with AI technologies. By openly discussing how AI can improve diagnostic accuracy, personalize treatment plans, and enhance overall care efficiency, healthcare providers can help alleviate fears and misconceptions that patients might have about AI. Transparency goes beyond just obtaining consent; it involves an ongoing dialogue with patients about how AI technologies are being used and developed in healthcare settings. This can include sharing information about safeguards in place to protect patient data, the measures taken to ensure AI systems are unbiased, and how AI findings are integrated into clinical decision-making processes. By prioritizing patient consent and maintaining high standards of transparency, healthcare providers can foster a climate of trust and cooperation, which is essential for the ethical and effective use of AI in healthcare. This approach not only addresses public concerns but also enhances patient engagement and confidence in the healthcare services they receive.

Interoperability among Diverse Systems

Interoperability among diverse systems is a fundamental requirement for AI technologies in healthcare. AI systems need to be capable of working across various healthcare IT systems and platforms to ensure an efficient exchange and use of health information. This capability is crucial for facilitating better coordination of patient care, as it allows different systems to communicate seamlessly and share information without compatibility issues. For AI to be effective, it must integrate smoothly with the range of electronic health records, diagnostic tools, and management systems currently in use. This requires standardized data formats and protocols that enable data from one system to be understood and used by another, regardless of the software or technology platform. Achieving this level of interoperability often involves collaboration between technology developers, healthcare providers, and regulatory bodies to ensure that all systems adhere to common standards. The benefits of such interoperability are profound. It allows for a more holistic view of a patient's health history and current condition, enabling healthcare providers to make more informed decisions. This can lead to improved treatment outcomes, more personalized care plans, and a reduction in errors or duplicated efforts. Additionally, interoperable AI systems can help streamline operations across different healthcare facilities, improving efficiency and reducing administrative burdens.

Therefore, prioritizing interoperability in the development and implementation of AI systems in healthcare is essential. It not only enhances the functionality and effectiveness of these technologies but also supports a more integrated and patient-centered approach to healthcare delivery. By ensuring that AI systems can communicate across different platforms, healthcare providers can offer more coordinated and efficient care to their patients.

Continual Learning and Adaptation

AI systems in healthcare must be designed with the capability for continual learning and adaptation. This is essential to ensure that they remain relevant and effective over time, as medical knowledge and clinical practices are constantly evolving. AI tools that can adapt to new data and incorporate the latest medical discoveries and changes in clinical practices provide more accurate and up-to-date support for healthcare professionals. Continual learning in AI involves algorithms that can update themselves as they receive new data, without the need for human intervention. This feature allows AI systems to refine their models and improve their predictions based on the latest information, whether it's emerging trends in patient data or new treatment protocols. For instance, an AI system used in oncology might learn from recent clinical trials and automatically adjust its recommendations for cancer treatment. The ability to adapt is particularly important in a field like healthcare, where new diseases can emerge and existing conditions can evolve. AI systems that are flexible and can quickly adjust to new healthcare challenges are invaluable, helping providers stay on the cutting edge of medical practice. However, ensuring that AI systems continue to learn and adapt in a controlled and reliable manner requires careful oversight. This involves regular updates and checks to ensure that the learning process aligns with ethical guidelines and clinical standards. It also requires the systems to be transparent enough that healthcare providers can understand and trust the basis for AI-generated recommendations. Incorporating continual learning and adaptation capabilities in AI tools is therefore crucial for sustaining their usefulness in the dynamic field of healthcare. It helps ensure that these technologies continue to support healthcare providers by providing insights that are both current and clinically relevant, ultimately leading to better patient outcomes.

Measuring Outcomes and Impact

Establishing clear metrics to measure the outcomes and impact of AI in healthcare is crucial for understanding its effectiveness and refining its applications. These metrics should encompass evaluations of improvements in patient outcomes, cost savings, and operational efficiencies. By setting up these benchmarks, healthcare organizations can not only assess the performance of AI tools but also demonstrate their value and justify further investments in AI technology. Measuring patient outcomes is one of the most critical metrics. This involves tracking how AI implementations affect the accuracy of diagnoses, the effectiveness of treatments, and overall patient health improvements. For example, an AI system designed to predict patient deterioration can be evaluated based on its ability to reduce adverse events and improve patient survival rates. Cost savings are another essential metric, particularly in today's healthcare environment where budget constraints are a significant concern. AI tools can be evaluated based on their ability to streamline administrative processes, reduce the need for unnecessary tests or treatments, and decrease hospital readmission rates, all of which contribute to financial savings. Operational efficiencies are also vital to measure. AI's impact on reducing the time healthcare professionals spend on administrative tasks, improving the speed of patient data processing, and optimizing resource allocation are all crucial metrics. For instance, an AI-driven scheduling system can be assessed by its ability to minimize wait times and enhance patient throughput. Regular assessment of these metrics is important for continuous improvement. It allows healthcare providers to identify areas where AI tools may be underperforming and make necessary adjustments. Regular evaluation also helps in demonstrating the tangible benefits of AI to both stakeholders and regulators, supporting broader adoption and investment. Overall, establishing and regularly assessing outcome and impact metrics for AI in healthcare not only ensures that the technology meets its intended goals but also fosters an environment of continuous learning and improvement. This approach is essential for maximizing the benefits of AI in enhancing healthcare delivery and patient care.

Balancing Automation with Human Oversight

While AI can automate many tasks within healthcare, maintaining a balance with human oversight is crucial, especially in critical decision-making processes. This balance ensures that AI assists healthcare professionals rather than replacing the essential human elements of patient care, such as empathy, ethical judgment, and interpersonal communication (Mhlanga 2023a; Mlanga 2023c). AI technologies have the capability to streamline various healthcare operations, from diagnostic processes to administrative tasks, enhancing efficiency and accuracy. However, these systems operate based on algorithms and data patterns, which, while powerful, lack the nuanced understanding that human professionals bring to patient care. For instance, while an AI might accurately diagnose a disease from imaging data, a healthcare professional can better understand and manage patient concerns and expectations about their diagnosis and treatment. Human oversight in AI-driven processes ensures that decision-making remains grounded in clinical expertise and ethical considerations Mlanga 2023c. It allows healthcare professionals to review and interpret AI-generated recommendations and decide whether they align with individual patient needs. For example, a doctor might use AI recommendations as a second opinion but will make the final treatment decision considering the patient's medical history, personal preferences, and overall health context. Maintaining this balance also safeguards against potential errors or biases that AI systems might propagate. Human oversight can identify anomalies or ethical concerns that AI might overlook, providing an essential check to ensure that patient care remains safe and effective. Thus, integrating AI into healthcare requires a careful approach where automation is used to enhance, not replace, human skills and insights. This synergy between human oversight and AI capabilities can lead to improved healthcare outcomes, where technology supports professionals in delivering more personalized, efficient, and compassionate care.

Developing Collaborative Frameworks

Developing collaborative frameworks is essential for the successful implementation of AI in healthcare. Effective collaboration among healthcare providers, AI developers, regulators, and patients ensures that AI technologies are designed, deployed, and monitored in ways that maximize their benefits and minimize potential risks. Creating such frameworks involves establishing channels and protocols for continuous communication and cooperation among all stakeholders involved. This collaboration can facilitate the sharing of best practices, resources, and expertise, leading to more innovative and effective AI solutions. For instance, healthcare providers can share insights on clinical needs and practical challenges, while AI developers can provide technological expertise to address these needs efficiently. Regulators play a crucial role in ensuring that AI technologies adhere to safety and privacy standards, offering guidance on compliance issues. By being part of the collaborative framework, they can help shape the development of AI tools to align with legal and ethical standards from the outset, rather than attempting to retrofit compliance after development. Involving patients in these frameworks is equally important, as it ensures that their needs and concerns are considered in the AI development process. Patient involvement can help tailor AI systems to be more user-friendly and focused on improving patient outcomes, enhancing acceptance and trust in AI technologies. Such collaborative frameworks also provide a platform for sharing resources, such as data for training AI systems, and expertise in managing and analyzing this data. This shared approach not only improves the quality and efficiency of AI development but also helps in overcoming common barriers to AI implementation, such as data silos and lack of interoperability among different healthcare IT systems. Overall, developing collaborative frameworks is key to fostering a cooperative environment where the benefits of AI in healthcare can be fully realized. This approach ensures that all parties contribute to and benefit from AI innovations, leading to more effective healthcare solutions and better patient care outcomes.

Conclusion

To overcome the obstacles to AI implementation in healthcare, a thorough strategy is needed that tackles the technological, ethical, regulatory, and cultural difficulties. Technological progress, such as enhanced algorithms for safeguarding data privacy and novel integration protocols, is crucial in promoting the acceptance of AI. Additionally, collaborative frameworks guarantee that the creation of AI tools is a cooperative endeavor including all parties involved. Furthermore, the provision of government assistance through policy modifications and economic incentives is essential for establishing an environment that fosters the integration of artificial intelligence. Periodic evaluations of AI's results and effects are crucial for improving these tools and showcasing their worth, guaranteeing that AI functions as a powerful catalyst for promoting global health and well-being. By effectively navigating the intricacies and utilizing interdisciplinary collaborations, the healthcare industry can fully utilize the power of AI to revolutionize the way treatment is provided, improve patient results, and optimize operational effectiveness. This chapter not only identifies the challenges to implementing AI in healthcare but also offers practical advice and ways to effectively overcome these obstacles.

References

Achour, S.L., Dojat, M., Rieux, C., Bierling, P. and Lepage, E. (2001). A UMLS-based knowledge acquisition tool for rule-based clinical decision support system development. Journal of the American Medical Informatics Association, 8(4), 351–60.

Alowais, S.A., Alghamdi, S.S., Alsuhebany, N., Alqahtani, T., Alshaya, A.I., Almohareb, S.N., ... and Albekairy, A.M. (2023). Revolutionizing healthcare: The role of artificial intelligence in clinical practice. BMC Medical Education, 23(1), 689.

Alloghani, M., Alani, M.M., Al-Jumeily, D., Baker, T., Mustafina, J., Hussain, A. and Aljaaf, A.J. (2019). A systematic review on the status and progress of homomorphic encryption technologies. Journal of Information Security and Applications, 48, 102362.

Anderson, L.A., and Dedrick, R.F. (1990). Development of the Trust in Physician Scale: A Measure to Assess Interpersonal Trust in Patient-Physician Relationships. Psychological Reports, 67(3_suppl), 1091–1100. https://doi.org/10.2466/pr0.1990.67.3f.1091

Arora, N.K., Fatima, T., Mishra, I., Verma, M., Mishra, J. and Mishra, V. (2018). Environmental sustainability: challenges and viable solutions. Environmental Sustainability, 1, 309–40.

Bianco, M. (2021). *Overcoming the Social Barriers of AI Adoption*. Master Thesis, Eindhoven University of Technology.

Bodorik, P., Pyra, J. and Riordon, J.S. (1990, July). Correcting execution of distributed queries. In Proceedings of the second international symposium on Databases in parallel and distributed systems (pp. 192–201).

Burger, J., Chapman, R. and Villanustre, F. (2011). Parallel Processing, Multiprocessors and Virtualization in Data-Intensive Computing. In Handbook of Data Intensive Computing (pp. 235–248). New York, NY: Springer New York.

Castañeda, H., Holmes, S.M., Madrigal, D.S., Young, M.E.D., Beyeler, N. and Quesada, J. (2015). Immigration as a social determinant of health. Annual review of public health, 36(1), 375–92.

Coppola, D., Lauritano, C., Palma Esposito, F., Riccio, G., Rizzo, C. and de Pascale, D. (2021). Fish waste: From problem to valuable resource. Marine drugs, 19(2), 116.

Dai, A. (2013). Increasing drought under global warming in observations and models. Nature climate change, 3(1), 52–58.

Davenport, T., Guha, A., Grewal, D. and Bressgott, T. (2020). How artificial intelligence will change the future of marketing. Journal of the Academy of Marketing Science, 48, 24–42.

El-Sappagh, S.H. and El-Masri, S. (2014). A distributed clinical decision support system architecture. Journal of King Saud University-Computer and Information Sciences, 26(1), 69–78.

Garrison, L.E. (1970). Development of continental shelf south of New England. AAPG Bulletin, 54(1), 109–24.

Gupta, A., Gonzalez-Rojas, Y., Juarez, E., Crespo Casal, M., Moya, J., Falci, D.R., ... and Shapiro, A.E. (2021). Early treatment for COVID-19 with SARS-CoV-2 neutralizing antibody sotrovimab. New England Journal of Medicine, 385(21), 1941–50.

Haider, H. (2020). Barriers to the adoption of artificial intelligence in healthcare in India.

Jha, A.P., Morrison, A.B., Parker, S.C. and Stanley, E.A. (2017). Practice is protective: Mindfulness training promotes cognitive resilience in high-stress cohorts. Mindfulness, 8, 46–58.

Jung, H., von Sternberg, K. and Davis, K. (2016). Expanding a measure of mental health literacy: Development and validation of a multicomponent mental health literacy measure. Psychiatry research, 243, 278–86.

Langer, J.A. (2011). Envisioning knowledge: Building literacy in the academic disciplines. Teachers College Press.

Manvelidze, A.B. (2013). The use of multi component software solutions in distributed information systems. In Information Technologies in Economy, Education and Business (pp. 5–6)

Mathur, P. and Geerts, B. (2023). *Barriers and Solutions to Adoption of AI in Healthcare*. In: *Translational Application of Artificial Intelligence in Healthcare* (pp. 71–81). Chapman and Hall/CRC.

McHenry, H.M. (1994). Behavioral ecological implications of early hominid body size. Journal of Human Evolution, 27(1-3), 77–87.

Meng, F., Hennink, W.E. and Zhong, Z. (2009). Reduction-sensitive polymers and bioconjugates for biomedical applications. Biomaterials, *30*(12), 2180–98.

Mhlanga, D. (2021). Artificial intelligence in the industry 4.0, and its impact on poverty, innovation, infrastructure development, and the sustainable development goals: Lessons from emerging economies? *Sustainability, 13*(11), 5788.

Mhlanga, D. (2022a). The role of artificial intelligence and machine learning amid the COVID-19 pandemic: What lessons are we learning on 4IR and the sustainable development goals. *International Journal of Environmental Research and Public Health, 19*(3), 1879.

Mhlanga, D. (2022b). Human-centered artificial intelligence: The superlative approach to achieve sustainable development goals in the fourth industrial revolution. *Sustainability, 14*(13), 7804.

Mhlanga, D. (2022c). The role of financial inclusion and FinTech in addressing climate-related challenges in the industry 4.0: Lessons for sustainable development goals. *Frontiers in Climate, 4*, 949178.

Mhlanga, D. (2023a). Financial Technology, Artificial Intelligence, and the Health Sector, Lessons We are Learning on Good Health and Well-Being. In: *FinTech and Artificial Intelligence for Sustainable Development: The Role of Smart Technologies in Achieving Development Goals* (pp. 145–170). Cham: Springer Nature Switzerland.

Mhlanga, D. (2023b). Block chain technology for digital financial inclusion in the industry 4.0, towards sustainable development? *Frontiers in Blockchain, 6*, 1035405.

Montague, E.N., Winchester III, W.W. and Kleiner, B.M. (2010). Trust in medical technology by patients and healthcare providers in obstetric work systems. Behaviour & information technology, *29*(5), 541–54.

Najjar, M., Alsurakji, I.H., El-Qanni, A. and Nour, A.I. (2023). The role of blockchain technology in the integration of sustainability practices across multi-tier supply networks: implications and potential complexities. Journal of Sustainable Finance & Investment, *13*(1), 744–62.

Pan, X., Slater, M., Beacco, A., Navarro, X., Bellido Rivas, A.I., Swapp, D., ... and Delacroix, S. (2016). The responses of medical general practitioners to unreasonable patient demand for antibiotics-a study of medical ethics using immersive virtual reality. PloS one, *11*(2), e0146837.

Patokar, A.M. and Gohokar, V.V. (2018). Precision agriculture system design using wireless sensor network. In Information and Communication Technology: Proceedings of ICICT 2016 (pp. 169–177). Springer Singapore.

Pesapane, F., Codari, M. and Sardanelli, F. (2018). Artificial intelligence in medical imaging: threat or opportunity? Radiologists again at the forefront of innovation in medicine. European radiology experimental, 2, 1–10.

Pinto-Coelho, L., Laska-Leśniewicz, A., Pereira, E.T. and Sztobryn-Giercuszkiewicz, J. (2023). Inclusion and adaptation beyond disability: Using virtual reality to foster empathy. Medycyna Pracy, *74*(1), 171–85.

Richmond, J., Boynton, M.H., Ozawa, S., Muessig, K.E., Cykert, S. and Ribisl, K.M. (2022). Development and validation of the trust in my doctor, trust in doctors in general, and trust in the health care team scales. Social science & medicine, 298, 114827.

Robie, D. (2012). 'Drugs, guns and gangs': Case studies on Pacific states and how they deploy NZ media regulators. Pacific Journalism Review, *18*(1), 105–27.

Stylios, G., Katsis, C.D. and Christodoulakis, D. (2014). Using Bio-inspired intelligence for Web opinion Mining. International Journal of Computer Applications, *87*(5).

Thom, D.H., Wong, S.T., Guzman, D., Wu, A., Penko, J., Miaskowski, C. and Kushel, M. (2011). Physician trust in the patient: development and validation of a new measure. The Annals of Family Medicine, *9*(2), 148–54.

Thrall, J.H., Li, X., Li, Q., Cruz, C., Do, S., Dreyer, K. and Brink, J. (2018). Artificial intelligence and machine learning in radiology: opportunities, challenges, pitfalls, and criteria for success. Journal of the American College of Radiology, *15*(3), 504–508.

Tyson, R.V., Treadwell, D.D. and Simonne, E.H. (2011). Opportunities and challenges to sustainability in aquaponic systems. HortTechnology, 21(1), 6–13.

Verykios, V.S. and Gkoulalas-Divanis, A. (2008). A survey of association rule hiding methods for privacy. Privacy-Preserving Data Mining: Models and Algorithms, 267–89.

Yang, C., Park, H. and Heo, J. (2010). A network analysis of interdisciplinary research relationships: the Korean government's R&D grant program. Scientometrics, *83*(1), 77–92.

Yates, P. M. and Bishop, I.D. (1998). The integration of existing GIS and modelling systems: with urban applications. Computers, environment and urban systems, *22*(1), 71–80.

Yesha, Y., Janeja, V.P., Rishe, N. and Yesha, Y. (2014, September). Personalized decision support system to enhance evidence based medicine through big data analytics. In 2014 IEEE International Conference on Healthcare Informatics (pp. 376–376). IEEE.

13 | AI in Hospital Administration, Revolutionizing Healthcare
A Conclusion

This chapter presents a thorough summary of the significant influence of artificial intelligence (AI) in hospital administration, examining its use in several areas of healthcare management. The incorporation of AI technology into hospital settings is transforming several procedures, ranging from patient care to resource management, as the technology continues to improve. This chapter provides an overview of the book's organization, emphasizing important chapters that examine the incorporation of AI in many domains, including patient scheduling, electronic health records, medical imaging, and clinical decision support systems. The chapter also addresses the difficulties and moral deliberations involved in applying AI in healthcare settings. This chapter provides a glimpse into the ideas and in-depth debates presented in the book. It serves as a conclusion to the book, emphasizing the importance of AI technologies in improving operational efficiency and patient outcomes in hospital management.

Introduction

The book *AI in Hospital Administration Revolutionizing Healthcare* investigates the transformational potential of artificial intelligence (AI) in the field of hospital administration and the enormous impact that AI has had on the process of redefining healthcare. AI has emerged as a powerful instrument in the healthcare sector, with the capacity to enhance and optimize numerous areas of healthcare administration (Le et al., 2018; Santosh and Gaur, 2022; Harry, 2023; Mhlanga, 2024). This is due to the fact that AI has the ability to improve and optimize a number of different parts of healthcare administration. According to Mhlanga (2021), Santosh and Gaur (2022), and Mhlanga (2022), these components include the following: the provision of medical treatment to patients; the distribution of resources; the methodologies used to make choices; and the efficiency of operational procedures. There are considerable opportunities and problems for healthcare systems on a global scale that are presented by the extensive integration of AI in hospital administration (Li et al., 2021; Yaqoob et al., 2021). In order to maximize the outcomes for patients and effectively distribute resources, healthcare organizations need to implement management and decision-making processes that are simplified. This is because of the complex and ever-changing nature of these companies. When it comes to achieving these criteria, however, standard administrative procedures can often be difficult to implement. This can lead to problems such as extended waiting times, inefficient scheduling, erroneous projections, and inappropriate resource allocation.

The possible applications of AI in the healthcare industry have been thoroughly investigated by researchers who have published their findings in academically scholarly journals. To be more specific, researchers have focused their attention on the medical imaging, clinical decision support systems, and illness detection applications that could potentially benefit from AI. According to the references Mhlanga (2023a, b, and c), these studies were carried out by Yan et al. in the year 2006, Malmir et al. in the year 2017, Sutton et al. in the year 2020, and Mhlanga in the year 2023. The role of AI in hospital management has not been adequately examined, despite the fact that there have been substantial breakthroughs and achievements in these sectors. Providing unique insights into the specific challenges encountered by hospital administration and how AI can be effectively deployed to address these problems is the goal of this book, which intends to overcome the information gap by delivering valuable insights. A comprehensive analysis of the existing hospital management practices is carried out in this book. This analysis is carried out by analyzing the academic material that is already available and identifying the most pressing difficulties and constraints. In this article, the complications of managing patient transportation, optimizing resource allocation, assuring effective staff scheduling, and building decision-making procedures that are driven by data are discussed. Furthermore, it investigates the ways in which AI-powered solutions could potentially ease these issues and undergo a revolution in the healthcare industry. This book makes use of research from a variety of fields and conducts an in-depth investigation into an array of advanced AI technologies, including machine learning, natural language processing, and predictive analytics, as well as their practical applications in the management of hospitals. In addition, the essay examines the ethical implications and potential difficulties that are involved with the implementation of AI in the healthcare industry. These difficulties include concerns around privacy, data security, and the human-machine interaction.

Through the presentation of real-world case studies and successfully implemented instances of artificial intelligence in hospital management, this book offers valuable insights that may be put into practice. This program provides healthcare workers, administrators, legislators, and academics with the information and skills necessary to effectively harness AI, stimulate innovation, and facilitate positive transformation in healthcare organizations. It is addressed in the book *AI in Hospital Administration: Revolutionizing Healthcare* that there is a dearth of academic material on the impact that AI makes on hospital management. The purpose of this book is to encourage additional research, provide a platform for making decisions that are well-informed, and build the basis for a future in which AI plays a significant role in improving hospital management. This objective is accomplished by putting emphasis on the description of the problems and providing solutions that are practical.

The book titled *AI in Hospital Administration: Revolutionizing Healthcare* investigates the revolutionary potential of AI in the field of hospital administration and the tremendous impact that it has on the process of modernizing healthcare. In order to investigate cutting-edge AI technology and how it may be utilized in hospital administration, this book makes use of both established scholarly literature and research from a variety of disciplines. Following an explanation of the fundamental principles of AI, the book delves into the pressing difficulties that hospital administrators are confronted with. These challenges include waiting times that are too long, scheduling that is inefficient, erroneous forecasting, and inadequate resource allocation. An emphasis is placed in the statement on the significance of utilizing efficient management and decision-making processes in order to maximize the outcomes for patients while simultaneously ensuring that resources are utilized in an appropriate manner. The application of AI in hospital management has received limited amount of research attention, despite the fact that major improvements have been made in AI in fields such as clinical decision support systems and medical imaging. The purpose of this book is to address this deficiency by analyzing the complexity involved in managing patient mobility, improving resource allocation, assuring optimal staff scheduling, and developing decision-making procedures that are driven by data. Machine learning, natural language processing, and predictive analytics are just some of the AI-driven solutions that are investigated in this book. The book also examines the capacity of these solutions to address the difficulties stated above. In addition to this, they address the ethical concerns and potential obstacles that are involved with the implementation of artificial intelligence in the healthcare industry. These concerns include issues pertaining to privacy, data security, and the relationship between humans and technologies. The book contributes to the dissemination of pragmatic ideas by incorporating concrete case studies and examples of successful applications of AI in hospital administration. This effort provides healthcare practitioners, administrators, policymakers, and researchers with the information and tools they need to effectively deploy AI, stimulate innovation, and drive innovations that are beneficial to healthcare organizations. The absence of scholarly literature on the influence of AI on hospital administration is the focus of the book *AI in Hospital Management: Revolutionizing Healthcare*, which aims to overcome this literature gap. This resource provides a full overview of the opportunities, constraints, and issues that are currently present in this sector. It encourages further exploration and makes it possible to make decisions based on accurate information. Throughout the course of the book, a hypothetical future is presented in which AI significantly improves the administration of healthcare.

The author of this book presents a comprehensive review of the substantial impact that AI can have on the management of hospitals. The various applications of artificial intelligence, the potential ramifications that it may bring, and the future of healthcare management are all topics that are discussed in this article. A brief introduction to the fundamental principles of AI is provided at the beginning of the work. This introduction covers a variety of significant concepts, including machine learning, deep learning, and natural language processing. These fundamental components provide the framework for comprehending how AI might be utilized to improve hospital management and the care that is provided to patients. Following the chapter that serves as an introduction, the book delves further into a number of applications of AI in the medical field. When it comes to patient management and scheduling, this essay takes a look at the most advanced AI systems now available, stressing their ability to improve efficiency and optimize resource allocation. The purpose of this analysis is to investigate the mutually beneficial relationship that exists between AI and electronic health records (EHRs), with a particular focus on how the integration of these two technologies improves data management and encourages better informed decisions regarding patient care. In addition to this, the book dives into the vital significance of AI in the field of medical imaging and diagnostics, highlighting the profound impact that AI has on enhancing diagnostic accuracy and operational efficiency.

In the following chapter of the book, the author discusses how AI can be utilized in predictive analytics and risk assessment. This article shows the ways in which these technologies can improve the proactive management of patient therapy and predict the consequences of healthcare delivery. In addition to this, the essay dives into the considerable impact that AI has had on the distribution and enhancement of resources in hospitals, including case studies and examples of successful applications. The implementation of AI into clinical decision support systems is the subject of this book, which also provides an illustration of how AI assists medical professionals in making more informed decisions on patient care. Disease diagnosis and the application of AI in hospital management are both topics that are covered in this text. The text places an emphasis on the ability of AI to simplify procedures and enhance the precision of diagnoses. In the field of healthcare finance and billing, AI is being utilized to improve efficiency, accuracy, and compliance with regulatory standards. Additionally, the book investigates the ethical implications and difficulties that are linked with the implementation of AI in the healthcare industry. Issues such as privacy, data security, and the requirement for transparency are among the themes that are examined. Towards the end of the book, the author performs an analysis of the difficulties that are encountered while applying AI in the medical field and offers suggestions for how these obstacles might be addressed. The following article makes forecasts on impending developments and emerging trends in AI-powered healthcare, and it projects the potential impact that these advances may have on hospital operations and the healthcare industry as a whole.

Presented below is a comprehensive synopsis of the book, with the initial chapters laying the groundwork for a better understanding of the role that AI plays in the medical field. In this essay, the potential of AI to increase both efficiency and patient care is presented. An overview of the subsequent chapters and the primary themes presented in them is provided here. The fundamental concepts of AI are discussed in this text. Some of the topics covered are machine learning, deep learning, and natural language processing. It is possible to gain a solid foundation for comprehending the more complex applications that are discussed later on in the book by utilizing these notions. Following that, the focus shifts to the particular applications of AI that enhance the functioning of hospitals. The essay places an emphasis on the substantial breakthroughs that have been made in patient management and scheduling, describing how these technologies have improved the efficiency of operating procedures. The investigation into the possibility of incorporating AI into EHRs is being conducted with the intention of enhancing patient care and data management. Throughout the course of the article, the enormous impact that AI has had on medical imaging and diagnostics is discussed. The potential of AI and predictive analytics in the healthcare industry is also investigated, specifically with regard to risk assessment and the early diagnosis of diseases. The influence of AI on the distribution of resources and the optimization of those resources in hospitals is investigated in this article. Moreover, it investigates the ways in which AI might enhance clinical decision support systems, hence resulting in more accurate decision-making in clinical contexts.

Following that, we talk about the greater significance of AI in the healthcare industry as well as the challenges that come along with its application. It is proved that AI can be utilized in disease identification, which results in an improvement in the efficiency and accuracy of medical diagnostics. The topic of discussion centers on the application of AI in hospital finance and billing, with the objective of improving financial operations and streamlining administrative procedures. This article deliberates upon the ethical implications of AI in the healthcare industry. It includes a discussion on the challenges that arise, issues over privacy, and the necessity of maintaining transparency and accountability in the implementation of AI. In the later chapters, the attention shifts to the future and the tactics that might be used to overcome the challenges that are preventing the widespread use of AI in the healthcare industry, and answers to these challenges are offered. At the end of the book, a concise overview of the discussions is presented, and the author emphasizes the key role that AI plays in the transformation of hospital administration.

Conclusion

This chapter finishes by restating the important role of AI in revolutionizing hospital administration. The book has provided a comprehensive plan outlining the material, with a focus on each chapter exploring distinct AI applications and their effects on healthcare administration. The capacity of AI to tackle conventional issues in hospital environments, such as ineffective distribution of resources and patient administration are highlighted. Additionally, it emphasizes the need for continuous research, ethical deliberations, and strategic execution in order to effectively utilize the full potential of AI. The final chapter not only introduces readers to the concept of AI in hospital management but also prepares them for a more thorough examination of its practical applications throughout the book, ultimately illustrating the crucial role of AI in molding the future of healthcare.

References

Harry, A. (2023). The Future of Medicine: Harnessing the Power of AI for Revolutionizing Healthcare. *International Journal of Multidisciplinary Sciences and Arts*, 2(1), 36–47.

Le, D.N., Van Le, C., Tromp, J.G. and Nguyen, G.N. (Eds.). (2018). *Emerging Technologies for Health and Medicine: Virtual Reality, Augmented Reality, Artificial Intelligence, Internet of Things, Robotics, Industry 4.0.* (297 pp.). Texas USA: Scrivener Publishing, LLC.

Li, J.P.O., Liu, H., Ting, D.S., Jeon, S., Chan, R.P., Kim, J.E., ... and Ting, D.S. (2021). Digital technology, tele-medicine, and artificial intelligence in ophthalmology: A global perspective. *Progress in Retinal and Eye Research*, 82, 100900.

Malmir, B., Amini, M. and Chang, S.I. (2017). A medical decision support system for disease diagnosis under uncertainty. *Expert Systems with Applications*, 88, 95–108.

Mhlanga, D. (2024).Generative AI for Emerging Researchers: The Promises, Ethics, and Risks. *Ethics, and Risks* (February 24.)) *SSRN*, 4737492.

Mhlanga, D. (2023a). Artificial Intelligence in Elderly Care: Navigating Ethical and Responsible AI Adoption for Seniors. *SSRN*, 4675564.

Mhlanga, D. (2023b). Financial Technology, Artificial Intelligence, and the Health Sector, Lessons We are Learning on Good Health and Well-Being. In: *FinTech and Artificial Intelligence for Sustainable Development: The Role of Smart Technologies in Achieving Development Goals* (pp. 145–70). Cham: Springer Nature Switzerland.

Mhlanga, D. (2023c). FinTech and Financial Inclusion: Application of AI to the Problem of Financial Exclusion What are the Challenges. In: *FinTech and Artificial Intelligence for Sustainable Development*. Sustainable Development Goals Series. Cham: Palgrave Macmillan. https://doi.org/10.1007/978-3-031-37776-1_14.

Mhlanga, D. (2022). Human-centered artificial intelligence: The superlative approach to achieve sustainable development goals in the fourth industrial revolution. *Sustainability*, 14(13), 7804.

Mhlanga, D. (2021). A Dynamic Analysis of the Demand for Healthcare in Post-apartheid South Africa. *Nursing Reports*, 11(02), 484–94.

Santosh, K.C. and Gaur, L. (2022). *Artificial Intelligence and Machine Learning in Public Healthcare: Opportunities and Societal Impact*. Springer Nature.

Sutton, R.T., Pincock, D., Baumgart, D.C., Sadowski, D.C., Fedorak, R.N. and Kroeker, K.I. (2020). An overview of clinical decision support systems: Benefits, risks, and strategies for success. *NPJ Digital Medicine*, 3(1), 17.

Yan, H., Jiang, Y., Zheng, J., Peng, C. and Li, Q. (2006). A multilayer perceptron-based medical decision support system for heart disease diagnosis. *Expert Systems with Applications*, 30(2), 272–81.

Yaqoob, I., Salah, K., Jayaraman, R. and Al-Hammadi, Y. (2021). Blockchain for healthcare data management: Opportunities, challenges, and future recommendations. *Neural Computing and Applications*, 1–16.

Index

A

Accountability 13, 24, 101, 102, 137, 138, 180, 181, 184, 186, 191, 203, 219
Administration 1-5, 31, 45, 71, 87, 109, 116, 130, 143, 144, 154, 175, 187, 190, 215-217, 219
Adoption Barriers 194, 200
AI Adoption 194, 198, 200
AI Algorithms 21, 22, 36, 38, 40-45, 52-57, 60, 61, 64, 73, 74, 78, 80-83, 85, 91-93, 96-98, 101, 106, 107, 112, 116, 120, 123, 125, 129, 136, 140, 145, 151, 165, 169, 203
AI Applications 5, 24, 64, 68, 75, 101, 102, 145, 147, 154, 163, 181, 184, 190, 199, 201, 205, 219
AI Challenges 85, 89
AI Ethics 13, 24
AI History 36, 168
AI Impact 4, 7, 13, 43, 76, 203
AI Implementation 2, 3, 191, 197, 209, 211
AI in Healthcare 1-4, 6, 53, 55, 61, 69, 89, 90, 112, 125, 128, 135, 137, 144, 150, 159, 161, 169, 175, 177, 183-188, 195, 196, 200, 203, 205
AI in Radiology 76
AI Integration 145, 191, 195, 197, 198
AI Models 15, 56, 62, 74, 86, 98, 115, 123, 126, 130, 137, 149, 151, 152, 163, 182, 189, 199, 206
AI Revolution 6, 80
AI Solutions 28, 32, 34, 36, 201, 204, 205, 207, 211
AI Tools 39, 41, 43, 57, 64, 74, 77, 85, 94, 97-99, 131, 135, 145, 146, 148, 152, 170, 171, 184, 185, 190, 191, 201, 205, 208, 209
AI Transparency 207
Artificial Intelligence (AI) 1, 4, 6, 7, 15, 16, 28, 49, 52, 68, 72, 73, 89, 112, 120, 123, 143, 159, 180, 194, 211, 215
Assessment 3, 8, 12, 30, 39, 78, 83, 85, 86, 89, 90, 123, 125, 136, 168, 180, 183, 190, 218

B

Background 19, 35, 62, 86, 131, 160, 186, 188, 190, 204
Barriers 20, 21, 33, 61, 64, 100, 124, 139, 194, 198, 199, 211
Bias in AI 101, 137, 183
Billing 3, 4, 43, 50, 159, 161, 175, 176, 200, 218, 219
Billing Systems 160, 162, 165

C

Change Management 135, 195
Clinical Decision Support 1-4, 33, 60, 94, 95, 120, 122, 123, 130, 196, 216-218
Cost Reduction 107, 133, 164, 172, 173, 174

D

Data Analytics 96, 108, 117, 120, 123, 139, 161, 169
Data Governance 90, 101
Data Management 3, 49, 51, 52, 65, 162, 195, 201, 218, 219
Data Mining 68, 122, 196
Data Security 2-4, 49, 51, 74, 136, 148, 154, 175, 176, 180, 191, 196, 198, 217, 218
Decision Support 1, 2, 33, 51, 54, 60, 94, 95, 120-125, 128, 130, 131, 140, 165, 196, 215, 216
Decision-Making 1-3, 6, 12, 16, 23, 28, 40, 43, 50, 54, 63, 64, 73, 75, 78-81, 89, 91, 94, 101, 105-107, 117, 120, 122-125, 127, 131, 135, 138-140, 143, 145, 164, 173, 180, 181, 184, 186, 196, 197, 203, 204, 206, 207, 210, 215-217, 219
Deep Learning 3, 4, 6, 7, 13-16, 60, 72, 74, 82, 88, 91, 92, 123, 127, 144-147, 149, 150, 152, 154, 218
Definition 7

Diagnosis Accuracy 146
Diagnostic Tools 38, 44, 77, 181, 184, 188, 200, 208
Diagnostics 3, 4, 41, 44, 54, 68, 69, 74, 75, 77, 78, 84-87, 95, 105, 127, 128, 132, 143, 146-148, 153, 164, 162, 184, 200, 218, 219
Disease Diagnosis 3, 63, 89, 143-145, 152, 154, 218

E

Efficiency Improvement 164
Electronic Health Records 1, 3, 30, 44, 49, 50, 52, 74, 79, 94, 112, 115, 133, 150, 161, 181, 208, 215, 218
Electronic Health Records (EHR) 1, 3, 30, 44, 49, 74, 79, 94, 112, 133, 150, 161, 181, 208, 215, 218
Ethical AI 4, 56, 100, 180
Ethical Considerations 1, 3-7, 15, 24, 54, 55, 74, 89, 101, 128, 134, 138, 143, 151, 169, 187, 189, 191, 194, 195, 210

F

Fraud Detection 159, 160, 163, 166, 176
Future of AI 9, 13, 102, 139, 146
Future Trends 35, 95, 96, 117, 163, 167, 173
Futuristic Perspective 120, 121, 123

H

Healthcare 1-5, 80, 82, 83, 95, 108, 109, 131, 144
Healthcare Analytics 84
Healthcare Data 40, 49, 50, 52, 53, 169, 199, 201, 206
Healthcare Efficiency 45, 58, 122, 133, 134
Healthcare Finance 3, 4, 159, 161, 163, 164, 166
Healthcare Forecasting 61
Healthcare Innovation 61, 110
Healthcare Management 1, 3, 5, 31, 93, 113, 117, 128, 129, 150, 215, 217
Healthcare Predictive 53, 84
Healthcare Regulation 163, 167, 174, 205
Healthcare Transformation 2, 3, 51, 159
History 29, 36, 37, 40, 50, 54, 55, 92-94, 100, 122, 123, 125, 134, 136, 146, 153, 164, 166, 171, 208
Hospital 1, 2, 75, 92, 96, 105, 107, 182, 187
Hospital Administration 1, 2, 143, 154, 187, 215
Hospital Management 1-3, 6, 39, 110, 143, 216

I

Image Recognition 15, 18

Informed Consent 137, 185, 186
Interoperability 50, 51, 58, 65, 129, 151, 196, 199, 208, 211

M

Machine Learning 2-4, 6, 9, 10, 13, 16, 21, 60, 62, 63, 71, 88, 90, 92, 107, 109, 112, 114, 121-123, 125, 143-145, 150, 167, 169, 173, 185, 195, 199, 216-218
Management 1-6, 24, 28, 29, 30, 32-34, 37-40, 59, 63, 65, 74, 78, 81, 83, 89, 91-99, 105-107, 109-115, 128-131, 159, 160, 173, 175, 180, 195
Medical Imaging 1-4, 68, 71, 72, 75, 124, 127, 146, 163, 173, 195, 200, 215-219

N

Natural Language Processing (NLP) 2-4, 6, 10, 19, 53, 123, 131, 165, 216-218
Neural Networks 7, 9, 10, 12-14, 16, 72, 153, 154

O

Operational Efficiency 1, 28, 32, 33, 35, 39, 45, 69, 84, 94, 95, 105-108, 110-114, 116, 135, 161, 164, 166-168, 171, 173-175, 202, 204, 218
Optimization 4, 31, 33, 81, 89, 95, 96, 101, 105, 107, 109, 219

P

Patient 1-7, 16, 22, 24, 28, 29, 72, 74-81, 101, 149, 160, 161, 170, 182, 190
Patient Care 1, 3, 4, 29, 31, 34, 38, 64, 65, 69, 72, 75, 79, 82, 87, 89, 92, 94, 95, 99, 102, 105, 109, 111, 135, 139, 143, 145, 149, 151, 154, 161, 162, 164, 166, 172, 173, 177, 180, 184, 186, 188, 190, 191, 194, 195, 197, 198, 203, 204, 207, 208
Patient Data 40, 49, 51, 52, 54, 55, 59, 60, 74, 81, 82, 91, 93, 94, 98, 99, 101, 112, 121, 124, 130, 133, 150, 162, 173, 176, 181, 182, 191, 197, 200
Patient Monitoring 44, 85, 97, 109, 121, 130, 173, 200
Patient Outcomes 1, 2, 6, 16, 22, 29, 33, 37, 40, 49, 50, 54-57, 60, 72, 74-78, 80, 84, 86, 88, 90, 92, 95, 96, 150, 151, 163, 173, 180, 183, 185, 188, 191, 195, 196, 199, 202, 203-205, 209, 211, 215
Patient Privacy 56-58, 74, 101, 135, 147, 148, 151, 181, 182, 191

Patient Scheduling 1, 28, 29, 31, 133, 202, 215
Predictive Analytics 2, 3, 4, 28, 34, 35, 45, 53, 56, 57, 59, 83, 84, 87, 89, 114, 115, 124, 125, 129, 130, 131, 140, 144, 160, 167, 173, 176, 182, 195, 219
Predictive Modeling 60, 71, 91, 92, 98, 106, 120, 139
Predictive Models 34, 60, 89, 96, 123

R

Radiomics 128
Regulatory Compliance 137, 159, 161, 162, 176
Reinforcement Learning 17, 18
Resource Allocation 2-5, 31, 34, 38, 39, 45, 58, 84, 91, 105, 106, 109, 110, 113, 117, 130, 133, 134, 168, 173, 174, 209
Resource Management 1, 28, 38, 45, 84, 105-107, 109, 114, 117, 131, 168, 215

Revenue Cycle 159, 160, 164
Revolutionizing 1-4, 39, 43, 49, 52, 57, 71, 76, 77, 82, 84, 87, 91, 110, 112, 163, 165, 195, 215-217
Risk Assessment 3, 89-91, 151, 153, 183, 218, 219
Risk Prediction 146, 180

S

Strategic Planning 96, 106, 160
Supervised Learning 17, 18, 71
Supply Chain Management 111, 114, 115

U

Unsupervised Learning 17, 18, 71

W

Workflow Optimization 133